SELL AND GROW RICH

SELL
AND GROW
RICH

by
FRED R. KISSLING, JR., C.L.U.

Introduction by
WILLIAM T. EARLS, C.L.U.

Foreword by
ROBERT E. DINEEN

 LEXINGTON HOUSE, LEXINGTON

Copyright 1966 by
FRED R. KISSLING, JR., C.L.U.

First Printing 1966
Limited Edition

Library of Congress Card Number 66-30545

PRINTED IN U.S.A.

To my mother

S A R A H

and

SARAH and "CARLIE" our pre-school girls who contributed every type of noise and distraction known to Jane and me, as we worked to complete this book.

FOREWORD

ROBERT E. DINEEN

I AM HONORED that Fred Kissling has asked me to comment about this collection of biographies. You too will be impressed with the story of youth and vitality that it tells. Our business is richer for this sensitive account of what some of the younger producers have accomplished - - in what seems to be an unusually short time.

It is my hope that the chief use of this book will be to educate the youthful searchers - - those who want to know what can be done and something of the whys and the hows. Any experienced man in the life insurance business owes a debt to men who are starting or who may start along our path. As I read this manuscript, it appeared particularly suited to such a role of encouragement and inspiration.

Finally, while there is variety in the lives and characters of these men, the reader cannot escape the realization that owning one's own life insurance agency is not for everyone. Questions of temperament, attitudes, and general motivation surround a decision to make a career of doing the life insurance man's job. Fred's book provides a valuable reference for general agents and managers as a reminder of the qualities we all seek. There are common denominators here, to study and to seek among those about whom such a book may again be written ten years from now.

I hope as you read it that you will find these things and many more.

ACKNOWLEDGMENTS

IT IS IMPOSSIBLE to pay tribute to all the people who directly or indirectly affected the writing of this book; thus, a few will be mentioned but many more unfortunately must remain unnamed.

First of all I want to acknowledge the help given me by Alden H. Smith, C.L.U., who brought me into the insurance business in 1953, and to his two partners, Joe Thompson, Jr., C.L.U., and Arthur D. Reed, C.L.U., who were with me during my four and a half neophyte years.

Also of great importance to me was the help and encouragement of my two general agents, E. T. Proctor, C.L.U., (deceased), and Starkey Duncan; and the opportunity to learn given me by C. P. Edwards, Jr., and his organization. All of these men left their mark on me and thus were indirectly responsible for this book.

For the actual writing of this book, I wish to pay tribute to my wife, Jane Kirkpatrick Kissling, who, when the going got rough and I ran out of time, took over the project under my supervision and wrote the biographies from outlines I gave her.

I would also like to acknowledge the help of the companies who cooperated with me in this project by sending me the names of their agents who might qualify for this book. I would also like to thank the men themselves who appear in this book for the tedious long hours they spent answering the lengthy questionnaire and compiling materials, including everything from special selling forms to speeches.

I would also like to mention the tremendous contribution the Million Dollar Round Table made just by being in existence, because this was the basis of the selection for all of the young men. Among the actual members and officers of the Million Dollar Round Table who gave me inspiration for this book were Quaife Ward and Don Shephard.

I would also like to thank Howard Sigmond, public relations counsel for the M.D.R.T., who gave me excellent suggestions on the manuscript.

I want to thank Dave Behling of the Northwestern Mutual Life Insurance Company for the excellent suggestions he made along the way, and also for the encouragement Neal Creswell of the Northwestern gave me from time to time.

Instrumental also were the helpful comments given to me by Charles Reid and Dan Haught of LIAMA.

I also appreciate the many points that Bob Mecklenborg, former editor of the *Diamond Life Bulletins*, made to me about the handling of *Sell and Grow Rich*.

Here in my own Lexington General Agency, I wish to thank my associates who acted as critics and made contributions to this book, notably Richard Hulette, Hugh Hines, Gerald Wise, and Waller Jones, who was my first associate to qualify for the Million Dollar Round Table.

And finally, I want to acknowledge the impact Bill Earls had on my life through his *Million Dollar Profiles*, the book that actually inspired me to compile this set of biographies of young men, and to thank him for his specific counsel, guidance, and suggestions for my book.

FRED R. KISSLING, JR.

CONTENTS

AUTHOR'S PREFACE

HOW AND WHY THIS BOOK WAS WRITTEN

MY LIFE INSURANCE CAREER and in effect this book actually began on a snowy January night in 1936 when a trolley car traveling without lights ran down and killed my father. Insurance stepped in at that point and enabled my mother to stay at home when I needed her as a youngster, and later gave me the opportunities of a college and graduate school education.

Thus in June of 1953 when I entered the life insurance business, I had a Bachelor's Degree and a Master's Degree from Vanderbilt University. I had spent a lot of time during my five years in college to prepare myself for my profession, and now here I was entering the life insurance business and very eager to succeed. I knew that if I could last it out and do the things that other successful men did, I would succeed; so I began to search out the methods of outstanding men in the life insurance business.

One of the first things I read was a section from the *Diamond Life Bulletins* entitled "Methods of Outstanding Men." One man who was written up was Alden H. Smith, and Alden H. Smith was the man who brought me into the insurance business. His methods had been analyzed along with many other outstanding men who were in our business. The only problem was that the men who were analyzed were much older than I, since I was only twenty-three.

I began to search continuously for articles or biographical sketches of young men in their twenties or early thirties who were successful and were members of the Million Dollar Round Table; because, from the very beginning, to make the Million Dollar Round Table as soon as possible was my goal.

In 1957, Bill Earls' articles appeared in the *Insurance Field*. A little later, his book, *Million Dollar Profiles*, was published. And this book, along with the section from the *Diamond Life Bulletins* (which by that time had been discontinued), became my reading night after night, until the pages became yellow with wear. The men described were older than I and had had much more time to be a success, and I found difficulty in using their methods. I was still searching for methods I could adapt as a young agent when the idea of writing, researching and copying other young men, who like myself were struggling to become members of the Million Dollar Round Table, came into my mind. But at that moment I did not have the time to devote to such a project.

Time passed and I made the Round Table and became a Life Member before I was thirty thanks to the teachings of Alden Smith, the encouragement of my General Agents, E. T. Proctor and Starkey Duncan, my association with C. P. Edwards, junior, and *Million Dollar Profiles* and the *Diamond Life Bulletins*. Eager to help other young life insurance men to make the M.D.R.T., I began making speeches as often as I could to tell them anything I might have learned along the way.

In 1960, still at the age of thirty, misfortune struck. I developed a throat ailment and on doctor's orders had to be on voice rest for a year. (I did write a million that year, however, by using pencil and pad to conduct my interviews.) During this period, I was stricken with another illness which put me in the hospital for two weeks. While lying in the hospital bed, unable to talk, my doctor told me that I could never make a lengthy public speech again. I realized that many things in my life would have to change. And as I lay there thinking how I could now ever make a real contribution to the life insurance industry, the idea for this book came into my mind. If I could analyze the methods of the most outstanding young life insurance men in the United States under age thirty-five, and put them in a book that all could read, I might be able to pay back the life insurance business for the great opportunities it had given me.

I could hope that such a book would inspire college men to choose the life insurance business as a career, because they would see that it was possible to be productive and successful in their twenties and early thirties. I could hope that any man who entered the life insurance business, if they were exposed to enough successful biographies of young men, could identify with some of these men in such a way that the biographies would serve as a guiding light to lead them into membership in the Million

Dollar Round Table or at least upgrade their production.

And I could hope this book might serve as a guideline to general agents and managers in helping them to see what made some of the outstanding young men in the insurance business tick, and thus possibly they too could pass on some of these ingredients to young men in their organizations.

And finally, I could hope it would be a stimulus to upgrade our profession of life insurance among the younger generation of our country.

In planning this book, I decided first I would contact all companies who might conceivably have had members under age thirty-five in the Million Dollar Round Table. And secondly, I would write these young men and ask them to co-operate in my undertaking by giving me thorough answers to a questionnaire, and any additional information in any area I needed to study more fully, to accurately present their methods of operation in biographical form.

Over 200 companies were written asking that they furnish me the names of young men who might be representative of their particular company and whose production had qualified them for the 1962 Round Table or who were writing a sufficient volume in 1962 to qualify for the 1963 Round Table. In response to my letters I had practically unanimous replies, many companies stating frankly they did not have anyone who qualified, many companies recommending only one, still others recommending three or four.

With the company recommendation, the choice was mine as to who would be picked to represent that particular company. I tried to base this, first, on the agent's consistency of production both in volume and lives; and secondly, on his reputation in his area of operation or within the industry. The project was then underway. My master list was narrowed down to approximately sixty young men; and this was the year 1962.

These men were contacted and sent a questionnaire, a copy of which is in the appendix. All agreed to furnish the information I required, holding back nothing. Their material actually turned out to be so voluminous that at this time I have about thirty-five loose leaf notebooks of the material gathered from the fifty-seven young men who are represented in this book and this does not include a number of tapes from the men which go into still greater detail. In addition to this, there are two file drawers of miscellaneous information, which I felt was not as significant as the information that we analyzed and placed in notebooks.

The biographies were, in the most part, written in 1962 and 1963 and rewritten in 1964, 1965, and 1966. They have been updated approximately eight times per person over the course of the period. These biographies are current as of this date.

It is my wish and hope that reading this book can help our industry as much as knowing these men has helped me for I have now personally met and talked with the majority of these men, and they are a fantastic inspiration.

For they have crossed most bridges that will face the young agent or the older agent and the man deciding on life insurance as a career. In the concordance, we have tried to cite certain questions and problems that have been met and solved by these young men. In this way we believe that almost any man can not only identify with a particular individual, but, with the use of the concordance, can quickly find the answers to his own problems or the things that are bothering him.

Therefore, we hope this book can be of lasting value as a guideline for the life insurance industry and give a better understanding of how a young man can attain greater heights and how general agents and managers can help the agent and himself.

SELL AND GROW RICH

INTRODUCTION

WILLIAM T. EARLS, C.L.U.

IT HAS BEEN my privilege to read in advance a copy of Fred Kissling's engrossing biographical study of a great number of outstanding young life insurance men in America.

All these men have written a million of life insurance prior to reaching age thirty-five. They have been recommended by their companies as being outstanding young performers. Most of them have already been recognized in the industry and in the Million Dollar Round Table for their accomplishments.

Fred presents here a series of biographies of men from all parts of the country and from different companies, who operate, as you will observe, dissimilarly but nevertheless all of whom are eminently successful. For someone who was thinking about a career in life insurance or for someone who is now in the business but who would like to improve his results in order to move ahead faster, a study of these biographies would prove richly rewarding.

Fred Kissling, with the aid of his wife, Jane, has been gathering this material, editing and re-editing these stories for five years. Just to have learned about the methods of these youngsters has been a wonderful experience for him and invaluable for use in his training of young men under his direction. It should be an even greater bonanza for the wide reader audience that this series is bound to attract. The biographical background, the procedures, the motivations, and the assistance each gained from others—all should be interesting and helpful to prospective and active young underwriters.

CHAPTER 1

LADD ALEXANDER, C.L.U.

LADD ALEXANDER is a philosopher. So deeply imbued in him is the Greek quest for truth, the Socratic drive to know why and have the questions answered, that his entire approach to life insurance is colored by these ideals. These were taught him by his father, who for over 35 years was Head of the Department of Languages at Northwestern State College. It is sometimes difficult to believe that Ladd has three times written over a million dollars of life insurance in one month. What burning fires of Olympus have sparked this man to achieve such gigantean feats?

Much of Ladd's motivation comes from his father, who is now deceased. "I want to give my late father some of the recognition which is due him. He was awarded a contract to translate seven volumes of philosophic works written by the Greek philosopher Apostle Makrakis. Dad worked every night from 10:00 P.M. until 1:00 A.M. for six years in this translation. But from all this work, he never received any recognition. Perhaps, some of my work can reflect honor on him."

Ladd is also very thankful for his complete and unshakeable faith in God made possible through the teachings of his mother and the Baptist Church. "Without it," says Ladd, "Life has no purpose or reward." Also, Ladd's mother, he relates "taught me to follow my convictions regardless of possible consequences, for being true to yourself is indispensable to happiness and success."

Ladd remembers with gratitude a happy childhood. But Ladd also recalls that he wasted no time in starting his selling career as a grammar school boy in Natchitoches, Louisiana. He remembers winning a hunting knife for selling the most subscriptions to a magazine, selling small painted turtles to college alumni visitors, and selling Kool-Aid and turtles from the same stand and same container.

After graduation from Kemper Military School, he enrolled in Northwestern State College. Here he took part in debating which has since served him immeasurably well. For through it, he learned to think on his feet, remain fluid and flexible in a hotly contested event, and not to fear mental combat. Ladd also served as President of the Junior and Senior Classes and was narrowly defeated for President of the student body in a runoff. Through these extracurricular activities Ladd met people who have since become his clients.

After earning his B.A. in Speech, Ladd taught school; but this was short-lived. Ladd's brother-in-law, a life insurance agent, wrote and suggested that Ladd come into life insurance. And Ladd turned to a career in life insurance without taking any aptitude tests or engaging in extensive conferences.

During his first years Ladd's wife Flo, and insurance men, Mr. R. R. Davenport, Mr. Jeff Nickelson, and Mr. Don E. Williford gave Ladd inspiration and guidance. However, a chance encounter with one of his ex-students, who was about to become a urologist, brought Ladd to his moment of truth.

After six years as a life insurance agent, after ten years out of college, with perhaps half of my normal life gone—where was I? How far had I come? To what thus far could I point with pride and say I had done that was mine?

I asked myself where I wanted to go, and if my pace thus far would get me there in time. My answer to these questions were somewhat terrifying. Nowhere could I find a reassuring thought to cling to—to derive some comfort from.

And the thought occurred to me, "What must it be like for a man to reach his golden years and have nothing to hold onto, nothing at which to point to represent his youth."

And so, as a result of that talk with myself, and many since, and I'm sure, many more to come, I know where I want to go. I'm convinced that knowing where you want to go is the key to success.

Where has Ladd wanted to go? Perhaps his biggest accomplished goal was winning the Southwestern Life Insurance Company's Grand Challenge Award, which goes to the leading company agent. In 1964 he received Life Membership in the Million Dollar Round Table and the C.L.U. designation. Ladd also found time for insurance association work, serving as

President of the Shreveport Association of Life Underwriters in 1964. In addition, he has been a Regional Vice President of the Louisiana Association of Life Underwriters.

And what of future goals? Ten million dollars of life insurance a year is his major one, for Ladd frankly believes that the best contribution a life insurance agent can make to his community, his family, and himself is to sell more life insurance in his city.

Ladd's own insurance program is planned out and expressed with a warmth few fathers and husbands manage to convey to their families. This is a sample of one page in a completely planned estate program:

Anniversary Gifts to Flo: On the 12th of September of each year Flo lives, $100.00 shall be payable to her.

Birthday Gifts to Tommy: On the 20th day of October of each year until 1980, $50.00 shall be paid to Thomas Bryant Alexander.

Christmas Gifts to Marie Angelique: On the 15th of December of each year until December of 1981, $50.00 shall be paid to Marie Angelique Barnes Alexander.

And so Ladd has managed to cheat death of its final victory by guaranteeing to his wife and each of their five children his interest and thoughtfulness as well as security, even after death.

Like his insurance program, Ladd's own daily planning is intricate. He does most of it Friday afternoon and Saturday morning. For each day he plans three closing interviews, three service interviews, and three picture taking interviews. At each interview he prospects for the fifteen new names he needs each week. Between 4:00 and 6:00 P.M. each work day, Ladd is in his office attending to details and getting the next day's interviews arranged, mainly with people in the oil industry and in professional groups.

All the while Ladd is cognizant, perhaps even fearful, of the rapidity with which the years pass and the relatively small amount of time he has to contribute something worthwhile. "I look around and observe men who are my age or older, who don't realize this or do not care about the fact that their lives thus far have contributed nothing of note to society, to themselves, or to their families." Ladd continues, "I have been blessed with wonderful opportunity, and I want to repay life and strengthen the heritage I received from my family." Ladd believes that life insurance has brought to him an early maturity, a sense of responsibility toward other people, and a more accurate picture of what this life is all about—in short, a more accurate sense of values. Among these is the great necessity of having a goal for which to strive, without which Ladd believes, a man will never reach anywhere near his maximum potential. The desire for the attainment of his goal must be all consuming to the point that, by comparison, all of those things we genuinely dislike become readily acceptable.

Ladd knows that having a clear plan of what you want to accomplish is as important for his policyholders as it is for himself. Ladd always emphasizes the fact that settlement options are dangerous unless the policyholder's program is reviewed each year to keep abreast of his changing situation. Ladd will never allow a client to move out of town without first taking out all settlement options in the policies and returning the settlement to lump sum, unless the client is willing to assume the responsibility and the risks which Ladd is relinquishing.

Ladd believes that, for a man choosing life insurance as a career, definite plans and goals are the most important things to his success. Otherwise, he will wander aimlessly. Ladd has thought out specific steps to help a new man make his choice of future goals wisely.

His first step should be to choose the company, and the best way is to look at the caliber of producers in the company being considered. Then the prospective agent should note what help the average producers are receiving—not what the highest producers are receiving—for this will give the most valid indication of the assistance a new man can expect to get.

After the new man has definitely established these facts of training, etc. and has chosen his company, Ladd would advise the man to "give himself completely, unquestionably, and without hesitation to the people working with and for him. He should do everything that he is told to do, when he is told to do it. Few men would fail in this business if they did this."

To a man coming into life insurance after previous business experience, Ladd would sound the warning that "few businesses, if any, require the individual discipline, study, and perseverance that life insurance requires. I believe that if a man will read

Carroll C. Day's *Little Red Wagons and Little Red Boots,* and read it again and again until its contents become a part of his very soul, he will be much better equipped to survive and derive satisfaction from this business. We all need a constant program to strengthen our convictions."

If the agent, after setting goals and making his plans, still is not succeeding at a satisfactory pace, Ladd believes that the goal itself may be the problem. "It may be too far in the distant future to offer any present incentive, and it may not *really* be the thing that the agent wants most. The young life insurance agent, I am firmly convinced, will amount to exactly what he wants to amount to. If he really wants to increase his production and is eager for greater success, and wants it badly enough, he will find a way. It may take him a little longer, and his method may be trial and error; but, if his desire is strong enough, he will make it. Whereas, the man that readily states he wants to do better, but never does, in my opinion, remains exactly at that point where he really wants to be."

To overcome one of the greatest problems in life insurance selling—the no's—Ladd emphasizes that the "no" in this business is not a personal rejection, but a rejection of the idea of life insurance. "The new man must realize that we are in a crusade to educate people to the benefits of life insurance and that abruptness and unwillingness to talk or grant an interview are more than likely an indication of ignorance of life insurance. He must realize that incidents and eventualities in his everyday operation necessarily divide themselves into two categories—those things over which we have control and those things over which we have no control. We must do everything possible to change the first, and learn to forget the latter."

A close which often helps Ladd in overcoming objections and getting the sales interview back on the right track contains these direct and concise thoughts—"regardless of the objections that you have raised in this interview, Mr. Prospect, the fact remains that, if you died today, there would not be enough money to take care of your family. Now the question is—and it is the only question—are you concerned enough to do something about it today? If you are, money is no object, for there is a plan of insurance that you can afford; but if you are not, then I am wasting your time."

At the annual meeting of the Mississippi Association of Life Underwriters in 1962 Ladd elaborated on coping with the "no's" and "yes's" in selling life insurance in a talk called "The Problems of Re-Entry." Ladd notes that the "ups" represent the meeting of opportunity with preparation and that the "downs" come as a result of our own shortcomings rather than the shortcomings of our business. When everything is going exceptionally well, we tend to coast and think this business is easy. "This business is anything but easy!" Ladd emphasized. "Only by surviving the lows of selling can we go on to our next highs. And of great importance is to realize that highs and lows characterize the operation of every life insurance man in the field today, for a complete absence would indicate perfection, and we are only mortal men."

Of certainty and security, Ladd knows the life insurance man has more of it than practically anyone, for "certainty or security, call it what you like, is nothing more than a man's confidence based on his ability to be ever aware of basic truths. This is the only real security. And the man leaving the life insurance business because of such insecurity and uncertainty will be plagued by this same insecurity and uncertainty wherever he goes."

In a speech to the Lamar Life Convention in New Orleans in 1962, Ladd defined what selling life insurance really means. "Would you like to know what we really sell? We sell dignity. We sell self-respect. We sell the assurance that families will never have to surrender their dignity, their self-respect, or their economic or political freedom. We sell self-sufficiency. We sell Americanism."

Ladd has made numerous other speeches as a member of a caravan that appeared in Shreveport, Lafayette, and New Orleans in 1959; to the Houston Association of Life Underwriters on their Million Dollar Round Table Day in 1961; and to several other groups in Mississippi, Texas, and Arkansas.

He is also a prolific writer. His articles have appeared in the *Southwestern Life News*, *The Insurance Salesman*, and in *The Gold Book of Life Insurance Selling*. His *Gold Book* article was entitled "A Guaranteed Income Monopoly." In this, Ladd asserts that "programming offers the greatest leverage available to life insurance salesmen today, because it spotlights the monopoly that life insurance men have on guaranteed income." For illustration Ladd tells of the case he credits with making him a life insurance agent. It was a decreasing term applicant whom Ladd's Company rated substantially to more than double the premium. Ladd decided to go for broke and ordered out Whole Life which had over a 50% increase in premium. After a four-hour interview with the man one afternoon and a four-hour interview with the man and his wife that night, and after which everything that could have possibly been said was said, Ladd delivered the case and the man begrudgingly wrote a check for the semi-annual premium. Thereafter, for the next 18 months, every time Ladd saw the man, he asked when the Company was going to take off the extra premium. Ladd always replied, "When you take the extra weight off." Eighteen months later the man died of a heart attack, and Ladd delivered a check for $25,000 to a semi-invalid wife and three young children. The only other insurance the man had was a $3,000 Group Plan and no other appreciable assets.

"When I delivered the proceeds check, I understood why an agent is told that he is not in the business, really, until he has his first death claim. This experience gave me impetus which has yet to fade!"

And at the rate Ladd is going toward well defined goals, it would seem the impetus will never fade.

CHAPTER 2

BOBBY D. ANDERSON, C.L.U.

"THE FASTEST WAY to overcome discouragements in this business is to make a sale," says Bobby Anderson, who made enough sales in his first year at the age of 23 to take home $10,000.

Today Bobby Anderson is District Manager for the Mutual Benefit in Macon, Georgia. He entered the life insurance business in February of 1958. In his first 10 months of production his volume was $1,150,000. He has been a member of the M.D.R.T. every single year he has been an agent, and each year his volume has increased along with his average size case. He has also earned membership in the National Associates which is the exclusive group of Mutual Benefit salesmen who rank in the top 25 in earnings in the whole United States.

Was this easy for Bobby? He told us "I have had so many discouraging experiences I can't recall which one was the most discouraging." To overcome discouraging experiences he recommended the following to us. "They work!" he promised.

1. Keep the faith that people will buy insurance, if they are appealed to properly.

2. Remember that this is a business in which we must play the averages.

3. Read and study.

4. Immediately after having a discouraging experience, call on a new prospect.

5. The fastest way to overcome discouragement in this business is to make a sale.

Perhaps Bobby began to learn how to overcome obstacles as he was growing up on a farm in a small town of approximately 5,000 people. In high school Bobby participated in all the sports and earned a scholarship to play basketball and baseball at Southern Tech in Atlanta, Georgia. "Had it not been for sports and my being able to obtain an athletic scholarship to college,"

Bobby states candidly, "I doubt very seriously that I would have been able to attend college."

To get an interview with a prospect, Bobby uses lead letters, approach letters, and cold calls. He has also used a movie on estate planning. His approach to a complete stranger, who he has reason to believe would be a good estate planning prospect would be as follows: "I am Bobby Anderson with the Mutual Benefit Life Insurance Company of New Jersey. Our Company has recently produced a movie entitled *According to Plan*. It is an estate planning film and deals with the importance of having a properly drawn will. It touches lightly on trusts and brings out their use in planning a man's estate. It brings out some of the latest tax changes that have come about in Congress affecting a man's business as well as his estate. It takes approximately 27 minutes to view, and it cost our Company a quarter of a million dollars to produce. While I am in this section of the city, I would like to make the film available to you."

What other approaches does Bobby use? Sometimes he shows a sample of the type of work he does and then proceeds to get the fact-finding information necessary to prepare his case. Other times he shows the film, explains generally the type of work he does, and then asks questions which will give him the information about this specific prospect that he will need in preparing his case. He solves his client's problem with a written proposal and/or a modified estate survey or analysis. Illustrations are prepared individually for each specific case. In addition, Bobby prepares what he calls *A Memorandum of Property Settlement* booklet.

Bobby creates his image in several ways: by using Tax letters, Million Dollar Round Table announcements, newspaper ads, and by showing a sample of the type of work he does for a prospect, using his own personal audit. If Bobby is dealing with a total stranger, he sometimes shows the prospect a booklet that contains a number of letters of recommendation and testimonials. These are letters from clients who have done business with Bobby or from influential people in different towns and cities throughout Georgia.

Bobby, during his first year, averaged three interviews per day. He worked six days a week from ten to twelve hours per day and always four nights a week. At the present time his system of work organization is based upon the fact that he calls on prospects three days a week and spends two days a week planning and preparing proposals. In this way, he has been able to keep up his momentum in the field and at the same time do the type of estate planning that he provides for his clients.

As for market areas, 50% of his business comes from business insurance, 40% from estate planning, and 10% from package sales.

Bobby credits his General Agent, William N. Thurman of Atlanta, with being the reason he went into the business insurance market at such an early age. Bobby especially likes the monthly meetings that Bill Thurman holds in Atlanta which is approximately 100 miles from Macon. At these meetings, the agents throughout Georgia gather to discuss any changes made in the insurance industry as well as changes made within the Mutual Benefit which might effect the agents themselves or their clients. "These agency meetings have been of great value to me from a standpoint of increasing my knowledge about the business as well as providing me with the encouragement and inspiration to continue to grow in our business," says Bobby enthusiastically. "Our agency meetings serve as a filling station for me. I usually go to the meetings empty and return filled up."

Bobby chose the life insurance business for a lifetime career because of the long range potential of earnings as well as an opportunity to do a very worthwhile thing with his life. He was quick to realize the potential that the life insurance business offers to the young man who wants a real opportunity.

"My suggestion to a young man who is at a standstill in his life insurance career—who is eager for success—is to find the most successful life insurance man that he possibly can within his community, or go to the most successful agency within his community and tell them his story. Simply say, 'I want to achieve great success in the life insurance business, and I am not happy with my production as it now stands, and I am determined to go forward or out. I am willing to pay the price, whatever it is, to succeed in this business. Will you help me to help myself?' If this is not the answer and a man wishes to remain with the organization that he is currently with, then Bobby would suggest that the agent upgrade his thinking, upgrade his prospecting, increase his knowledge daily, and drill for skill to improve his sales ability. This could possibly be in the form of finding a good sales track to run on as a general rule and drilling for skill for that particular track. This does not mean that the agent would have to use this sales track in all cases; however, it would give him a firm foundation to rely on in those cases where he finds himself without words.

Bobby's advice to those who enter the life insurance business upon graduation from college includes: Accepting the fact that success in this business demands that you pay the price, just as you must do in any other profession such as medicine, law, etc.; not expecting great earnings in your first year; thinking in terms of long range objectives; building a clientele, and growing with the clientele; being a sponge to absorb every bit of information you can about the life insurance business (There is no substitute for knowledge in this business.); working no less than 10 hours per day 6 days a week in the first year. That is no more than any young doctor or lawyer does in preparation for his future profession.

Bobby believes strongly in two basic concepts:

First, a man will sell approximately 10 times the amount of life insurance he owns. If he wants to sell a million he must own at least $100,000. I am sure there are exceptions to this rule, but this will hold true in the majority of cases. How can a man sell to others an idea or concept that he has not accepted for himself? If it is good for the people you call on, it is good for you. If you want to improve or increase your production, increase your own life insurance program.

And, secondly, I believe strongly in the human life value concept. The greatest asset of most men is their economic value. When you project a man's average earnings times the number of years remaining between his present age and age 65, you come up with a figure that will represent most likely an asset that is greater than any asset which he now has. The very first thing that any man should do is protect that asset. I have never met a man that was over-insured, even though I will admit that I have met some who had about as much as they could pay for.

These are the most important thoughts that I could pass on to other underwriters: In summary, they mean sell yourself. I would suggest the underwriter sit down and project his own economic life values, multiply his annual income times the number of years remaining between now and his age 65. At that point he will come up with an asset that is probably larger than any other asset he can point to within his estate. If he doesn't have this asset adequately insured then he should do so. Then he should go out and tell others what he did.

I know that if a man firmly believes these two points and accepts them as a part of his own personality and constitution, and if he is willing to do the routine things a life insurance agent must do to stay in the business, then he is capable of becoming a successful life insurance producer.

Instead of prospecting for problems, Bobby prospects for money. He believes that if you find enough people with money, you can show them problems which they have and are capable of doing something about.

From his first year Bobby Anderson has made the Million Dollar Round Table and prior to his thirtieth birthday received confirmation of Life Membership in MDRT, having qualified eight consecutive times. Like all other underwriters who have gained membership in the Million Dollar Round Table at an early age, he paid the price. But it was worth it! What higher honor and what greater financial rewards can a young man and his family obtain for seven years of work, than to become a Life Member of the Million Dollar Round Table before that thirtieth birthday.

CHAPTER 3

RICHARD WILLIAM ANDREW, C.L.U.

"A FELLOW PHONED ME at 11:30 one night. I was asleep and thought I was dreaming, for I had been trying to sell him for some time. He said he was leaving on a plane trip at 6:00 A.M. the next morning and had meant to call me all day. He wanted to buy some insurance—at least $50,000. I roused a doctor out of bed to examine him at midnight, and I placed $100,000." Few of Bill Andrew's cases are this exciting—"thank goodness"—but his life in Canada has been colorful!

Born in the gold mining district of Northern Ontario at a place near Timmins, Bill spent his boyhood at the Dome Mines. He won a hockey scholarship to the University of Michigan, Ann Arbor. But he chose to go to the University of Toronto, and graduated with a Bachelor of Commerce Degree in 1952. The hodge podge mixture of fellows Bill lived with in the college residence taught him many things about people. College also helped Bill to have a questioning attitude and a desire for some of the better things in life.

Although Bill had considered the life insurance business from the time he left college, he worked for four years—first at the Ford Motor Company and then at the Trans Canada Pipe Lines for the controller—before becoming a life insurance salesman.

And what made him a life underwriter?

I read Frank Bettger's book the year after I graduated from college. I had also seen the tremendous help that insurance had been for us when my father died. I can also remember life insurance men in our home, talking with my father. One was a friend, a salesman with the London Life, to whom my father gave a number of leads.

Also, my father was a strong believer in life insurance. These things all helped to get me thinking about the life insurance business.

13

I chose it as a career, because one has to analyze what ability he has and see what business offers him an opportunity to exercise these abilities.

I wanted to be in finance. And I wanted to be my own boss, for my father had impressed me with the importance of this. In addition, I wanted to do something that was worthwhile, something that had a future and something that was profitable. A career in life insurance proved to be my answer.

When Bill became affiliated with the London Life Insurance Company while living in Calgary, Alberta, he decided almost immediately that he wanted to be a top man in Canadian life insurance and in Calgary's life insurance circles. He is well on his way for he has qualified six years for the Million Dollar Round Table and will be a life member as soon as the application papers are accepted; he was the 1964 President of the Calgary Life Underwriters Association; he is President of the University of Toronto Alumni, Calgary Branch, chairman of Committee of Stewards of St. Andrew's United Church for 1964 and again in 1965, an Executive of a twelve man Clients' Advisory Committee of the London Life; and in 1964 he was named Man of the Year by London Life.

And this is how Bill does these things, as well as spending time with his wife, Nancy, and their four daughters.

Practically all of Bill's appointments are arranged via the telephone. Bill also uses the telephone to prospect, for he often calls his clients when he needs help to get introductions for leads, etc. At his interviews, Bills uses the London Life's confidential specification sheet to get his information. Depending upon the information, he then goes into his "Five Main Money Needs" sales talk which Bill developed, after hearing Jack Nussbaum speak at a Life Underwriters Sales Congress on the "Four Main Money Needs." Bill encourages the prospect to talk about the concepts in which he is most interested, in order of importance to him—money in the event of premature death, money in the event of disability, money for retirement, money for education, or money for business opportunity. Then Bill and his prospect measure the job the prospect wants to accomplish under these five main money needs.

Bill recommends to his prospects and clients what he himself would do in the same situation. He has this philosophy which he explains to them: "If you have provided what you want for your family in the event of premature death, provided what you want in the event of your disability from sickness or accident, and you are setting aside for retirement the amount that you want, then you are free to spend every other dollar you earn any way you choose."

Another very successful idea that Bill uses when discussing Estate Taxes with a business man is to ask the man if he would be interested in setting up a loan to pay his Estate Taxes, a loan that would be available at an unknown date in the future, one that would never have to be repaid, and a loan on which all he would have to do is to pay interest in advance at the rate of say 3% per year. This idea has made his work with business men so profitable that over 50% of his production comes from this market.

Bill says that his manager, Harry Dalgleish, gave him a great deal of help and inspiration, and that Al Clapp was the person most instrumental in starting him in the business. Mr. H. C. Dalgleish (now deceased) pointed out that Bill was a believer in owning life insurance prior to coming into the business. "Bill already owned considerable permanent insurance and knew the value of it. He took some time to decide and wanted to know the answers to all his questions before joining the company. He asked many questions and studied many books about life insurance right from the start of his career. The success pattern was there on the day he entered the business. His progress in the business was consistent each year. The conservation of the business written by him was remarkable, for his business has shown a conservation of 99% even with his production of well over one million a year. His clients think highly of him and know he places their interests first. He has always been a tremendous worker with a lot of desire."

His secretary describes Bill as "always busy and keeps me busy. He appreciates everything you do for him. He often gives me new work, so I can learn more about the business—something new and different to do every day. Sometimes he expects a lot, but this keeps me on my toes. He is quiet, and never flies off the handle, when I make an error."

Bill also expects and gets a lot from his clients. One client and his wife gave up their present needs such as better furniture, in order to begin saving money for retirement and for the education of their children, and in providing money in the event of disability and premature death. These people made real sacrifices to purchase $100,000 of Whole Life.

Another man told Bill on the phone that he could come to see him if he wished, but that it wouldn't take long—he wasn't going to buy any insurance. "I told my wife when I went out at 8:30 that evening I would only be gone about half an hour. I ended up writing an application for $100,000 Whole Life with an annual premium and got home at midnight."

Not all of Bill's appointments have such happy endings, but as a six times member of the MDRT, he has maintained consistent high production. He has found his gold, not in the Dome Mines of Porcupine, but in the human minds of the men and women of Calgary.

CHAPTER 4

FRANK E. BAKER

AT 28 YEARS OF AGE Frank E. Baker is a very, very young million-dollar producer in Seattle, Washington. On his two acre country estate in suburban Seattle he has a horse stable, raises sheep for a hobby, and in addition to his home he has a guest house. He has the opportunity to do a great deal of boating in the Puget Sound area and takes long week-ends aboard his boat—an opportunity which would most likely be impossible in a more conventional type of job or profession.

Frank's civic activities are many, including the Washington Athletic Club, Seattle Yacht Club, and the Toastmasters. He is an active participant in the Big Brothers Program and President of the Board of Directors of his college fraternity. Of his activities, Frank says, ". . . perhaps Toastmasters helps you a great deal in your ability to communicate with others, and the Big Brother Program has made me more aware of the true value of life insurance, since my little 'brother' came from a family of six who lost their father in an aviation accident some eight years ago."

Frank's interest in the insurance business began in the summer of his junior year in college. At that time, one of the leading agents of a casualty firm died, and Frank went to work for this casualty agency in his home town servicing renewal accounts during the summer. Frank says that it was here he gained his first really practical experience in the casualty field and became very intrigued with the insurance business. His casualty experience made him decide that this was not the field he was interested in, so he entered part-time life insurance selling during college mainly in order to earn some extra income to support his new bride. However, he became more and more intrigued with this line of insurance. But before he entered graduate school at the University of Washington, Frank decided to have several interviews with major corporations; he found very little challenge and very little indication that extra effort in a job would be recognized. This tentatively confirmed his belief that the life insurance business offered to a young man a rather unique career: "I know of very few businesses where a man can enter with merely an investment of himself and a fountain pen, have complete freedom, and also be reasonably free from outside influences which directly affect his income."

Frank has never worked on a full-time basis in any occupation other than selling life insurance; but, because of his college training, he has often been able to recognize complicated financial problems that insurance could solve and to work out solutions that the neophyte agent ordinarily would not have the knowledge to do. This has given Frank a terrific beginning in our business.

Having decided early that life insurance is a great business, Frank also decided that he would be outstanding in it. He credits the Million Dollar Round Table as being one of the greatest stimuli to his success in life underwriting.

He tries to stay away from the conventional methods of selling life insurance and relies basically on a more candid and everyday approach to people. He does not sell any particular life insurance company or plan, but tries first to sell himself, recognizing that most people of character realize they have a problem, and it is just a matter of their accepting him to work out a solution to their problem.

Frank and his associates have merchandised an entity to the people which is called The Financial Planning Clinic, Inc. Frank says of his associates: "We have a group of people within our organization who each specialize in different areas. We are associated with a stock broker and a casualty man who has his own business but with whom we work very closely. We have an attorney who has a wide background of tax planning. I look at our basic job as that of selling the work of our associates. I am a salesman and not a technician. Technical knowledge is easy to purchase, but the ability to sell seems to be a rare commodity."

Frank thinks the most unusual facet of their operation is the fact that they merchandise to professional people a comprehensive financial planning service and sell them a concept of one-stop financial planning.

They try to project to their clients an image of a comprehensive financial planning service. It is called a new concept in financial planning for the professional man.

They advertise in many of the professional journals and send tax letters and special letters that they have developed themselves to the particular markets in which they are working. They have, for example, sent formal invitations to people which state simply, "An invitation to discuss personally with The Financial Planning Clinic, Inc. a new concept in financial planning." They try to apply many of the basic marketing principles to the life insurance business, forgetting the conventional type methods, and using their own ideas developed through creative thinking.

Frank uses this procedure to get an interview with a prospect: "Practically all of the people I approach receive a pre-approach letter stating a particular idea or ideas I hope will be stimulating to them. Then I give them a call referring to the letter and ask for an interview. Obviously, I think the invitation is rather a unique method of reaching people and, normally, it is the last piece of mail that reaches the prospect prior to our call. After we have obtained an initial interview with the prospect, we go to him and show him a sample of the type of work we do. We have an attorney, a stock broker, and a general insurance man in our organization; and we show the prospect a particular folder we have prepared for someone else. In this case, it is a hypothetical person. We show him how we scientifically determine the amount of insurance he should own, and that we can handle his casualty insurance for him, and also through our brokerage facilities help him invest his dollars to the best advantage. We normally illustrate to the prospect some of the advantages of a testamentary trust and some general estate planning techniques to pique his curiosity, and encourage him to think that perhaps we can do for him something he hasn't seen before and should have done to save taxes or put his affairs in better order."

Frank explains that practically all of the cases are written on a two interview basis with a completely typed proposal being submitted in the closing interview. In many cases, it is an estate survey, and often where there is not a tremendous amount of other property, it is just an intelligent summary of all the benefits that he receives by taking action on their particular solutions to his problem. Frank uses the Mutual Benefit Life's analagraph a great deal and thinks it is a tremendous tool for helping people solve the basic problems on an impartial, unbiased basis.

Since they use a two interview programing approach, they leave with the prospect a complete written analysis for his situation. Thus when they see him for the review, he already knows the problem they are going to solve, and it is simply a matter of bringing his situation up to date. In addition, they send everyone the usual birthday card and also they send a brief, bi-monthly mailing piece. "Whenever I receive some sort of honor I always make sure they know what it is, whether it is the Million Dollar Round Table announcement, 'Man of the Year' award, or whatever comes my way."

This unusual young man who came directly from college into the life insurance business has developed a clientele of physicians and dentists in the Seattle area that is outstanding. He still averages at least three selling interviews a day and works at least two nights a week.

"My goals have changed very little since I entered the life insurance business. I knew at the inception that Million Dollar Round Table status was almost a necessity. My goals are basically just that, a matter of amounts. Every year I try to add a new market and shoot for a higher goal in production. There is no substitute for production as far as I am concerned, and this must be achieved."

Frank says that Francis Merritt has given him the greatest inspiration in the life insurance business and tells us something about this famous person. "I have always admired Francis Merritt a great deal for his ability to inspire the new man. At the time I entered the business he was Director of Training for the Mutual Benefit Life. A few months after becoming a full-time agent, I had the opportunity of spending two weeks with him in what the Mutual Benefit calls a career school. Since I already had quite a bit of part-time selling experience, he was able to communicate to me many valuable ideas and philosophies which I still maintain to date. One phrase, for example, which I think is tremendously important is, 'When in trouble run for protection.' Francis Merritt, in his basic philosophy, felt that getting title to property was the most important function. If there is one thing a person can't argue with in a life insurance policy, it is the fact that if he dies in the first year, he will have acquired more money than he possibly could in any other investment. Many times we forget and argue with the prospect that he cannot earn more on some other form of investment, and we lose our perspective of what life insurance does best—that is deliver money at a time when his family needs it most."

Another aspect that has helped Frank attain success is the stimuli he receives from being a part of a successful agency team. "My particular General Agent is always making sure that my goals are high enough and is constantly urging me on to greater heights. My agency itself is continually helping me set a pace. Environment to me is most important, and the pace set by others around you is an extremely important factor in growth."

As for encouraging other young men to become life insurance agents Frank says that in the past he has often advised young men to join his agency, and he feels quite strongly that for the person with the particular abilities to sell and the desire to succeed, there is no finer profession. "What other industry can you enter with a total investment of $1.98, which is the purchase price of a ball point pen, and have the opportunity to earn as much income as your ability will allow you to produce?" Frank asks. "Also, you obviously have complete freedom; and, essentially, you are in business for yourself." Many men search for an opportunity such as this, and Frank believes many walk by the life insurance industry, because of their personal bias, without stopping long enough to analyze what the life insurance business can offer them in return for a substantial amount of dedication.

Frank makes these suggestions to a young man who is at a standstill in his life insurance career: "Mental attitude is certainly a tremendous factor in creating a successful image with people. People like to do business with successful people, and many times I think men hesitate to think large enough. Study certainly gives a man a great deal of confidence; and reading articles, which build a larger mental image as to how one looks at himself, can be tremendously important. Study as far as technical aspects of the business are concerned enables one to be more confident in answering objections and gaining the respect of the people you are doing business with. Methods of operation can be important. In my own personal case it was a programming method in addition to my package selling that put me in the Round Table. It raised my average size case from $10,000 to $20,000, and this on a slightly greater number of lives enabled me to write over a million dollars. Currently, my average size case is $45,000. Many times a simple change in procedure, in addition to what you are doing presently, can produce tremendous results. A 10% change in methods has many times resulted in 40% to 50% more success in a given market."

Mr. Clifford E. Bertram, C.L.U., Frank's former General Agent with the Mutual Benefit in Seattle, says that Frank is restless for a big future and is not satisfied to sit back and rest on his oars. "As George Bernard Shaw said, 'People are always blaming their circumstances for what they are.' I don't believe in circumstances. The people who get on in the world are the people who get up and look for the circumstances they want, and if you can't find them, make them." That describes Frank Baker to a tee.

Frank's secretary emphasizes an attitude which could account for much of his success: "Working for him has taught me that life insurance is not just something for an individual to pay for until he dies, but an instrument in planning for the future and retirement." How true this is and yet so many life insurance men fail to get this across to their clients and even to the people they are associated with from day to day.

"The real turning point in my career," says Frank, "was when I began talking to people on a needs basis and using a basic programming system. This did wonders for my average size case. An earlier turning point occurred when his General Agent gave him a book on selling life insurance. In it was the idea of going to the reverse telephone directory, copying down all the phone numbers in a large commercial building in town and copying all the names from the building listing on 3" x 5" cards, and calling people on a cold canvass telephone approach. "From this I learned a great deal about telephone technique which has become increasingly valuable over the years."

Also, it has helped him secure prospects, for Frank came to Seattle with absolutely no contacts and, as his former General

Agent said, he is a product of the circumstances which he has created. Here is a young man who spent two and a half years in studying about the life insurance business before he entered it. This, obviously, has helped him immeasurably in getting started early on the road to million dollar production, and he has continued through the years to study everything within reach that would help him grow in his organization and help him fulfill the needs of his clientele.

In working out a survey of his business for the five years he has been a life underwriter, Frank has found that 92% of his policyholders are still paying premiums, and one-half of the 8% of lost volume is from death claims. In this period of time he has built around himself a successful organization which undoubtedly will continue to grow throughout the years into one of the most unusual and unique organizations of its kind in the Northwest.

CHAPTER 5

WILLIAM R. BALLARD

"PLAIN OLE VANILLA SALESMAN" is the way William R. Ballard—who sold a million dollars of life insurance during his first seven months in Houston, Texas, where he knew no one—describes himself. Today, at age 34 he is a life member of the Million Dollar Round Table with production in excess of $1,500,000 a year. Some vanilla salesman Bill is!

Mr. Benjamin N. Woodson, President of American General Life Insurance Company, described Bill's workings in a recent article entitled "Return to Fundamentals."

Bill starts his day early enough to get in a half-hour of study and life insurance reading before the business day begins. He plans each day's activity before he goes out on the street. He disciplines himself to make sure that each day and each week, he will complete the required number of calls, face-to-face interviews, closing attempts, and prospecting interviews.

His sales presentation is simple and convincing. It is based on family need and on the proposition that when a young man buys whole life insurance for the protection of his family, he spends only 10 cents on the dollar, saves the other 90 cents during the first 20 policy years, and saves his entire outlay and more besides in later years.

He requires himself, without fail, to secure at least two brand-new names or situations each business day; and he tries to get a replacement name for every person whose name goes out of his prospect list for whatever reason.

These activities produce an average of two sales a week, averaging a little more than $15,000 per sale, and totaling about $1,400,000 per year.

Everything this young man does can be found in the first chapter of any of a hundred life insurance sales training courses!

All he is doing is carrying out the simplest and surest of the fundamentals of life underwriting.

And all he is doing in consequence is $1,500,000 a year!

From the President of one's company this is indeed praise.
Bill believes what really makes him go is complete happiness with his job. "Every day is like a holiday. I get so much fun out of my work, that it does not seem like work at all!"

Bill grew up on a farm in West Texas where he spent ten years in a 4-H Club. He made his own money from age nine onward by selling show animals. He raised Abilene's Grand Champion calf in 1949, and showed seven championship pigs in succeeding years. He netted $3,000 his senior year in high school from these endeavors.

Bill received a football scholarship to Texas A & M College where he was a varsity letterman. When he graduated in Animal Husbandry, Bill looked forward to a career as a professional agriculture man.

In college, however, Bill had noted that one of his college friends was making a great deal of money as a part-time life insurance agent. While waiting to go into the service, Bill tried selling life insurance, and he loved it. His insurance career had begun!

While he was in the Air Force, Bill spent lots of time studying Napoleon Hill's *Think and Grow Rich*. He planned out his life insurance career as the book suggested, and he still keeps a year to year analysis of the progress, for "this one book has done more to initiate drive and success in my thinking than any other single thing."

From his very first day, he has used only one method of prospecting and interviewing. He sends no mailing pieces and does not advertise in newspapers, preferring to be just plain Bill working in his client's behalf. Upon completion of an interview, he asks for the name of the prospect's best friend and always gets it! He then calls the friend about 5:30 P.M., just after he gets home from work, asking for an appointment later that night or in the future.

His interview is simple programming using the LSU Formula taught at the Institute of Insurance Marketing. Bill colors the program with crayons as he goes over it with the prospect, and he leaves this program with the prospect. American General is able to furnish him with proposals in ledger form for almost every insurance plan, and Bill uses this service whenever possible.

After, or sometimes even before the sale has been made, Bill makes up an analysis folder; this has been most favorably received through the years. Originally Bill's idea, today a good number of men with American General have adopted it.

Bill visits with each policyholder—a social call—about three times a year. He sends birthday cards to every member of the family, and Christmas cards to each family. Bill gives away several hundred ball point pens each year, sends flowers to everyone who becomes hospitalized, and gives Christmas presents to his bigger policyholders. Every family also receives a metal policy box with a combination lock. About 65% of his business comes from these policyholders and another 25% from their referrals.

Bill's favorite sales idea is explaining how life insurance works by using a 2¢ stamp on a $1.00 bill. It goes as follows:

Mr. Prospect, instead of thinking about this $10,000 policy and this $200.00 premium, let's look at it on a $1.00 basis. Here is the way it works. You put a 2¢ postage stamp on this $1.00 bill. If you die during the year, we furnish the $1.00 and mail it to your family just because you paid the postage on it. The next year we will ask you for another postage stamp; in fact, each year we ask you for one. But that's not the miracle. After 18 years there is no way you could have invested more than $ .36 in postage. Thank God, you didn't need the insurance anyway, so now you start worrying about how to educate little Joey. If you need the postage, we will give you back all the postage to help put him through school. This plan we are discussing would have enough cash value in 18 years to furnish $50.00 per month for nine months for four college years. Mr. Prospect, this is so wonderful you just cannot afford to be without it.

And enough of Bill's prospects agree with him to give him the fantastic closing ratio of one sale to every one and a half interviews.

Bill's long range objective is to continue writing as many lives as possible for about five more years to get ten million in force, and then spend his time servicing these policyholders. Bill now has 700 policyholders and 90% are within five years of his age. They are just now ready to start making good money. And Bill plans to grow with each of them.

Bill is in a unique position to understand the situation of men becoming life insurance agents. He has served on the faculty at L.S.U. Institute of Insurance Marketing since 1958, and he has spoken every year to each of its six classes. He has also spoken extensively to Life Underwriters Associations in Oklahoma, Louisiana, and Texas.

Bill believes that the first thing a new man in life insurance should do is to learn his product, preferably at the L.S.U. or Purdue Insurance Marketing schools. After a new man is properly educated to his product and is still experiencing difficulty, Bill believes he is just not making enough calls.

"If you will work! work! work! for five years, you should have the world by the tail with a downhill swing," Bill emphasizes.

Bill has found a tape recorder indispensable to his career. He has a library of tape recorded talks made by outstanding life insurance men at meetings Bill has attended. "I often play a tape, while I am doing paper work in the office," he explains. "These talks serve as a great inspiration for me, especially when I am down." He would encourage every life insurance man to buy a tape recorder at any sacrifice, and then record and re-record his sales talk until it is perfect.

Bill notes that in his case there have been three other important factors in his unusually successful career—two men and his wife.

Bill calls his manager, Al Pratka, "the most generous guy in the world"; and he notes that Al himself regularly produces over a million, and his Houston Agency produced 14 million in 1964 with 16 full time agents. Another man who has often helped Bill by giving him advice on his most complicated cases is Charles E. Gaines, C.L.U., Director of the Institute of Insurance Marketing at L.S.U.

Bill calls his wife, Junita, the perfect insurance wife. She helped organize the Ladies Auxiliary of the Houston Underwriters Association and has served as an officer of the organization, while caring for their four children. "We attended high school together and dated all four years," Bill recalls. "She was valedictorian of her high school class, very active in all sports, and was a class favorite. She attended McMurray College for two years before we married, then worked two years while I finished Texas A & M. During my first two years, when I was working every night of the week, she never once complained about my being gone so much. She has always put my business first and family pleasures second."

Thus, today they can both take pride in Bill's outstanding success.

CHAPTER 6

HOWARD C. BUSBEY, C.L.U.

"I WAS LOOKING for a profession in which I could grow when I chose life insurance," recalled Howard Busbey, C.L.U., recently at a M.D.R.T. meeting. And in twelve years he has pushed his production well over $2,000,000, and led his Company, the Guardian. In addition, he is a past president of the Guardian's Leaders' Club which means he was elected by a committee comprised of leading producers in the United States. Here is Howard Busbey's work philosophy: "There is no grand slam effort that will put you in the Million Dollar Round Table. It is the combination of many small victories that have been attained by a lot of everyday hard, drudgerous work. It is the daily activity and the hard work that makes a million dollar producer in our business."

Howard C. Busbey worked his way through night school at Georgia State College, had it interrupted by military service, and had other crises that would have sent most men into eclipse. Nevertheless, in twelve short years this man has risen to the position of leadership in his Company, and lives in a fine home on Fox Croft Road in Atlanta, equipped with a full-size trampoline and swimming pool which he and his family use the entire year to keep in shape.

Howard, like so many other agents in this book, believes that our business offers everything for which a young man could ask. "I cannot be too emphatic in advising young men to come into life insurance. I can't understand why so few people are convinced that this is a fine business. To me, it has all the advantages of being in business for yourself with none of the hazards. You do not have a penny invested, and yet you can make more money than in almost any other profession that I know of. The prestige that can be built up in the community from a good quality operation is almost unbelievable, and yet, in spite of this, men will still pick the job with a limited future in a large corporation."

Howard gives some important advice to anyone entering the life insurance business from college. "I believe programing, theories of the business, pension plans—all of these things are important. But the most important thing to *begin* with is (1) survival, (2) getting yourself known by writing a large number of lives, and (3) getting into as many situations as you can expose yourself. The really important thing to do when you come into our business is to develop a method of operation. You cannot flounder. You must have an operation and know that the law of averages will take care of you. I know that if I make that luncheon date the afternoon before, call on two or three people, and have a coffee break interview with the person the next day, I am going to turn up business, if I am saying the right thing."

A method of operation is something, believe it or not, few people ever develop in our business. Let this be a word to all aspiring candidates for the MDRT. Develop a method of operation.

This amazing young man can best be described as a hard worker, who is well organized and who has developed a persuasive sales appeal that deals with people's emotions. It is his conviction that emotion is the thing that sells life insurance, not facts and figures. He suggests that you watch people for their reaction to forms of motivation. Howard has perfected through concentrated effort a system of operation and a persuasive technique that has led him to a production greater than $2,000,000.

What really makes this young man tick? He states it is a drive for money, money that he never enjoyed as a child, and for prestige that he never had during his early life. Because of these drives, he is willing to pay the price to earn them, not only for himself but for his children so that perhaps they will not have to drive quite as hard as he did. He goes on to add, "I also believe that God never intended for man to be lazy or unproductive, and you are happiest when you are the busiest. Unless you can leave your mark on something, then you have wasted a lot of valuable time on this earth. I cannot help but believe, however, that it is fear, and I hate to admit it, that makes me go. It is fear of going back to the life I knew in my earlier years. I suppose the one thing you can say about me all the time is that I run a very scared race. The rich man, I find, is more afraid of poverty than the poor one, for he has further to fall."

With an average number of 125 lives for the past two years, Howard is really running a race, but he is also doing a real service to the life insurance profession and to his clients.

What does he use in his approach? In practically every instance he makes a call to a referred lead, and he tries to make the call brief and to the point. He says, "I tell him how I got his name, that the individual wanted me to meet him, and that 'the person referring me did not tell me you were in the market for life insurance; however, I wanted to get a chance to meet you and was wondering, if, sometime when I am downtown, I might give you a buzz and grab a bite of lunch with you, or at least have a cup of coffee so that we may chat and get a chance to know each other.'" He does not attempt to show the prospect anything at this particular point; he only strives to get him to see him at a later date. This is a simple approach and one that few people could turn down, yet it is very straight and to the point. When he does secure this interview at a later time he stresses three things. He sells the professional concept of insurance. He explains what a life insurance policy really is —"you would be surprised how little even intelligent people know about it." He motivates the man to save money on a systematic basis to solve the problems that need solving.

An interesting thing about Howard is that he does a very thorough and deep analysis of all of his clients' insurance; yet, he presents his proposals and resumes in long hand. He finds that a client seems to appreciate this more than if the work is typewritten: "If proposals and surveys are typewritten the client thinks some secretary did it and that little time has been devoted to it, but when they are in my own handwriting the client knows better."

Here is a young million dollar producer that is using an informal presentation in long hand, and it is working to the tune of $2,000,000 a year. This only goes to prove that the young man going into the business without adequate capital does not need a full-time secretary in order to build up his production for qualification in the Million Dollar Round Table.

This is Howard's organization pattern. "On Friday afternoon before I leave the office, I fill out a sheet which lists all of the people I intend to keep in mind during the week. I keep a calendar at hand, then when people tell me they want me to contact them in the future, I will list this on the activity sheet and it shows up for a week in the future. I take this activity sheet home with me over the week-end, along with the alphabetical file of all my prospects and policyholders. During the course of the week-end, I will flip through this and try to imagine sales situations with anyone that I have already sold, and people that I have called on previously but have not sold. If any of these situations look good, I will pull the card out and list it on the activity sheet for the next week. My whole day is built around a luncheon appointment. I try to secure this luncheon appointment the afternoon before the day I am going to see the man. That gives me at least one interview for the day, and I try to see two other people in addition to this. This interview might be a closing interview, it might be a fact-finding interview, or it could be a sales interview."

Howard Busbey is a young man who was looking for a profession in which he could grow; and, as the twelve years have passed, he has proved to himself and to the world the life insurance business is a profession in which a young man can grow to astronomical heights.

CHAPTER 7

ARCH W. CASSIDY, C.L.U.

To MAKE the Million Dollar Round Table and to be selected the Life Insurance Man of the Year by the General Agents and Managers Association were two milestones Arch W. Cassidy, C.L.U., passed his first year in the business. He began his full time career in 1958 when he wrote $1,250,000 with premiums of $16,000. Today he is a Life and Qualifying member of the Round Table and in 1963 he wrote $2,200,000. On October 1, 1963 he took on managerial responsibilities with his company, the Equitable Life Assurance Society of the United States, but he kept his personal production at $1,750,000 on 92 lives in 1964 (no health or group).

A 1955 University of Florida graduate, Arch had majored in Life Insurance and Business Administration, had been active in the Insurance Society at the University, had held a football scholarship, and upon graduation he had served as a U. S. Naval Officer for three and a half years before becoming a life insurance man.

Arch chose this career because of three main influences: a college professor who encouraged him in life insurance; his father who was a successful life underwriter; and, of most importance, the fact that life insurance was one of the few careers in which he alone would be responsible for climbing as high as he wanted to go. "There were no fixed territories, no fixed income, nothing fixed. The better you did, the greater reward you would receive. When I entered the life insurance business, my goals were to have a successful, prosperous, happy home life, to be a million dollar producer, to some day have a reputation as a very competent and successful underwriter in my area; and to be the number one underwriter in my city. My goals haven't changed, but rather have become more and more a burning conviction."

For prospecting, Arch uses the newspapers. He also uses an endless chain referral, primarily working from one person to another. He tries to make sure that the prospect knows who he is, what he does, and why he is there prior to talking to him. Arch uses a form letter for service personnel based on Social Security which has been effective.

Arch generally uses the first meeting as a fact-finding interview. His fact finding involves the use of a blank piece of paper on which he writes the man's full name correctly spelled, his date of birth, occupation, title, present life insurance, life insurance companies he does business with, mode of premium payments, and types of insurance. Arch finds out if the prospect owns his home, what his plans are, what his retirement ideas are, and what fringe benefits he receives from the company he is associated with, if he is other than the proprietor. If time permits, Arch goes into a short sales demonstration, usually involving uses of life insurance. Arch, a firm believer in keeping the presentation simple, believes that as soon as you get the problem too detailed, you lose the prospect.

Arch attempts to get the man examined and to get a commitment from the medical department before going any further. "We do not know whether the proposed idea is workable, until I get the man examined."

Arch's unique way to follow up is to use "Half Happy Birthday" letters. He mails this letter to his clients just prior to their age change. Arch points out to them that the period just prior to the age change are life insurance bargain days, and that within the next few days Arch will get in touch with them to see if they want to take advantage of this.

Arch uses the Guaranteed Insurability Options that are now available, and he has had approximately 90% persistency on exercising these options for the people that were buying their first basic policy. The idea that a man can create an immediate estate through life insurance, tax free, is a powerful selling point.

To organize his work, Arch uses a two by four inch book which he carries with him. This book contains a list of appointments for each day and the hour of the appointment. The right-hand page is used for appointments; the left-hand page is used to list people to call and reminders. "I have found that if I write it down in a book, I'll do it, and I get a track to run on rather than trying to leave it to memory. I strive at all times to see at least three or four people a day for sales interviews, and I try to work on an appointment basis as much as possible."

The greatest percentage of Arch's business comes from people between the ages of twenty and forty—the young college graduate that is either in a professional occupation or in sales. Arch has done extensive work and had great success with young lawyers who have turned out to be tremendous centers of influence for him.

Arch would advise any young man, who is willing to work, to choose life insurance as a career. Arch believes that in life insurance a man can set his own goals, be his own boss, have unlimited opportunity, and have no inventory requirements or big cash layout or money tied up in business investment. In no other business can you have so little money tied up and produce so much net profit.

And Arch believes in setting those goals. He suggests that the agent who has stopped progressing should set a short range definite goal, such as two applications a week, 100 paid cases a year, etc. Arch is a firm believer that, if the average producer would set a minimum goal of a certain number of applications paid for each year, he could make the living that he would like to.

Arch also recommends a twenty point per day game system of achievement. A man who gets twenty points each day based on the following evaluations will be a success in this business. Arch emphasizes, however, that it is necessary to get the twenty points each day, not forty points one day and none the next day, but twenty points per day five or six days a week. Here's how they are figured:

One point for a telephone call to make arrangements for an appointment.

Two points if the telephone call is completed and the appointment is arranged.

Three points for an interview in which you cannot see the man, or the interview is not concluded.

Four points for an interview that necessitates a call back or a non-closing interview.

Five points for closing the interview and taking the application.

Arch also emphasizes the importance of the young underwriter working under and talking to men who are already experienced, successful underwriters. "Later each young agent can develop his own techniques, but not in the beginning."

Arch maintains that when you enter the life insurance business you have to remember that you are your own boss. "It's like a proprietor; you must keep the door open so many hours a day and be productive. You can't just put the time in, because without productivity you will be out of business. You can't expect to work four days a week and be a success in this business in the early years, and even in the later years. You have to put the time in and make that time productive for you."

Arch believes that the first thing a young potential agent should learn is organization in his work habits. He needs a track on which he can run. A man needs to know what he has to do and where he is going in order to be a success. He should learn, above all, how to prospect. "Once you get in front of the man, you know what to say. It's the ability to prospect that divides the men from the boys. It's like the fisherman; he knows how to catch the fish; the problem is to find them. Our problem is to find the man who can be motivated to buy."

Arch had very early experience with the life insurance business. "My father was a life insurance agent, and I grew up knowing life insurance. He provided me with a fine life, and I wanted to provide the same kind of life for my family, which I am glad I have been able to do. I believe that it is a fine life for any young gentleman to have."

Arch knows a young man starting in the business will hear several objections over and over. These include: I'm insurance poor; I have been programmed; Joe Smith handles my insurance; or, I have a friend or a relative in the business. Probably the most frequent objection, Arch believes, is that I am insurance poor, or I have all the insurance I can afford. Arch has found that it is quite effective to reverse this and ask the prospect several questions.

By asking questions you will have his attention, and most gentlemen will answer any questions you ask them. After you have talked to the prospect a bit ask him, "Would you like to know the minimum amount of insurance a man of your income should carry?" I am amazed at the reactions I have gotten, and to this day I have never had a negative one. This question enables the agent to find out the man's present life insurance program, his desires, his aims, and his needs for additional insurance. Very rarely will a young agent find the prospect who has all the insurance required to fulfill his wishes.

Therefore, this question opens the door to every type of life insurance sale there is. Every day you hear people wanting to know how much they should have, and by stressing what would be the minimum amount a man would need in the income position he's in, this question becomes an excellent attention getting device, and one that will make the man sit up and listen to you.

In a speech Arch made at the President's Council of the National Leaders' Meeting of the Equitable, he explained how he goes about increasing the average size of his cases and the number of cases written: The first time Arch talks to a man who is non-policyholder, instead of talking in terms of $5,000, $10,000, or $15,000, he talks in terms of $50,000, $75,000, or $100,000. This will open the prospect's eyes and make him think a lot bigger. Arch has found it much easier to climb down the ladder than up. "You may be talking in terms of $50,000 and $75,000 and still get the $5,000 or $15,000, but the door will open for you to go back for a second sale." Arch says that you can also take the figure of the premium where you sold $10,000 or $25,000, and if it is an odd figure you can round it out. If it is $602, see if you can push it to $650 or $700, and you will build up quite a sizeable amount over a period of years.

"When I put my head down on the pillow at night to go to sleep there is nothing better than to know what I am going to be doing tomorrow." This is the philosophy that has allowed Arch to continue to achieve the tremendous production goals he has set for himself year after year.

CHAPTER 8

DONALD E. CHARNLEY

FOUR APPLICATIONS each and every week is old stuff for Don Charnley, young Qualifying and Life Member of the M.D.R.T. and a star Mutual Life of New York agent living in Kalamazoo, Michigan. How can one do this, we asked him. "Show your sincerity and convictions, sell a service, and expect to sell," he replied, summing up in one sentence the philosophy behind his outstanding record.

Don graduated from Western Michigan University in 1952 and received his Masters Degree in Business Administration from the University of Michigan in 1954. He qualified for the M.D.R.T. his third year as an underwriter, led MONY in applications in 1958 and has been no lower than fourth in the company for the past eight years. He has made numerous speeches, the most noteworthy being his talk to the 1964 M.D.R.T. meeting on package selling entitled "My Method of Operation." He has made company records with one application or more a week for the past eleven years, writing over 2,200 life applications in this period, plus many personal Health and Disability Income policies as well as several group programs.

Don's father has been with MONY as a part-time agent for over forty years and together with his first manager, Charles E. Brown (deceased), they were the men most influential in Don's choice of a life insurance career. Both Don's father and Mr. Brown took an interest in Don and started educating him in this great business while he was still in high school. Then in college, Don pursued a business course of study, taking all the insurance subjects available and attending all agency meetings he could manage.

When Don did start his life insurance career in Kalamazoo, Michigan, he sold strictly with cold calls, averaging fifteen to twenty interviews a week. Today 70% of his business is from former clients, and he now has ten interviews a week. His original goal was an application a week every week of the year. Don says that this quite naturally over the years has turned to an average of nearly four applications a week." In his early years he was on the company training program being guaranteed $4,200. At the end of the second year he was $8,400 ahead of the training program.

Don calls his third year the turning point of his career: "I qualified for the M.D.R.T. that year and each consecutive year thereafter, thanks to a great manager, Daniel P. Cahill, C.L.U., who has since passed away."

Don also credits his present manager, Delmar D. Stevens and cashier Dan Starmann with helpful assistance. Of Starmann Don says, "He has given me my greatest help in daily problems. He is the best cashier in my company—a real salesman's helper."

At home Don has also been blessed; he has an understanding wife and five children. He pays his wife Cynthia this high tribute: "Cynthia's calmness and understanding are the steadying influence of my career. She never has questions or complaints about my hours, whereabouts, or lateness . . . she just understands."

Don's present method of operation is described in his M.D.R.T. talk entitled "Setting Goals and Keeping it Simple." He maintains that a goal is of primary importance, whether it is two applications a week, $25,000 of volume per week, $100,000 of volume per month, the M.D.R.T., etc. Don also names three areas in which an agent must be proficient to be successful: Prospecting, sales presentation, and organizing for effective operation.

And what does Don name as the most important work of the agent: "Seeing people and writing applications." Don tries to see ten people a day, thirty to forty a week. He makes a concentrated effort to obtain an application on Monday, so his week can start with a positive accomplishment.

In order to reach his primary goal of three or four paid applications a week, Don keeps a steady stream of carefully qualified names and prospects moving through his plan book each week. He sends one thousand birthday cards a year, mails six hundred copies of *MONY Points*, and puts ads in the Civic Theatre and Summer Stock Theatre programs to keep his name before the public. An often overlooked source from which Don gets many prospects is his own mailing list. By watching for address changes, Don was able to sell four mortgage policies in one month! From term conversions came thirty-three per cent of his production in 1963, twenty-five per cent of his production in 1964, and twenty per cent of his production by September of 1965. Don gleans most of his new prospects from young college graduates who are now in the business field and who will increase their programs as the years pass. And over seventy per cent of his business is on his old policyholders whom he calls on regularly. He keeps a continuous check on these other sources: Policy record card file, age changes, birthday books, and purchase options.

Armed with a qualified prospect, Don's next step is to get a yes answer for an interview. At the interview Don establishes the financial ability of each prospect to spend additional money. Most of Don's sales result from using a "Family Program Kit" for package selling to fulfill these needs: Quick cash fund, readjustment fund, mortgage cancellation, or income for the critical income period of the family. The sale will depend on the importance the prospect places on a particular need. Don says that "we can usually spend his present insurance on one or two needs and then go right into the next most important one."

Don does a lot of package selling. He believes it is an excellent method, because it is simple and easily understood; it is quick and not complex; it readily enables Don to obtain his goal of three or four paid-for applications a week; it keeps him on a planned activity schedule; it eliminates time-consuming color charts and diagrams, and yet it gives him an entree to simple programming.

You can read Don's entire sales talk in the *Proceedings of the 1964 Million Dollar Round Table,* so we will only briefly mention two points of it here. Don always asks the prospect how much he can save rather than how much he can spend. And for the beginning of his close, Don refers back to the amount the prospect says he can save. If the prospect objects, Don reverts to the advantages of the contract. "Let objections go over your head. In other words, don't argue yourself out of a sale," Don emphasizes. Don also tries to stress the importance of first covering the prospect's needs before showing him what the contract will provide at age 65 in addition to his Social Security, company pension, etc.

Don has always been generous in sharing his ideas with others. His articles have appeared in the 1957 *Life Insurance Salesman,* the 1957 *Life Leaders,* the 1964 Million Dollar Round Table publications, the 1964 *National Underwriter,* and the 1964 *Diamond Life Bulletin.*

What do others say of this exceptional young man? Dan Starmann, Agency Cashier, gets directly to the point with his description of Don:

Deeply religious in background, thoughts and action. A perfectionist in every way—in his personal, family, social, and business life. Very humble and modest, yet egotistical, but just to a beautifully palatable degree. Demanding, but generously considerate and thoughtful of others; kind to everyone. Absolutely dependable in any and all commitments. Forceful, determined, and merciless on himself to make goals, to succeed in a big way, provided it is deserved, earned, and without favors, without shortcuts of any kind, without evading or breaking any rules, or taking advantage of anyone else. A stickler on details. Painfully honest in every way and with everyone with whom he comes in contact. Insists upon having a personal knowledge and understanding of necessary technical information and of all Company rules and requirements. Keeps up on all changes. Generous with his time and activities to help others in his agency, his company, and community: Jr. Chamber of Commerce, First Congregational Church Board of Trustees, hospital drives, former Vice President, P.T.A., speaker at Million Dollar Round Table, Michigan Sales Congress, numberless meeting programs of Life Underwriter Associations, local and national level, agency meetings of his own Company at local and national level.

Don's minister, Dr. William A. Keith of the First Congregational Church describes Don as "one of those personable, warm people who communicates easily with other people. As I have observed him, he may excel where others fail just by sheer hard work, seeking out every lead and following it up." Don and his family regularly attend Church, and he has served on the Board of Trustees and Chairman of the Finance Committee.

Thus Don Charnley emerges as a many sided man—one whose pattern of living has made for him a life of benefit not only to himself but also to the many people he serves.

At the climax of his M.D.R.T. address, Don gave this pattern in an admonition to us all:

Finally, you must know yourself, your family, and your associates, your clients and your fellow men; and you must trust in God, for in our business more than in any other, God is our Partner. Be fair with him, and he will be more than fair with you. Love and serve people, and, if you sincerely do, they will buy from you again and again. They will respect you and make your associations through life happy and prosperous ones. Thus, as I lay out my work from day to day, I look forward to carrying out these plans. And the Bible tells us that, "As a man thinketh in his heart, so is he."

CHAPTER 9

WILLIAM E. CHOATE, C.L.U.

COULD YOU set up your schedule a year in advance: Bill Choate not only can but does, for he almost has to. He sold over $11,000,-000 in 1964, $8,000,000 in 1965, and will write close to $12,000,000 in 1966. A highly regarded young corporate executive, Bill also serves as First Vice President of the Allen T. Archer Co. where he is the principal in their Life Insurance Department. This is a prominent Los Angeles firm of insurance brokers in which all of the principals of this Company hold either the C.P.C.U. or the C.L.U. degree. Bill also serves his community as an active member of various boards and civic organizations. For recreation, he and his wife, Mary, spend their hours at tennis and paddle tennis.

Bill entered the insurance business in 1956 with the New England Life, and his very first year's production was $1,200,000. He continued to be one of their leading producers over the years, and set their all-time company production record in 1964.

After graduating from Stanford University in 1953 with a B.A. Degree in Economics, he served three years as an officer in the U.S. Navy where he completed a number of legal and insurance courses. He has worked diligently and studied hard ever since, and attained his C.L.U. degree in 1959. Since that time, he has become one of the best known and most respected young men on the West Coast, specializing in the corporate market.

Today the Allen T. Archer Co. serves as General Agents for the National Life of Vermont with Bill Choate as its principal. The Archer Co. demonstrates one of the rare instances where a complete professional insurance service is rendered by one firm. This Company provides excellent counsel and guidance for the client's entire insurance needs, handling virtually all phases of general and life insurance both on business as well as personal matters.

The brochure given to policyholders and prospects describing the Archer Co. is one of the finest we have ever seen. Its layout and text demonstrates without a doubt that this firm is the epitome of professional excellence. Its services are too numerous to name, but it provides analysis, programming, and competitive placement for all types of coverage. Bill's work as First Vice President in charge of the Life and Pension Departments is concerned with all areas of corporate dollar as well as personal insurance planning. For example, the function of the Life Insurance Department is "to work in close harmony with our client's lawyer, accountant, and other advisors in arranging a program to attain his personal and business objectives." Then the additional services and continuing services are described in detail. After reading this brochure and listening to a description of the firm, you almost know that you wouldn't want to talk to another insurance organization concerning any of your insurance needs. You can't help but think to yourself, "This firm is for me. They can provide whatever I need." The brochure itself sells while appearing not to sell at all, and it is done in such a way that you want to do business with Bill and the Archer Co. Working jointly with the other departments, Bill has achieved coordination to an extent that is very unusual in a firm of this size. It has been developed in such a way that the firm, in most instances, handles the client's entire insurance needs.

About 70% of Bill's time is spent in the corporate dollar area and the balance in personal and estate planning. In addition, he has a number of group insurance cases and does a substantial amount of pension and profit sharing planning. Since all members of the firm work together as a team, certain of Bill's clients are referrals who come to the firm for complete service of their insurance needs. In contacting individuals, Bill's approach is to explain his function in the Company and to offer his services in the area the prospect may have a problem. This procedure is followed by a fact finding interview, written proposals, and arrangement of a sound insurance program. All clients are approached at least once a year through personal contact or letter, depending upon the needs of that client. This firm delivers the services they have promised. They make it a point to keep up with their clients throughout the year and maintain routine contact through their own newsletter, as well as specialized tax letters.

Bill, being a very intelligent and well-organized life insurance man, has constantly endeavored to study in order to keep abreast of all current developments. Obviously, his tremendous production shows that he can handle the most complicated situations. In fact, he has been able to master every situation in which he has found himself in the field of life insurance, often turning to recognized leaders such as Ben Stern, Howard Neal, and Bob Lawthers, for inspiration and knowledge.

He also ferrets out the patterns of other successful insurance men and uses their ideas and patterns of operation, and he strongly recommends this to the newer life insurance agent. Naturally, these thoughts should be adapted to the young man's individual situation and meshed with his own ideas and approaches to life insurance problems.

Bill emphasizes that a young man should never apologize for being a life insurance salesman, because the life insurance business is a profession, and the newer agent must not forget this. Bill has certainly contributed his part in making it so through his many talks before Life Insurance Underwriters Associations as well as the Million Dollar Round Table.

Several years ago, Bill devised a basic estate planning presentation that he refers to as his Coordinated Estates Proposal. Although a majority of his efforts are now expended in the corporate dollar field, he still refers to this as the "bread and butter" business and its format is as applicable today as when Bill was spending all of his time in the personal insurance field. A quote from the last paragraph of this proposal may help you understand why Bill has risen so fast in the life insurance business, and even more important why he can be expected to continue in this rapid growth. "I hope you will think as we do that this program will intelligently preserve your goals for your family. Also, we believe our periodic reviews will be of immeasurable help to you in insuring that you will always be obtaining the best of advice and service." The Allen T. Archer Co. is certainly striving to do this in all its operations.

Their repeated sales to policyholders as well as their yearly increasing new sales seem to say: "Bill, you have attained your purpose!"

CHAPTER 10

DONALD H. CRAWFORD, C.L.U.

FROM a fire and casualty agent to a million dollar life and pension agent is a quick summary of Donald H. Crawford's life, thus far. The third generation of an outstanding life insurance family from Toronto, Canada, Donald is now aiming for two million dollars of production.

Donald entered the life insurance business on a full time basis after having a casualty license for seven years and writing an average volume of $350,000 of life insurance each year on the side. He eventually decided that he could not do justice to both life and casualty insurance, so he became a full time life agent. "I only wish I had decided to do so much earlier," Donald recently told us. "It is my firm belief that there is so much to learn in both businesses, it is impossible for one to do the best possible job for his clients and himself, while trying to do both. It is exactly the same as a doctor practicing medicine and dentistry, or a lawyer attempting to practice law and accounting, at the same time."

Donald says that he chose life insurance as a career mainly because his father had had a most successful and enjoyable career in the business, and Donald believed that he too could have some success in it. The fire and casualty field was too slow for Donald and did not offer him the same feeling of accomplishment. In addition, he liked dealing in human life values rather than buildings and cars. Finally, Donald knew that the income from selling life insurance was as good and that it came quicker.

Thus Donald and his father formed the partnership of Crawford and Crawford. Ninety-five per cent of Donald's business is secured by his own efforts while approximately five per cent consists of split cases which he and his father work on together. Mr. S. Hume Crawford, Donald's father, has been a life insurance agent with Manufacturers Life for over forty-five years and he is considered to have one of the best approaches and closes in life underwriting. During his fully active years he wrote up to three million a year. Donald's grandfather, also an outstanding agent for Manufacturers Life, makes three generations of agents from one family in this company, something which had never before occurred. Donald appears to have inherited his father's ability to approach a prospect for Donald has a knack for obtaining information from people concerning their affairs, mainly by asking questions. He is usually able to get the facts quite easily, perhaps because he is very sincere regarding the prospect's affairs and the life insurance business.

Donald's immediate goal on becoming a full time life underwriter was to earn a lot more money than he was making in the fire and casualty field, although his casualty business was growing nicely, but slowly. His long range goal was to make the Million Dollar Round Table. But to Donald "this seemed so far away that I did not think too much about it." Now that he is a member of the Million Dollar Round Table, and the Two Million Dollar Club his goal is to make the Big Three "by working smarter but not harder." Donald credits Mr. W. J. H. Chittick, Toronto Manager for Manufacturers Life, with helping him over the MDRT hurdle.

Donald finds that a great deal of his business is done with people he meets through clubs. He is a member of the Granite Club, the Georgian Peaks Ski Club, the Toronto Board of Trade, Kappa Alpha Alumni Society, Lambton Golf and Country Club, and the St. Clair Reservoir Angling and Upland Game Club. He finds this a most enjoyable way to prospect and in 99.9% of the calls he makes to people he has met through these avenues, he receives a most hearty welcome. "I have tried to work on an extremely low pressure basis, so that I could not be criticized for using the clubs for business. It has certainly paid off, for I have many friends who approach me with their life insurance or pension problems, and with referred leads," says Donald.

Perhaps the comments of Donald's secretary may explain part of his prospecting success. She notes that "Mr. Crawford is an attractive man with a dynamic personality, very popular with both sexes. He is not fond of routine office work, but is very able in selling life insurance and pensions."

To secure an interview, Donald uses the most direct method possible. "I call the prospect on the telephone and ask him for an appointment. There are no frills or deceptions, and I rarely fail to get an interview with anyone that I call. If the prospect says he has an agent looking after him, and I know the agent is a good one, I thank the prospect and hang up. If the prospect hesitates, I sincerely say I would just like to meet him even though we cannot do any business. I find there are very few businessmen in our city who do not have the courtesy to let you introduce yourself to them."

On the first interview, Donald's aim is to get the prospect's confidence, and then subsequently have the prospect relate his situations. Donald does this by asking leading questions, which as far as he is concerned, is the only successful method of obtaining the facts. After the prospect has told Donald about himself and his views and aims, Donald then tries to sell the prospect on an analysis of his estate or his business insurance or his pension problems. If the prospect agrees for Donald to do this, he fills out a form or information sheet, securing all the necessary data. Donald keeps the survey he prepares as simple as possible so that the prospect can understand it as he goes over it with him. "We have found that, if the survey is complicated, the prospect will ask us to leave it with him to study which leads to further procrastination by the prospect, and we lose the opportunity of selling him on the first selling interview."

During the past two years Donald has been specializing in group pension plans, and his secretary is now able to do many of the calculations for these plans besides completing the proposal.

To the young agent just entering the business, Donald would say: "Do not be over-anxious for sales, but aim toward developing a clientele. Help young people buy as much level term as they want, because most of it will be converted later on. If possible, steer away from selling reducing term or family income, for it is not a good contract, both from the standpoint of the client and yourself. Many young agents will try to steer a prospect away from term when it is the correct plan for him. Always help him buy what you would buy, if you were selling yourself and in a like position as the prospect. Join as many clubs and associations as possible, so that you will get to know good prospects; however, do not spread yourself too thin. Really learn our business and continue to study it, for without increasing your knowledge you will eventually reach a standstill."

Donald believes that one of the greatest handicaps most men have when they enter life insurance selling is the inability to express themselves adequately. Expecting to go into the insurance business upon graduation from college, Donald took at college general courses in psychology, philosophy, economics, calculus, actuarial science, and one English course. Donald now believes that, if he had taken more English courses, he would be better able to get his ideas across to prospects and client. He feels that the ability to express oneself really well is a tremendous advantage in any type of selling.

To an agent at a standstill in his career, Donald would suggest that "he forget about looking for volume and start looking for methods to increase the commission per thousand (e.g., Single Premium Immediate Annuity business). He should study his operation and find exactly why he is at a standstill. Talking to older and more successful agents to find out what they did to keep moving and to increase their success, and learning to work smarter instead of harder, may also enable an agent to get moving again."

Donald's father had a specific method for curing slumps, a method Donald has used successfully. He recommended this exact procedure:

(1) Clean out your desk.
(2) Clean up any loose ends on cases you have closed.
(3) Write out a list of all the good prospects you have, showing the amount of business you expect from each.
(4) Start going after them, working as consistently as possible.

Donald adds that the best feeling he receives from this business is not from closing a case, but from doing a good day's work, even without obtaining any business immediately. "We all know that if we do a full day's work, using some common sense and intelligence, that day's work must eventually produce some business."

Donald says he gets his drive to succeed mainly from the need for money, so that he and his family may live in the manner they wish. "The product that we sell cannot be questioned as to its usefulness and goodness to the public in general, and to the father in particular. Therefore, I believe any drive I have comes from a desire to increase my family's standard of living. We, in the life insurance business, are so fortunate that often we forget it. If we work harder, or smarter, it just naturally follows that we increase our income and subsequently our family's standard of living, and at the same time we are helping others. This is not true of many other jobs, positions, or professions."

Aside from success as a life underwriter, Donald is also a keen sportsman, an interest shared by his wife, Joan, and their five children which include twin boys. They have a ski cabin which is located ninety miles north of Toronto at Collingwood, Ontario, and they spend week-ends there during January, February, and March. In addition, they have just purchased a beautiful six acre island, three hundred miles north of Toronto, on Lake Temagami, one of Canada's best known fishing and camping areas. They are considering remodeling an old trapper's cabin there and plan to build a main cottage in the near future. For each of the past six years they have spent at least three weeks of the summer vacationing in this wonderful area.

In addition to these vacations, Donald and his wife usually ski for ten days during the winter at Stowe or Sugar Bush, and he fishes in Northern Canada for a week in the spring with friends of the St. Clair Reservoir Angling and Upland Game Club.

These sporting vacations of Donald's are not always all play and no work. One of these vacations did yield Donald's biggest volume case, although by no means his largest commission case.

I knew of two partners who needed a substantial amount of life insurance on a cross purchase in conjunction with a buy and sell agreement. One of them showed some interest when I was able to see him only briefly, but I could not get the two of them together to sit down and review the facts. After trying to see them for over six months without success, I went on a holiday for three weeks in Temagami. The fact that I was unable to get in to see them to- gether was preying on my mind, even while I was enjoying good fishing. I decided I would phone via radio telephone and ask for an appointment and for some reason, when I mentioned I was calling via radio phone, the senior partner was impressed. I arranged to fly down to Toronto, via amphibian, and left the island about 6 A.M.

the next morning, arriving back the same night. I was pretty excited, having placed $550,000 of business insurance on the two partners, plus $50,000 of personal insurance on the senior man. The actual interview took no more than one hour.

You know what they say: "Where there's a will, there's a way." And Donald has certainly shown that he has the will—and the way!

CHAPTER 11

EDWARD T. DANIEL

"I HEARD A DYING MAN PLEAD for the product I was selling, but I couldn't deliver it. I am thankful he can't look back and see what happened to his youngest son and widow. The son lost one million dollars of income and the 58 year old widow doesn't have one cent of income. These people were my father, mother, and brother."

Dedicated to seeing that others do not suffer in like circumstances, Ed Daniel has written over a million dollars of life insurance every year that he has been in the business, including his first year.

Both his past and present read like a modern-day Horatio Alger; in fact his very life, both past and present, contain motivating stories that all insurance men can call upon in their sale of life insurance. This young man and his family represent to his prospects everything that the life insurance business and life insurance property exemplify.

To understand how Ed goes about his everyday business of life insurance, we must first delve into Edward Daniel's past. He was born and reared on a farm in the hills of Tennessee. He stayed there for thirteen years, and during these thirteen years he knew nothing but poverty, and when we say poverty we mean it in the worst way. He attended a little country grammar school which was located four miles from his home. There were few days he went to school that he wasn't laughed at or criticized by his schoolmates, because of the clothes he wore and the food that his family couldn't give him for his noonday lunch. There was one time during the winter when he was forced to walk to school in six inches of snow without soles on his shoes.

This background of a young boy growing up in poverty has caused him to believe and to understand the great benefits of life insurance as we all know it today. His family's miseries started during the depression, when his father lost the dry goods business he had strived hard to build. Somehow, because of the collapse of the stock market and of his business, Ed's father lost some of the things we need in this life in order to have the will to win; so he took refuge on a farm back in the hills of Tennessee.

Thirteen years after Ed was born, his father decided that life wasn't so bad after all, and he started over again as the manager of a dry goods store in Earle, Arkansas. When the family moved to Earle, there was new hope and a promise of a happier life to Ed and his brothers. This was not true, however, in the case of Ed's mother. Because of the horrible beating she had taken in the past years, she could not get accustomed to the move from the country to the city. She developed a negative mental attitude toward everything; and this was something else that Ed and his brothers had to overcome.

Then Ed entered high school and his ability on the football field made him somebody for the first time in his life. When Ed finished four years of high school football, however, he found escape in the Korean situation, and he didn't graduate from high school. His mother had repeatedly told Ed that he would never graduate from high school or do anything. Nevertheless, while he was in the service, he did finish high school.

And he had plenty of time to decide just what he wanted to get out of life. He wanted a college education, and because he wanted to prove to his family that he was a man and could do things, he decided to graduate from college in two and a half years. And he did. He took a four year college course in two and a half years at the University of Arkansas and finished with a "B" average, and received the Outstanding Senior Award; and for those two and a half years he also lettered in football.

With this brief background, you can see why Ed Daniel believes in life insurance. We talk about educational policies, and we talk about savings. If Ed's father had been able to save through life insurance, young Ed and his mother and family could, no doubt, have had a childhood and a home life that was filled with pleasant memories instead of horrible nightmares. This early life gave Ed a deep compassion for people and especially a deep conviction that widows and orphans should have a right to "walk in the sunshine with their heads up." Ed has been able to do something about these beliefs in his life insurance programs for others.

After graduation from the University of Arkansas, Ed had another goal and purpose in life. He joined the Pan American Life Insurance Company and decided to finish his Company's salary plan with more money than any other previous agent. This he did, even though during this period of time he lost a business that cost him everything he had and his $25,000 home burned to the ground. Instead of quitting, he grew that much more determined to overcome everything that had happened to him, both past and present.

Here is a young man who entered the life insurance business in 1959 and made the Million Dollar Round Table in 1960, 1961, 1962, 1963, 1964, 1965 and 1966; and believe it or not, for his first full year in business which was from June 1959 to May 31, 1960, he wrote $1,200,000.

Ed had a purpose and goal. And four years later, he had a farm; he had Tennessee walking horses; he had cattle, and he had a life's dream. As a small boy he had always had to walk; today he rides in a Cadillac. But money is not Ed's sole goal; he feels that through life insurance, he is giving a greater service to mankind, than he is gaining personally through his commission statement.

I quote from a letter I received from Ed:

When I say life insurance, may I tell you one more story that will explain to you what life insurance really means to me and what really put me in the life insurance business. It is a good story about a grand little man and a little woman who are walking down the street called "the lonely street that has no end." This little man who, because of being uninformed and never stopping to think, or maybe too weak to make decisions for himself and for his family, let his wife make decisions, and the decisions were always, "No, we can't afford it," or "We don't need it." I received a letter from this little woman sometime ago telling me she was sorry for the mistakes she had made. She congratulated me for what I was doing and what I had accomplished.

This little man and woman are my father and mother. You see, my father entered the Veterans Hospital in Memphis, Tennessee on June 1, 1960, and died June 12, 1960. It was a horrible death, and I pray

54

to God his soul will rest in peace. I am thankful he can't look back and see what happened to his youngest son and widow: The son lost one million dollars in future income because he was forced to drop out of the University of Tennessee, just when he had started working on his degree in Medicine. He was going to be a doctor of internal medicine. The widow doesn't have one cent of income; she is only 58. She worked for my daddy in the store as long as he lived, but after he died Mr. Employer fired her, because he didn't want to be reminded of the fact that he was so cheap he wouldn't provide employee benefits.

I will never forget the day when my father died, not only because I lost my father, but because this was the day I really became dedicated to the life insurance business with all my heart; because, for the first time, I heard a dying man plead for the product I was selling, and I couldn't deliver it. As he was lying there in bed under an oxygen tent, he jumped up and grabbed me and said, "Theo, get the doctor—I can't get my breath! I am going to die! What will Mamma and Billy do?" Then, I watched him slowly grasp for his last breath and pass on into peace, but not with dignity and self-respect the way he would have wanted to die. With all due respect I have for my father, he failed miserably by not doing what he should have done the last thirty years, and that was saving one dollar a day or more and putting it into a life insurance policy—in order that he could have retired at age 65 and enjoyed the last few years of his life, in order that his son who had washed dishes in college for six years could have completed his education, in order that his widow could have lived on with dignity and pride. Yes, life insurance could have given him dignity and self-respect in these last few moments of life. Thank God for the life insurance business which makes possible my purpose—financial security and abundance.

Life insurance and the life insurance business have become Ed Daniel's cause in life. For this cause he has broken one record after another and his income is now one of the highest incomes of any young man in the United States with only six years of life insurance selling behind him.

Now, how did he begin selling? Ed made phone calls to referred leads. When making a call, he introduced himself and stated his business. He qualified himself by showing the prospect information on the Million Dollar Round Table and other material such as his "Man of the Year" brochure from the Company, etc., that would let the cold prospect know that he is a man worth talking to. He showed examples of services and work he had done for other people and the benefits that had occurred by his work. He always made written proposals and prepared estate surveys. He sent out birthday cards and followed them up from year to year; and, yes, he also worked four nights a week, and he spent two hours a day planning for the next day. He set up at least ten calls each day with at least four of these closing interviews. In order to get four closes he had to see seven people, and at the end of each week he tallied his records up to find out if he was on his mark.

Today, Ed Daniel is President of Pro-Pen, Inc., which is a company serving as consultants and providing actuarial services to employers on pensions, profit sharing plans, and employee saving plans. One hundred per cent of his business is now from pensions and profit-sharing plans, and he is assisted in this complicated work by his vice-president and counsel, tax attorney Milton W. Schober. Pro-Pen, Inc. is not bound to any insurance company and neither is Ed. He works on a fee basis in most cases.

What advice would this young man, who has paid the price to become a real success in our business, give to new agents? "Start with a rugged work schedule—at least ten calls per day— and stay with it. I would also advise him to educate his wife to the fact that she can make him or break him by not cooperating with him. I would advise him to start keeping records from the start and learn to control his time by having set times for everything and not to deviate."

If anyone's life could be put into a modern day Horatio Alger book, here is the top candidate. If you knew what Ed's income was last year it would be difficult for you to believe that only six years earlier this young man had had to work his way through college. Ed Daniel's life exemplifies the height of material achievement after coming from the very depths of material deprivation and hopelessness.

But this is only half of the story. Ed's life also exemplifies the finest spiritual qualities. Do you know that this young man goes to the Chapel which is in his building and thanks God at least once a day for being blessed with a wonderful wife, a fine family, and also the ability to help other people put their savings into the product that his mother and father needed so greatly but never were convinced that they should buy.

To be in a position to be able to recommend the life insurance that will exactly fulfill their needs, Ed studies hard to stay abreast of the latest techniques, and his friends say he buys more life insurance services and books himself than most entire agencies buy. Although he is successful, he continues to study, to build up his library, to read, to listen to motivating records, and to really spur himself into continuous action. He knows each hour of the day where he is going, whom he is going to call on, and what he is going to say.

You might think from what has been said here that Ed at first made all of his sales right from the cuff using motivational approaches, but he nearly always prepared written surveys; and his favorite approach was simply this: "Do you own your estate, or are you just leasing it?" If a man said he owned it, then Ed told him, "Well that is wonderful, but if you own it, why let the Government take 40% of it at your death?" The prospect usually asked, "What the heck do you mean?" And then Ed told him that if he did not have proper planning through life insurance, wills, etc. the Government would take as much as 40% of the estate for Federal Estate taxes. From that point on, he went into an estate tax approach and ended up asking for a financial statement, policies, and other necessary information.

Mr. W. S. Ray, one of Ed's policyholders is a well known real estate developer and contractor of Shreveport. He tells me that Ed planned his estate and showed him the many, many advantages of life insurance as a tax saving vehicle for estate taxes, and that he will be forever indebted to Ed for passing on to him his expert knowledge of the life insurance business.

Mr. Ray was especially impressed, when Ed's service did not end with the sale. With such continuing service and advice long after the sale, Mr. Ray says he is "always happy to refer my friends to Ed Daniel." What finer recommendation can one have than that of his policyholders!

Ed Daniel in a very short time—1959 to 1966—has become one of the great life insurance men in his State and has moved from the simple motivational sales to doing 100% of his business in the pension and profit-sharing area as President of Pro-Pen, Inc.

CHAPTER 12

DANNY DELL

"THE ONLY WAY to reach the top is to start climbing," observed Danny Dell recently. And since entering the insurance business in Cincinnati in 1954 to write $800,000, Danny's climb upward has never ceased. Today as a M.D.R.T. member, Danny writes a large number of lives, works hard, has fun, and is making a name for himself from the third floor of the Carew Tower, Cincinnati's tallest building.

His ability to sell is spectacular. Last year he made sales on over 100 different lives, and from the very beginning he has written in excess of 100 lives every year. He does this by having a pattern and by sheer hard work. He makes on the average seven telephone calls a day and works fifty hours a week.

Here in detail is Danny Dell's work pattern: He gets his prospects from direct mail, referred leads, personal observation, and friends; and from these sources he makes forty telephone calls a week for appointments. From these forty calls he gets an average of seven appointments and four sales. The interviews, appointments, and sales are obtained mostly from young men in their 20's and 30's. Danny feels that the way to become a success is to have a young clientele and grow up with them. And he is proving that this is true.

Danny advises young men just entering the life insurance business to contact a large number of good people and really believe in the law of averages. Work out a law of averages for yourself. In his case, he makes forty calls, gets seven appointments, and knows that four sales are going to result. This, in itself, is security for the life underwriter. Danny gets young men with promise on the books, and he sees them every two years until they own $100,000 of life insurance, or whatever they can handle in their particular financial situation. In other words, he has built and is building a clientele around young men in his age group.

Danny presents his clients with a proposal—nothing complicated—based on the programing concept, i.e., dollars for future delivery; and he tries to explain to his clients the type of plan he feels best suits their needs. His proposal is based around the ledger statement idea in which he has four columns—gross annual premium deposits, yearly increases in cash value, annual dividends, and the yearly cost of the plan. Then he summarizes the return at ages sixty and sixty-five. This is a simple illustration, easy to explain, and one that shows life insurance is good property to own with dollars available for future delivery.

Danny copyrighted a brochure entitled "Inflation, Life Insurance, and You." In a good looking layout, it explains with very simple terms why all of us should own life insurance in spite of increasing inflation.

He follows the book in keeping up with his clientele. He sends out tax letters, birthday cards, and Christmas cards. He takes prospects to lunch, and makes certain that he has telephone follow-ups every six months to two years, depending upon the situations of his clients. In other words, he believes in keeping up with these people to help them complete their insurance programs as their situations change.

Danny is an excellent golfer, and he is well known in Cincinnati for his game. Considerable social, fraternal, and country club exposure over the years, together with favorable publicity in these areas, have created good will and a source of prospects for Danny. "I would hate to be without the business that I have written directly and indirectly from golf, but with rare exceptions do I ever discuss the subject while playing," adds Danny. He has never let golf take the place of work however, for he still averages three night calls a week and fifty hours a week talking with clients and working on their changing situations.

In times of slumps Danny has made it a practice to double activity, spending the most time phoning for appointments. Thus he ends the slump, before it gets a firm hold.

Danny's final advice to the newer insurance man: "Talk at length to dozens of members of the MDRT and build a pattern of living applicable to your own special abilities. Consistency in work habits, properly carried out with dedicated enthusiasm, will bring success in our business to those who really want to succeed."

And Danny has proved that, at least in his case, this is certainly true.

CHAPTER 13

A. R. (BUDDY) DIKE, C.L.U.

MANY FAMOUS ATHLETES must envy Buddy Dike for his success-ful transition from athletic success to career and financial success. Buddy Dike was a college senior when he chose life insurance as a career—a career about which he can say: "The longer I'm in this business, the more excited I get. The opportunities, as I see them, are unlimited."

Buddy's boyhood family consisted of a sister sixteen months his senior and a brother eleven years his junior. His father was and still is an executive for Swift, Incorporated. Upon grad-uating from high school in Oak Park, Illinois, Buddy received a football scholarship to Texas Christian University in Fort Worth, Texas, where he was a member of the All-Conference Team, and captain of the football team in 1958 at T.C.U. Because of his participation in college football, Buddy had an opportunity to meet many people. After graduation from T.C.U. in 1958, Buddy entered the life insurance business in July of that year in Fort Worth. The leadership abilities and competitive spirit which he had already developed in sports now served him well in selling life insurance.

And Buddy has often compared playing football with selling life insurance. As a boy, Buddy loved football as a game; in high school, it got harder, but was still fun. After four years in college and a ruptured kidney, 36 stitches in his leg, and a nose that had been broken several times, football got to be a pretty tough job! Rather than become a professional football player, Buddy decided to sell life insurance. For careful evaluation of several careers made him believe that this one offered him the most opportunities.

"Believe me, those first few years in life insurance were as tough, if not a lot tougher, than football," admits Buddy.

There were many occasions in the early years that Buddy

considered getting out of the business. However, football had taught him that, if you get knocked down, you have to get up and work twice as hard to win. He used this idea successfully in selling.

"There have been bad times as well as good times. But as I have looked at other professions or businesses, whether law, medicine, or business, I realize that all of them require a time of apprenticeship, so I can't complain."

He wrote $1,091,000 his first year and received his Company's award for the leading first year agent in volume. The second year in the business, he attained membership in the Million Dollar Round Table. He received his C.L.U. designation his third year in the business at age 25, and is also a six time National Quality Award winner and a member of Connecticut Mutual's President Club. Last year he wrote over $2,000,000.

Buddy entered the business after graduation from T.C.U., under Connecticut Mutual's SMTP program. "After wandering around for three months, I decided to do what the Company suggested under their Time and Control Plan—so many calls, interviews, etc.—and it worked." At the same time Buddy also decided on a definite Sales Tract. Using this tract he began calling on as many people as he possibly could. The resulting sales—$75,000 in his first week alone—proved to him that a planned sales talk can control the interview.

As sales tools, Buddy was selling packages, using "You'll Earn a Fortune" technique about 80% of the time and the other 20% a programming sales method. He kept adequate records, planned his time, and set definite goals—Production, Income, Education, etc. "I averaged working at least 5½ days a week and two nights a week. Most of my prospects were obtained on a referral basis, with some direct mail. My main source of business came from young married couples and T.C.U. students. Here were the average results of that three years activity."

	Sales	Amount	New Prospects	Calls	Progress	Total Interviews	Service Calls Deliveries
Average Yearly (50 Weeks)	97	$1,223,284	633	1,348	804	315	230
Average Weekly	1.94	24,465	12.60	30	16.08	8	4.60

	Field	Planning	Study	Total
		Hours		
Average Yearly (50 Weeks)	1,324	797	255	2,375
Average Weekly	26.48	15.94	5.10	47.50

Active in the Kiwanis Club, the Breakfast Club, the Frog Club, and the Life Underwriters Association, Buddy is also currently an officer in the Life Underwriters Association, the T.C.U. Ex-Letterman's Club, the T.C.U. Ex-Business Students Club, and a committee chairman in the Downtown Kiwanis Club. Through these clubs Buddy meets many people who later become his clients, although Buddy's primary motivation in these activities is the enjoyment of participation.

Buddy's strongest career area is prospecting. He keeps complete records of what he has done and exactly what he wants to accomplish. To be successful has been a part of Buddy's make-up from his earliest years. Pride and wanting things for his family and himself have been contributing factors. When he first started, Buddy set his goal to write one million dollars of life insurance a year. Since achieving that goal he has continually upgraded his market and the average size of his case, and has averaged about 80 cases a year. His goal now is to sell two million of life insurance and more business insurance and pension plans.

Buddy uses a newsletter called "Business and Estate Topics" with his picture on the front cover. He also uses an approach letter and a telephone call to set up appointments, 90% of which are referred leads.

For handling the initial interview, Buddy usually uses a programming approach, dealing with the various needs for life insurance. He sometimes uses visuals. He solves the client's problems by using an estate analysis procedure, using either forms he has developed or Connecticut Mutual forms. After selling a case, Buddy sets up a permanent file on the client and calls him once every one or two years. About 30% to 40% of his new business comes from clients he has sold over the past six years.

Buddy made ten to twelve calls a day his first year in the business; today he makes four calls a day. He worked six days a week his first year, but now he works five and a half. Ten to fourteen hours made up Buddy's working day his first year; today he works eight to ten hours. His first year he worked four nights a week; now he works two nights a week.

To make two sales before Wednesday is Buddy's simple but effective work pattern. After these sales are made, he can then speculate with business insurance sales. His market is primarily businessmen and young professional men.

Buddy praises both his General Agent, Mr. Thomas Moody, and Mr. C. Frank Eastman, an outstanding Connecticut Mutual producer from Wilkes-Barre, for the help and inspiration that they have given him. He says that his General Agent showed complete confidence in him from the very beginning.

Buddy has spoken at the Omaha Association of Life Underwriters and the Regional Convention of the Connecticut Mutual. In these talks and in the various leaflets published by his company which contain articles by Buddy, he often explains the tremendous opportunities in life insurance for young men. He believes that to be happy and successful in selling life insurance an underwriter needs a definite pattern of operation. This means you must set goals and follow them, keep records, continually prepare yourself with education, prospect upward, and after experience in selling many kinds of prospects, begin to specialize —to pick and choose your prospects.

Buddy also believes that the young life insurance agent should call on large numbers of people and then let the averages work for him. By this, Buddy means that a young agent should call on as many people as he personally must, in order to make the number of sales that he sets for his goal. If a person does not have his own averages worked out, there are averages of other agents available, which a new man can use.

Only seven years in life insurance himself, Buddy Dike, C.L.U., Million Dollar Round Table Member, and consistent winner of the National Quality Award, is already well known for his outstanding achievement. And Buddy strongly believes "no other line of endeavor can offer a man the freedom, independence and satisfaction which can be derived from a life insurance career—if he is willing to work for it!"

CHAPTER 14

KURT J. FIXSEN

KURT J. FIXSEN began his insurance career in Germany with Allianz and Frankfurter, first as a special agent, then as city inspector, and finally as director of agencies. He also served his tour of active duty there as an airborne ranger with the United States Army and met and married his German-born, German-educated wife, Georgine.

He entered the life insurance business in 1957 and has sold more than $1,000,000 of insurance each year since that time. In 1960 Kurt became an agency supervisor for the Continental Assurance Company at their Garden City office. In 1961 he was promoted to Assistant Manager of the Long Island Branch office in Merrick. Finally, in 1962, he was appointed Agency Manager for the Continental Assurance Company with offices at Commack, New York.

Kurt has been the recipient of the National Quality Award and of the Health Insurance Persistency Award for four years, as well as numerous company awards.

Kurt's wife is actively engaged in a brokerage business; most of her contacts are from clients to whom Kurt has sold life insurance. In these contacts with her brokerage business, she has acted many times as a good will ambassador or has set up appointments to make life and A&H sales. In addition to her brokerage business, she has held a life insurance license since 1959, and she handles inquiries and questions as well as service calls for Kurt's life insurance clients.

Socially, Kurt and his wife are engaged in the German American Society of New York City where he has served as First Vice-President. Kurt is also very active in the Masons. He spends considerable time on fund raising activities as a Shriner and is also an officer of his Lodge.

Eighty per cent of Kurt's business is from referred leads and are from no particular market. He has been so successful in acquiring leads that he developed a referred lead questionnaire, which his Company has adopted for the use of all agents. It consists of a glued form 5″ x 7″ which says in effect that you, the policyholder, can help your agent by listing the name, address, phone, approximate age, marital status, and dependents of any friend, relative, acquaintance, or associate who has just married, been recently promoted, bought a new home, moved into town, or become new parents. Kurt now staples this referred lead questionnaire to the application, so that it will serve as a constant reminder. The idea of getting referred leads regularly was hit upon by Kurt when, early in his career, he asked his clients for their personal telephone directory so that he could enter his name and phone number on the appropriate alphabetical page. In doing so, he noticed that these books contained a lot of names, who had to be personal friends of the prospect. It was then that he decided to use this as a normal routine approach and get his referred leads by using this one method.

A typical approach would be, "Mr. Prospect, since you no doubt have already too many business cards and instead of my giving you another one for your collection, I presume that it would be much simplier if I would enter my name in your telephone book. Could I have your personal directory please?" As Kurt is making the entry he asks, "Incidentally, Mr. Prospect, who are these people listed next to my name? I am certain that some of these people would be interested in knowing about the service, that I just performed for you. Would you mind if I call upon some of them and use your name?" This method definitely works; and Kurt not only uses it himself, but he has taught it to new agents when he was a supervisor, and he is still using it today with his agents.

Kurt arrives at his office around 10:00 A.M. each day, and works until mid-afternoon finishing up paper work and setting up appointments. He then leaves for home, often dropping in on policyholders or prospective clients on the way. He leaves again at 6:00 P.M. and returns home at 10:00 P.M. after several appointments.

When Kurt obtains a referred lead, he generally gets information about the time the prospect can be seen and will be home.

Kurt then drops in on him, introduces himself as a friend of Mr. X, and explains briefly the service he performed for the man's friend. Kurt has found that personal appearances work better for him, than calling on the phone.

Kurt does not use any particular visual aid, but he uses what is called a policyowner's service chart, furnished by the Continental Assurance Co.

He keeps in contact with his policyholders by sending a thank you card for the business, then birthday and Christmas cards, and by telephoning them at least once a year.

Aside from the weekly planning booklet, he carries the names of all prospects or clients to be seen on a 3" x 5" card in his shirt pocket, so that he will be constantly reminded. After he has seen the people or taken care of their service work, he places their card back in the file.

Kurt often uses the Graduate Professional Program of the Continental Assurance, which is designed for financing insurance. It works especially well for residents and interns who are sought out as prospects, because of their potential buying power. In the East, especially, these men are approached regularly by life underwriters, and they have developed a defense against them. They have created a shell around themselves. Kurt has developed a very workable way for breaking this shell.

The method he has found most satisfactory and effective is through socializing with these men. He seeks out an intern or resident whom he can develop into a friend. The intern or resident, in turn, invites Kurt to the social functions of the hospital. At these social gatherings, the intern or resident introduces Kurt to other interns and residents. Referrals have always been Kurt's source of prospecting, and referrals in this market are no different than in any other market.

If a young man is considering life insurance as a career, or if he is already an agent and wants to achieve greater success, Kurt's advice is that he take stock of himself and then determine how badly he really wants success or greater success. After he sets his big goal he must break the goal down to weekly requirements, and then go to work and not stop, until these requirements are fulfilled.

Kurt considers his biggest accomplishments as selling more than a million dollars of insurance each calendar year, becoming a member of the Million Dollar Round Table, being the national leader for the Continental Assurance Company in 1960, and receiving the new N.A.L.U. sales award last year.

And these certainly are accomplishments any agent could be very proud of!

CHAPTER 15

HOWARD B. FRANKLIN, C.L.U.

HOWARD FRANKLIN has just completed his first $1,000,000 plus month, January, 1966; yet it was only a little over a year ago that he was hanging between life and death in the intensive care unit of a Chicago hospital. This younger member of the brilliantly working partnership of Schultz, Franklin, and Associates tells us that he had just over a million dollars in 1965 working only about six months because of his illness. But his plans for the future are unlimited. Before we get Howard's own description of his brush with death and the effect it has had on him, however, let's look at his background.

In the partnership of Howard Franklin, C.L.U., with Harry R. Schultz, C.L.U., we have working to the advantage of both the unusual union of an older and phenomenally astute man working with a young and highly energetic man. Harry and Howard formed their partnership on November 1, 1960. And you could almost add "they lived happily ever after," for Howard's description of the partnership reads just this way.

Basically, we operate as individuals, using each other as consultants, and to provide continuity in the business. We have found it extremely useful in larger group cases, business insurance cases, and particularly in pension planning; the ability for the two of us to provide services and knowledge to the client is quite reassuring to the insurance buyer. Last year, because of a serious illness, I was out for five months. Our setup which permits someone to service my clients and follow through on work which I had started was extremely useful.

Really, I think one of the more important aspects is the ability of the two of us to discuss cases and situations before coming up with some avenue of approach. This is a tremendous advantage. In addition, often we'll make an interview together with one of us doing the selling and the other one sitting back and observing the prospect. In this way, we're able to get a good feeling of what his thinking is and pick up any points the other one might have missed. Generally, I do more group business and I usually work up the group proposals as well as the disability insurance, having concentrated a little bit more than Harry in these areas.

Harry himself has set quite an example for Howard to follow, for Harry is a Life Member of the Million Dollar Round Table and has qualified for twenty-three years!

Howard keeps his entire work on a professional level. To be able to do a really professional job, Howard began working on his C.L.U. almost immediately after he became a life insurance agent. And in contrast to most of the other young million dollar producers, Howard lists as his greatest accomplishment in the life insurance field the obtaining of his C.L.U.

This attitude dates back to the professor at the University of Illinois who first interested Howard in life insurance. Howard admits that he was not particularly interested in any professional endeavor until "Dr. Robert Mehr spurred my interest in the field of insurance, at which point I developed excellent grades and a great interest in the field." He graduated in 1951 and received the award as the Outstanding Student of Insurance from the Illinois State Association of Life Underwriters.

Howard gets the greatest per cent of his business from the small business market, but when he started, he "certainly had no specific market." Looking for day time activity with people who came to Chicago for business reasons, he developed a nest of commercial artists. Later he began selling men who had just started in small businesses and since that time he has grown up with his clients.

Howard's sole mailing piece is, as we might expect, the C.L.U.'s *Query*. His first interview is a fact finding session. "You've got to find the problem before you can solve it," he notes. "It is important to consider the problems of the client and to be sympathetic to them, realizing that our product is not the only means of guaranteeing dollars, that there are many other forms of investment. Only one product, life insurance can really give him the guarantees in case of death, however. Be a good listener and let your prospect talk it out, but keep coming back to how you are solving his problem." It is at this point that Howard's greatest abilities come into play. With the facts in hand Howard goes back to his office to lay out and determine what the problem is and the solution to the problem.

The solution is always personalized, never put on forms, so that it will look professional and let the client know it was done specifically for him. Howard points out that he makes a real effort to be sure every proposal put out by his office is on excellent quality paper and typed perfectly.

To close most sales Howard brings the prospect to fully comprehend his problem and the impact on himself and others, if he does nothing about it. Howard then presents his suggestion for solving the problem situation: A life insurance trust with a review of the client's will instruments and a follow through on the legal papers.

Howard's percentage of closing at this interview is a high seventy per cent; his meticulous work and his lucid presentation of it spurs the prospect to take action!

Howard always makes one of these calls a day, and sometimes two. And this pattern has moved his production from $500,000 in 1954, his first full year in the business (when he was having four interviews a day), up to Life and Qualifying Membership in the Million Dollar Round Table.

Howard plans to bring his production to over $2,000,000, and he is doing this by finding more and more clients who can and will upgrade their thinking and aim toward $100,000 to $200,000 of life insurance. "My long range objective is to continue what I am doing, but be able to do it even better and smarter. My whole concept of work is to be able to do it better and not harder." Howard calls 1958, the first year he made the M.D.R.T., the turning point in his career, for this marked the beginning of large cases, especially in the business market.

Howard's own analysis of his particular assets and liabilities is this:

I think I'm smart and at the same time personable; just fairly well organized. I don't believe I'm a particularly charming person. I think I'm tactful in dealing with clients; just fairly persuasive, determined to see that the client does do what is best for him. I'm quite diplomatic and try to be a clear thinker; not as self-disciplined as I would like to be. My will to win could be greater—greater incentive. I'm fairly self-reliant, not too colorful. I'm willing to work long hours but don't have the tendency to do so. I am sincere, which I feel is extremely important, and I have a belief in the product we offer. I am knowledgeable, honest and trustworthy.

To keep at consistent top production, Howard must continually overcome discouragements, but Howard has a sure cure for all of them in hard work: "If you're not very busy and don't have enough people to see, work harder. If you get a medical underwriting rejection, work harder. Or if you were riding along, believing you had the business in the bag, and you didn't, work harder. Hard work will help you overcome these things, because enough activity will prevent you from making the mistake of putting all your eggs in one basket."

And Howard is far from putting all of his eggs in one basket, even outside his business. For relaxation he does a great deal of reading, including novels non-historical in nature. He also enjoys camping and tries to spend at least two to three weeks a year under canvas. He prefers to camp in remote sites with few people in the surrounding area.

Generally, about a week of this camping is with his family, his wife Elayne and their three children—Jody, age 10, Karen, age 7, and Marianne, age 3. Elayne was Howard's high school sweetheart and they also attended the University of Illinois together before they married. Howard says Elayne "maintains an excellent home, is an outstanding mother to the children, and works hard for her favorite charities."

All of this seems like a perfect kind of life to lead, doesn't it? But only a little over a year ago Howard was in the intensive care unit of a Chicago hospital. He had been rushed to the hospital from the same doctor's office where only three days before he had been given a clean bill of health with a suspected bleeding ulcer that had hemorrhaged. He developed pneumonia and a temperature of 104, and the last thing the doctors wanted to do was to operate. But finally the doctors had no choice. Howard was losing blood faster than they were able to replace it.

The operation lasted seven and a half hours, and confirmed a bleeding ulcer, and Howard was put in the intensive care unit. Here watched day and night by three nurses and a doctor, with the glaring lights, the moans and the horrible sounds of death, around him, Howard reached a moment of truth.

For the first several days there, I really didn't know what was going on and I really didn't care.

By the third night, the sedation had been reduced and my head cleared. I knew everything that was going on that night and the next day, and it wasn't pretty.

A man in his early forties was on the left of me. He received the last rites of the Catholic church early in the evening. He was delirious all night long. Sometime toward early morning he died.

All night, I heard a slapping noise—I didn't know what it was. It bothered the dickens out of me.

Later, I was told that a young housewife had taken an overdose of sleeping pills. She was brought into the hospital black as coal from toxic poisoning. The nurses were slapping her all night to keep her awake. By the time I left the room the next afternoon, she was sitting up and eating.

There was another man, middleaged, a few beds away on the right of me. He had undergone open heart surgery and was receiving constant attention. There was some device attached to him— probably a heart pacer.

The only other patient was a man close to eighty. He seemed to be quite comfortable, except that he kept asking for his brandy. He wasn't allowed any. I guess intensive care didn't have a liquor license.

At this point, I began to take inventory. My mind was clear enough to know that some of us weren't going to come out of this room alive and I was scared. I had heard a Catholic father give the last rites, seen a minister come into the room to attend to someone. Fortunately, I didn't see a Rabbi around because that would have really shook me up, for I am Jewish. I knew I was pretty sick. Just how sick I wasn't told, until sometime after I had left the hospital.

Each November, I review my insurance—all facets of it.

This last November, I had determined that I had adequate life insurance. My life insurance was set up in an insurance trust, using a corporate trustee and a pour-over provision in my will. The will makes full use of the marital deduction.

My renewals were set up under a spread payment method, wherein the payments would be spread equally over a period of ten years.

Within the trust, I had set up funds for my three daughters to allow them to go through college.

In case I didn't make the grade, I knew that my family would be able to live in much the same manner to which they were accustomed. So this wasn't a worry.

The medical bills, which I knew would be substantial, were being paid for primarily through the MONY group insurance plan. So this wasn't a worry.

In case I was ill for a long period of time, the loss of income wouldn't be crippling. Our deferred method of compensation of renewals and efficiency income would provide me with a substantial monthly income.

Besides, I did have an adequate disability program. In fact, in November, I thought there was a weakness here and I provided additional coverage with a company outside of Mutual of New York as I already had the maximum MONY would offer. This coverage provides first day hospital benefits. So, here again, this wasn't a worry.

What I want to emphasize is that I had provided the economic security that our product can offer.

Needless to say, at my age 35, I haven't been particularly concerned about the problem of retirement. It is interesting to note, if the contributions by myself and the company to the Mutual of New York Pension Plan should remain at the present level with no increases, and based on a 4% rate of interest, in 30 years, when I'm 65, my pension will have a value in excess of $210,000.00.

Recently, I heard Dr. David Gregg, President of the American College, use the Latin definition of security as, "without care."

Were the people on either side of me in the intensive care unit "without care" economically? Had they been prepared? Had some life insurance man sought them out and sold them on the values of our product? If not, they would have three strikes against them to begin with.

Strike 1—They would be worried about how their families would get along financially in case of their death.

Strike 2—They would be worried about how they were going to pay these tremendous medical bills. Unless you have major medical, no hospitalization coverage is going to pick up any sizable portion of this type of bill.

Strike 3—They would be worried about where income for self and family would come from in case of prolonged disability.

I laid there—certainly concerned about my family—but I knew I had done everything economically feasible that I could and I was able to concentrate only on getting better. I had purchased financial peace of mind.

Like everything else, you've got to fight. When you're laying there, very weak, you must have the desire and concern only of getting better, without the three strikes that many people have against them.

Once you're lying there, thinking about this under circumstances of death being really close to you, it's too late.

You've got to prepare now. You've got to make that will. You've got to analyze your needs and somehow, someway, fill them.

And if you do it for yourself, you've got to give the people you're calling on that same opportunity.

Can a more sincere and eloquent plea than this be made for the sale of life insurance?

CHAPTER 16

JOE GANDOLFO, C.L.U.

AT AGE ELEVEN Joe Gandolfo, C.L.U., lost both parents and felt the full impact of what life insurance can do—it paid for food, clothing, and an education for him and his two brothers through military school and college. This experience made Joseph M. Gandolfo a dynamic and loyal supporter of the benefits of life insurance. In fact helping others to see what insurance could do for them propelled Joe at such a rapid pace that in his very first year he wrote $1,990,000—$1,200,000 of it during his first six months—for an income of over $18,000. We know of no one else who can lay claim to that kind of production in their first year.

How did Joe do it? Warning us that he originally chose the life insurance business, because it enabled him to do something every minute of the day, we were nevertheless unprepared for the statistics he gave of his first year's work: Joe worked eighteen hours a day to have twenty-five interviews each week, and he did this seven days a week. Hard work, yes; but look at this first year's production and pay—almost two million for over eighteen thousand! Where else would hard work pay off so handsomely?

Joe has now cut his work day to fifteen or sixteen hours, four and a half days a week for ten interviews a week. However, he has continuously upped his production and goals. He paid for $2,200,000 on 245 lives in 1963. He paid for $2,700,000 on 236 lives in 1964; and in 1965 he paid for 5,110,000 on 410 lives. For the first part of 1966 he had written $5,000,000 on 380 lives. His early goals included becoming a C.L.U., a member of the M.D.R.T., winning the National Quality Award, and writing 100 lives a year before the age of thirty. He qualified for the M.D.R.T. in 1963, 1964, 1965, and in 1966; he qualified for the National Quality Award in 1962, 1963, 1964, 1965 and 1966;

and he received his C.L.U. designation in 1965. Having passed all of these milestones, he is now aiming toward five hundred lives a year and $10,000,000 production.

Why does he set and make these goals? Joe describes the reason as pride. How does he do it? By methods he describes as simple. And this pride, simplicity in methods, and hard work as an insurance agent netted Joe Gandolfo an immediate $18,000! And what kind of background inspires Joe to set and accomplish these high aspirations? For one thing Joe credits his four years of military school which taught him self-discipline, "for this self-discipline plays an important part in my success today."

Other factors in his years of education were also important. He went on to attend Vanderbilt and graduated from Miami of Ohio in 1958 with a B.S. degree in math. While in college, he also played football and baseball, and signed with the Dodgers upon graduation. Even though he had to give up pro ball later because of an arm injury, Joe says it served its purpose: "Playing football and baseball taught me how to win and lose."

At Miami of Ohio Joe met his wife, Carol Lorentz, who graduated Magna Cum Laude from the University and has since had three young Gandolfos—Michael Alan, Diane and Donna. Today she also plays brilliant tennis, and helped build their home which is situated in the middle of orange and grapefruit trees in Lakeland, Florida. In his address to the M.D.R.T. Joe calls Carol "a very valuable asset and a very valuable part of my ball club. She takes care of the home. She writes all of the checks. If the washing machine or dryer breaks down, she makes sure that it's repaired. She sees that the lawn gets mowed; she takes care of her car; and if the kids get sick, she calls the doctor; everything from A to Z. She never calls me at the office. I call her two and three times a day. She doesn't know a thing about the life insurance business, but once a year I sit down with her and review my will, life insurance program, and everything that pertains to my death. She is a very, very important part of my life."

With his mind freed from home worries by the competent hands of Carol and buoyed by her enthusiasm, Joe can devote his full energies to his even now fifteen to sixteen hours of work for ten interviews each week.

His offices are in the Florida Building located on one of the main streets of downtown Lakeland. "This makes it easy for clients to find," Joe tells us. His special clientele has been, even from the very beginning, the single man.

His methods appear in the many articles he has written: "Sell the Single Man," *Underwriters Review,* May, 1964; "The Single Man Buys Savings," *The Insurance Salesman,* April, 1964; "Borrowing Successful Ideas Helps Me Sell $4,000,000," *Life Insurance Selling,* December, 1965; and "A Presentation That Helps Me Sell Unmarried Men," *Life Insurance Selling,* April, 1964.

However, he has summed them all up in the speech which appears in the *1966 M.D.R.T. Proceedings.* The three necessary fundamentals which he lays down apply to success not only in the life insurance business but in all businesses.

"We hear a great deal about the word enthusiasm. It means 'God within.' I don't see how any man can concentrate on preparing a man's estate for death unless he is concentrating 100 percent, and he can't unless he is right with the 'Man Upstairs.' If your production is down, and you are having trouble prospecting and closing, this may be the reason." Joe's first fundamental then is to be right with God.

His second fundamental is having a domestic situation in which the wife is able to manage the household affairs competently—a situation like the one we have already described.

Joe believes that his third fundamental, a positive mental attitude, is nothing more than the first two items. "If you are right with the 'Man Upstairs' and if your wife is a valuable part of your ball club, and if you are not worried about anything domestically, you don't have anything to do but sell life insurance."

In his article "Sell the Single Man" which appeared in the *Underwriters Review* in May, 1964, Joe says:

If he is saving money in a bank, I recommend that he continue doing so but transfer $10 to $15 a month to this long-range plan that I have just shown. I also emphasize to him that his savings at the bank is for a short term emergency, and that his savings in any proposal is for a long term. I let him know that nowhere else can he invest his money and have a self-completing program, in the event he should become disabled.

Emphasizing the future, and how much more it will cost each year he waits, plus the fact that this money accumulates tax free makes the sale of a single man enjoyable and very lucrative.

Another article "Borrowing Successful Ideas Helps Me Sell $4,000,000 A Year" which appeared in *Life Insurance Selling,* December, 1965, is self-explanatory:

Ideas are a dime a dozen, but the man who puts them into practice is priceless. Oliver Wendell Holmes said, 'Many times ideas grow better when transplanted into another mind than in the one where they sprang up.'

I take this as full license to borrow, use and change to my needs any ideas that appeal to me. A good idea is an idea that I feel I have to show. That is, I must get into the field and show it to prospects or it is an unused idea. Often when I first try a certain new idea, it doesn't seem to ring a bell. However, after I have polished it up, used it and used it again, it becomes my idea, and it begins to sell a lot of life insurance for me—because I am sold on it!

His sharing of ideas has not stopped with articles, however. He has given speeches in over 37 states and in four countries. He gave the keynote speech at the September, 1965, N.A.L.U. Meeting in St. Louis, Missouri; he addressed the LIAMA Meeting in November, 1965, at Washington, D. C.; and he gave the inspirational address on the last day of the 1966 M.D.R.T. Meeting in Boston, Massachusetts.

Why is Joe willing to give so generously of his invaluable time to share his ideas and enthusiasm with others? Because he considers this his greatest accomplishment. For instance, showing his ideas to sales congresses throughout the world is of more importance to him than selling a million dollar policy with a $68,000 premium, a policy by the way his client called him for! As Joe modestly tells it, "The person called me on the phone. I had been doing work for the son. He recommended me. There was nothing to the sale; the attorney and accountant sold it!"

Sharing his ideas with others is also more important to him than the personal glory attached to having spoken to LIAMA, NALU, and the MDRT all within a year.

And if his goal does not change, and he becomes the president of an insurance company, he will be in an even better position to share his ideas with others.

Does Joe have an idea he can isolate for singular importance and pass along to other insurance men? "A career in life insurance enables you to be an individual businessman with no boss over you. Above all, there is no limit to your income. This gives one a great free feeling." Joe recommends this spur to get yourself moving—"Build yourself a new home and go in debt $30,000." As for the amount of work required for great success in life insurance Joe recommends "a minimum of 70 hours a week, 6 days a week, from 6:00 in the morning until 11:00 at night. Don't take coffee breaks and spend a maximum of 20 minutes a day eating lunch, breakfast and dinner. See people; see people; and see people! Have faith in ratios and get a lot of exposure." And, finally, Joe says, "Have faith in God and put Him above everything. In time of need, ask Him for help. I go to Church to just meditate. I did this when I started, and many, many times I get a great deal of strength from talking with God."

And this philosophy of life enables Joe, even with his vast amount of exposure, to truthfully say when asked about discouraging experiences, "I never had any!"

CHAPTER 17

J. ERIC GILLESPIE

J. ERIC GILLESPIE, tyrant and perfectionist, of Toronto, Canada, is the owner of his own consulting firm, J. Eric Gillespie and Associates. After a varied education in England followed by professional training as an accountant there, Eric immigrated to Canada in 1956. Eric is completely self-taught in life insurance, but because of his background, he does not have to limit his approach only to advising on life insurance matters. He is competent to advise on other business matters as well.

Eric says that the purpose of his estate analysis and planning service is to do everything in his power to make the particular client's estate serve him in the most effective way possible; that is, to guarantee the successful creation, correlation, and management of the property the client now owns or may someday own, and to take every available measure to conserve the man's estate for his family by limiting the depletion which it will suffer through taxes at death. Eric explains that the person, by providing the data needed, enables Gillespie and Associates to serve him with the same professional skill he would expect from his other professional counsellors. Eric adds that it is his desire to work in very close cooperation with these other counsellors, with, of course, all information held in strictest confidence. "No estate survey is worth more than the data upon which it is based," Eric emphasizes.

Eric does not solicit business at all, but he finds that after having completed the affairs of one person, this person speaks to others in his group; and they, in turn, contact Eric. His associates are life insurance agents who bring Eric their difficult pension and life insurance cases. Most of his business is on a split commission basis with other agents who only introduce him to their client. The business which results is either in the area of pension or medical plans, or large life insurance cases. It is usual for Eric to work on only ten life cases a year, and each case is a client and not a sale. Eric relies greatly on renewal income, and as yet no case has not been renewed. Much of Eric's business stems from employee benefit plans, pension plans, and medical plans; and because of the large premium involved, it allows him to look upon small life insurance premiums as a matter of course.

Eric views estate planning as strictly a business matter. Throughout the interview Eric attempts to impart sufficient confidence in his work so that the client will invariably ask, "What would you do?" He gives the client a written proposal outlining his whole situation. Eric then tells the man it is entirely up to him to decide to what extent he wishes to solve the problems Eric has outlined, and that he should make a decision in such matters in exactly the same way he would make any business decision.

Eric's closing ratio is around 80%. He adds, "I look forward to an increased income by continuing to approach my business in a professional way. I have seen it grow successively each year so that it now approximates $40,000."

Some of Eric's clients have included Babson's Canadian Reports Limited, the Canadian March of Dimes, and the Canadian Professional Golfers' Association. In the February 1962 issues of *Golf and Club News*, Eric wrote an article entitled "Golf Personnel Security Program" in which he explained the features of the security program he administers for the C.P.G.A. Thirty-five per cent of all eligible clubs and their professionals participated immediately. Today, there is 60% participation. A unique feature is that, as a professional moves from club to club, his pension moves with him.

Eric maintains that the proper business approach makes the proportion of sales to prospects two or three times as high as the average. Consequently, the successful agent can make an income disproportionate to his efforts as commission scales have been carefully selected to keep the average salesman just in the business. Therefore, he feels it is a must to analyze premiums in relationship to volume and lives in order that an agent's efforts be justly rewarded.

Last year Eric suffered a mild coronary attack which kept him out of action for three months. However, every case he had been working on prior to his disability has now been closed, and in no case did the clients turn elsewhere for advice. Thus this interlude from work appears to have had no permanent detrimental effect, for Eric's sales that year were his highest thus far—life insurance sales amounting to $500,000 (all permanent), six pension plans, and ten medical plans. Would that twelve months and perfect health could always yield so much!

CHAPTER 18

WALTER GREENBLATT, C.L.U.

WALTER GREENBLATT early knew the meaning of crème de la crème for his mother was a prominent New York lawyer and his father a well-known C.P.A. He graduated from the University of Pennsylvania's Wharton School of Finance, where he learned a concept that became the motivating force behind his early success in the life insurance business—the Human Life Value Concept as explained by Dr. Huebner himself.

Walter moved to Dallas in December of 1951. He had one casual acquaintance there. Undaunted, he leafed through the yellow pages of the telephone book to Estate Planners and selected at random the name of Stanley Martin. Walter called Stanley for an appointment, and from that day hence he has been associated with Stanley Martin and the State Mutual Life Assurance Company.

With Dr. Huebner's fundamental concept of human life values and Stanley Martin's guidance in estate planning, Walter had a head start toward becoming a life underwriter, who would specialize in personal programing and business insurance.

Believing that hard work along a prescribed plan and constant service to policyholders would be the way to build up a future permanent clientele, Walter set out this way and proved it worked for him.

He uses the Al Granum approach which he learned from Tom Wolff: "Would you have any objection in discussing your life insurance program with me?" Walter has found this to be a satisfactory approach to his friends and has built up a large clientele among outstanding Jewish businessmen in the city of Dallas, many of whom he has met from being very active on the Board of Directors of the Local B'nai B'rith Chapter, the Executive Committee of the Julius Schepps Community Center, the Preston Hollow Country Club, and A.E.P.I. Alumni Club.

Walter's approach has been mostly on a referred lead basis, using approach letters followed by the usual telephone call for an appointment. He sells the medical as a close and sets up a continuous year to year review of his client's program.

When approaching a new prospect, Walter sells them on the idea of his service as an agent with the facts that he is a C.L.U. and a member of the Million Dollar Round Table and by telling them of new tax savings ideas that he has to offer them.

Walter designed an eye-catching "Cost to Wait" illustration which he uses often and successfully to overcome procrastination.

Walter keeps up with his clientele by using a Company newsletter, *Query*, birthday cards, MDRT announcements, calendars, ads in the local paper, and age-change card notifications.

No one doubts that Walter is a well-organized agent. He has qualified for M.D.R.T. for the fifth consecutive year, and is now writing $3,000,000 a year. Since entering the life insurance business, he has put fourteen groups in force and two pension plans. We can see that he has built quite a production figure, maintaining a constant weekly production and with a year-by-year increase in the number of lives and in his volume. He has also been quite active in the State Mutual C.L.U. Agents Association, having served as president for 1962-64.

The turning point in Walter's career was, "Making up my mind to become a Million Dollar Round Table member." This seems to be the underlying motivation of nearly all the men in this book. They have made up their minds to become members of the Million Dollar Round Table and have worked consistently toward that goal. This was the goal each sought and worked hard to achieve. It is very interesting to note that not a single one of these men stated that his goal was to become a member of his own company's million dollar organization, leader's club, etc.; but in each case his goal was to become a member of the Million Dollar Round Table. What a motivating influence the Million Dollar Round Table is in giving us a definite goal for the future!

Walter has constantly sought to increase his production year by year and has dramatically driven to the top. He has just been honored as the State Mutual's leading producer in the United States for 1965. He is now seeking to become a life member of the Million Dollar Round Table. When we asked him, "What then?" he replied, "To become a life and qualifying member of the Million Dollar Round Table for another twenty years." And I am sure that twenty years from now, we will see the name of Walter Greenblatt on the MDRT Roster!

CHAPTER 19

JAMES S. HARDING, C.L.U.

THE BEST KNOWN of James S. Harding's more than 150 speeches is called "The Second Time Around." Jim delivered it at the July, 1963, General Meeting of the Northwestern Mutual Life Insurance Company and at life underwriters meetings throughout the country. He borrowed this title from Mr. Tom Proctor who, until his death in 1965, was considered by many to be "Mr. Northwestern" himself. Mr. Proctor used it when he reentered the field as a special agent after 32 successful years as Nashville's general agent. Jim Harding's talk described his highly successful re-entry into the field force after spending almost three years as an assistant superintendent of agencies. In 1961, as a Home Office official, he wrote nothing. In 1962, upon his return home to Portland, Oregon, he wrote $1,920,815 on 73 lives.

Jim's talk explained why he chose to go from management back to personal production and how he got set to write two million in one year. When Jim first considered life insurance as a career at age twenty-two, it had seemed an easy enough business. His father had been a highly successful agent for over 27 years, but after all Jim was bigger than his father; Jim was the product of a better educational system; Jim could beat his father on the golf course and in the family ping pong matches. It seemed like life insurance would be a cinch, and Jim expected to sell a million dollars of business right away. "It took me about six months to stop and analyze what had been a terrible job up to then. And the thing I became readily aware of was that my father had become very smart in a six month period."

In 1959 Jim was offered an opportunity in a Home Office job to travel 100,000 miles by air to talk with agents and general agents in the field force. Jim's sales philosophies and concepts about the business are a result of his having worked with these men in this job.

In weighing management opportunities against sales production opportunities, Jim stresses that "the good general agent, the dedicated general agent, gives more and does more of a service for this business than any other man, because he is the one who brings people in, trains them, and supervises them into big producers." He added that no one should consider management, unless they were so good as an agent that it would be a sacrifice for them to go into management, but they would still do it because of a liking for general agency work.

Of his decision to go back into the field as an agent, Jim says, "The challenge of managing yourself is difficult, but to me this is one of the big factors in personal production. You have the opportunity to build your business the way you want to build it." To decide between being an agent, a general agent, or a home office official, Jim recommends that you be honest with yourself, put the facts on the table, and move from strength, but never to solve a shortrange problem.

While still in the Ivory Tower of the Home Office, Jim had to make the decision about what he could do as an agent. Jim listened to John Todd and the greats on what the law of averages does to the life insurance man. But Jim didn't have a set of averages himself on which to work out a system of operation—a system that would bring him business so that he didn't have to worry about getting five or ten big cases during the year. Jim wanted to be able to depend on a system to bring him the business. Therefore, he borrowed the averages used by the Granum Agency. "I decided first that I would open cases on 20% of the people whom I contacted, open cases of the type that can be closed in sixty to ninety days. Secondly, I knew I wasn't going to be any red hot salesman—that I'd close one out of three of these cases in a year's time. I'd open 20%, close a third, and the average size case would be $20,000. This meant that in a year's time I would have to contact 1,500 prospects by phone, or 125 a month. If I did that, I would open cases on 20% or 300 a year, or 25 a month. I'd close a third of these, or 100 over a year's time. This is a little over eight a month. A hundred cases at $20,000 makes two million in production."

How did this plan actually work out for Jim? "I contacted 900 people; I opened 259 cases out of 900, or a little better than one out of four. I closed approximately one out of three—89 cases out of 259 openings. The big surprise was that the average size case was $24,700, which brought me to a volume of a little over two million paid for."

The important point of this is the way the averages worked out. Whether you want to write half a million or $750,000 or a good premium business, whether you want to make the Round Table, or you want to write two million or five million or ten million, Jim knows that it is your step by step plan of day to day work that gets you to your goal.

Jim uses the one card system; he finds the automatic aspect of it especially good. Most of the details—age changes, birth dates, appointment making—can be handled automatically by a secretary.

One of the hardest things for most agents to do without becoming discouraged is to call eighty people and open only twenty. Here is Jim's idea for making these facts a little more palatable.

You are only going to get a favorable reception from a certain percentage of people. Maybe the prospect wants to see you, but for some reason they are not going to let you get to them without doing a little work. So, on some of them, you're going to strike out, but I think you can do wonders by adding one simple question to your vocabulary: "Well, I can understand that, Mr. Prospect. It's perfectly all right. Tell me, would you have any objection to my staying in touch with you by mail?" "Well, no, but I'm not going to buy any insurance." "Well, I can understand that. That's perfectly all right. What's your residence address? What's your business address? What's your family situation? Your full name is John Q. Jones. What's your birthday, John?" Once you get his birth date you can get his age change, put him in a system to cultivate him automatically, send him something every month in the mail, and spend 20 or 25 cents for each man you put in there for mailing purposes.

Another 40%, or about 32 of the 80 can be added to your file each month by the use of this simple question: "Would you have any objection to my staying in touch with you by mail?" So now what do we have? We have 60% affirmative results. It's a kind of deferred affirmative, but I think it is affirmative. So now when you have this stack of 80 cards, you can look at it and say, "One out of every two of these is going to tell me yes some day." Finding out which ones becomes a real challenge.

One question that comes up a lot is, "Why should I spend money on this 40% of people that I have never met, people whom I just put into the system? Isn't this a waste of money?" My only answer is: In the 18 months I've been back in the field, I have had $12,000 of paid premiums which came from people I had added to my one card system by the mailing list approach.

How did it come? Just from people calling me on the phone and saying, "I've got a problem. Can you help me with it?" Or, people call me, saying that they have a client who has a problem, and would I come down and see him? These are the same people that were not favorable, when I called them at age change time, etc. But now it's open season. They have asked questions of me, and they are glad that I came. You can build a clientele in this way, and you don't have to keep waiting to see people a month from now or a year from now. You can automatically put them in the system, cultivate them, forget about them, and they will bring you big returns.

By doing this Jim recognizes the fundamental tendency of a prospect to avoid an agent. When Jim goes along with the person, and still sends him something in spite of his refusal, Jim is doing something few agents do, but something that has paid off handsomely.

Another point that Jim frequently emphasizes is that in life insurance we've got the marvelous combination of money for life and death through cash value life insurance, but we often sit back and don't tell people how we feel about it. As a result, we let people in mediocre types of saving and investment plans take money away from our prospects they should be putting into cash value life insurance. "Just your conviction, your sincerity in telling the story will sell cash value life insurance; and, if you don't believe it, try it!" challenges Jim.

For this is what Jim Harding has been doing, and this year he sold $2,000,000 again. He has revised his objectives based on his three years' production in the field and is successfully working toward a $4,000,000 year. His current M.D.R.T. classification is Repeat Qualifying. This is quite a change from his first year's production in 1953 of $150,000!

Jim's major motivation is "to truly realize my potential and to be successful in the eyes of my peers." Jim has established a ten-year plan of achievement in both recognition and financial gain, a plan he will complete by age forty.

Jim creates his image through a consistent mailing list including tax letters and other useful items for his prospects. Almost all of his work is with referred leads, so Jim tries to have his centers of influence work for him in introducing him to the referrals. This is done either with a phone call made by the center of influence to the prospect, or by the center adding a note on the approach letter which Jim sends to the prospect. Then Jim follows through with a telephone call for the interview, either shooting for the interview or for an opportunity to keep in contact with this man in the hope that Jim will see him at a future time.

Jim handles his initial interview with a brief statement of his philosophy and concept of the way he does business:

(1) I tell the prospect that I don't presume he is in the market for life insurance at this point.

(2) I tell him that my function is to give him ideas which have worked successfully for other people.

(3) I tell him that his plan is either perfect or there are some errors in it. In either case, he would profit from our discussion. Either he will find that his plan is perfect, and he will be happy about it; or I will be helpful to him by showing him where the errors are in his plan. Then I tell him that the way I work is to get the facts about his situation; then go back and give a very honest analysis and presentation of my recommendations for him, and follow through with a type of service work which few, if any, in our business provide for their clients—The Northwestern Mutual Million Book.

Through his age change interviews set up automatically by the one card system, Jim contacts his clients every year and keeps their Million Books up-to-date.

Jim now makes four calls a day; he made six his first year in the business. He has always worked five days a week. He now works from ten to twelve hours a day; his first year he worked eight to ten hours. He now works six to eight nights per month; his first year he worked four nights per month. Perhaps these statistics explains why Jim writes $2,000,000 now and wrote $150,000 his first year.

Jim runs his office with a full time secretary, a high school girl who does mailings, etc., and a service department within the agency, which he uses the equivalent of another three-fourths of an additional secretary. This department does all proposals and service work. His private secretary makes appointments for him and basically keeps him organized. Jim believes in hiring competent help, even before you can really afford it. "The agent needs to spend his time in the field doing what he is best qualified to do—sell—and not in the office doing the work that $2 to $5 per hour people can do.

His best single market, which accounts for one-third of his business, is the medical market. Jim got into this market by cold calls and a real effort to get there. It is now worked totally by referred leads.

To offer his physician clients the best possible services regardless of where they may move, and also a special newsletter, *The Physician's Guide*, Jim is active in Physicians Nationwide, Inc. In fact, he is Secretary-Treasurer of Physicians Nationwide, Inc., a national organization of highly competent men who handle financial planning for doctors all over the United States. Also in this organization is one of the two men who, Jim says, has shown him what a young man can really do in this business—Hugh Thompson, President of Physicians Nationwide, Inc. The other is Northwestern Agent Dave Hilton. Both are in this book.

To get started in the life insurance business, Jim recommends that you pick the young men who are going to be successful and sell them life insurance—"sell 100 lives per year to fellows who are coming up, and you can't help being successful. Sell life insurance as the heart of a financial program; sell the advantage of buying life insurance at an early age and life insurance as property."

Jim believes that if you want a business which offers unlimited opportunity and challenge in a professional atmosphere, life insurance is it. Men entering the life insurance field with previous business experience should capitalize on this experience and immediately learn planned incomes, simplified estate planning, and also have a simple package approach which will appeal to sophisticated people such as a good youth insurance presentation. "Every father is interested in talking about his son," notes Jim. However, a man should not come into this profession because he feels he can make a lot of money in a hurry. Rather, he should have an understanding that his compensation is spread over a ten-year period.

Dedicated and sincere with great motivation, well-organized and best at prospecting and opening cases, Jim Harding is well on his way to being another Louis Behr.

CHAPTER 20

SANFORD H. HARMELIN, C.L.U.

SANFORD H. HARMELIN, C.L.U., a million dollar producer who continues to study every day, is the General Agent for The Manhattan Life Insurance Company in Newark, New Jersey. Sandy specializes in pension trusts and other phases of estate planning, and he finds that most of his ideas come from his tremendous amount of reading. He gets up at 6:00 A.M. every morning to have at least an hour of study before he begins his day. He reads the *Million Dollar Round Table Proceedings,* services such as the *Prentice-Hall Pension and Profit Sharing Service,* the *IBP Service,* the *R&R Advanced Underwriting Service,* and periodical magazines such as *Trust and Estates, Current Comments, and Report Bulletins.*

Sandy's work organization pattern is based on meeting as many businessmen and accountants as possible, and then using the ideas he has gained in study for their benefit. Most of his production comes from businessmen primarily involved in close corporations.

Says Sandy, "I became interested in the corporate market, because I honestly believed I could do a better job there than in, for instance, the professional market. I find it easier to be understood by the businessman, and it is my opinion that corporations have more money to spend on life insurance and pension trusts than do other markets."

Perhaps Sandy's background has something to do with his approach. He received a B.S. from the Wharton School of Finance and Commerce. Largely because of the example of his father who was also a successful life insurance agent, Sandy says that he never really considered any other profession except life insurance. Therefore, he majored in Insurance at the Wharton School of Finance. At Wharton he was influenced and inspired by Dr. Huebner and the late Dr. David McCahan. Sandy recalls that Dr. McCahan's course was probably the most out-standing course given in the Insurance Department. "Part of the reason was the subject matter: Estate Planning, and what we today call Advanced Underwriting. A more important reason, however, was the fact that Dr. McCahan was an outstanding technician and a really wonderful gentleman. Many times at the end of the class, I would stay and discuss some aspects of estate planning with Dr. McCahan. I learned more from these informal chats than I did from the actual texts. In my opinion, he was truly a great teacher and a great man. He inspired his students to act and think as professionals."

This background set the pattern which now distinguishes Sandy's career, for he always does a highly professional job for his clients. "My father always believed, and I believe, that if you do the job right for your client and forget the commission, it will eventually result in more business than if you had thought only of commission dollars. A client's recommendations to his friends and business contacts are better than any other form of advertising."

To gain widespread publication of his ideas and of his work, Sandy has a luncheon meeting twice a year for about fifty ac-countants. He has a guest speaker, usually a tax attorney, who discusses a subject that is of interest to the accountants. Sandy then talks briefly about some phase of life insurance, such as "Qualified Pension Plans for the Close Corporation," etc. Within a month after the luncheon, Sandy tries to have a private luncheon date with each of the accountants that attended. He then makes a more detailed presentation to the accountant. Sandy also explains that his work is strictly professional, and the accountant's client will be in good hands, if he calls Sandy in to advise on life insurance matters. He makes it a point to present ideas to an accountant or to an attorney about three times a week.

"With nearly every sale of personal insurance for estate tax purposes or pension trust, I meet the man's accountant and lawyer," says Sandy. "The client normally will want me to discuss my recommendation with one or both of them. If I am successful in impressing the accountant and lawyer, he may call me in to serve other clients as well. This has happened on many occasions and substantial sales have resulted."

Most of Sandy's interviews are acquired through referred leads or from people who are already his clients. Sandy says that if he wishes to get an appointment with a referred lead, he calls the prospect on the telephone, explains who he is, and that Mr. Client suggested that he call him. "I was allowed to do some work for Mr. Client, and he was impressed with my services, and he thought they would be of value to you, Mr. Prospect. I have no way of knowing whether or not my services would be of value to you; however, I do have some ideas that have been of interest to many men in your position, and they may possibly be of interest to you." Continues Sandy, "I promise to take only fifteen minutes of your times. If my ideas are of interest to you, we can talk longer; if not, I shall leave. May I see you Tuesday morning at 10:30 or Wednesday afternoon about 2:00?" With a referred lead, Sandy usually gets the appointment.

At the appointment Sandy asks the prospect a few questions such as, "How did you get into this business?" This usually gets the executive talking for about five to seven minutes. Then Sandy explains that Mr. Client's firm entered into a Qualified Pension Plan and Mr. Client thought that such a program could be advantageous to Mr. Prospect and to his company.

Then Sandy explains briefly the advantages of such a plan to the corporation and to Mr. Prospect himself. Sandy shows Mr. Prospect the benefit schedule of a plan that he has handled. The names have been changed, but the figures are accurate. Sandy explains that these figures are only a sample, although a real life case, and the figures for his company will be different in many respects. Sandy tells him that in order to show him figures, he must have certain information regarding the employees of the company. Sandy leaves a blank census sheet for the bookkeeper to complete and return to him.

If Sandy cannot get the census information; or, if after getting the information, he fails to close the pension trust, he knows the reason why. The discussion usually brings out another need for either business or personal life insurance. This then is the area to which Sandy turns his attention.

Often, too, he turns to another area after talking to the prospect's accountant. The accountant may explain why a pension is not in the cards immediately. However, this discussion usually brings out the need for life insurance elsewhere.

On many occasions, before or after a sale is made, he gets together with the client's lawyer regarding estate planning for Mr. Prospect.

The simplicity of Sandy's work organization belies its effectiveness. "I try to meet as many businessmen and accountants, as I possibly can. I also try to study at least one hour a day. I try to think over in my mind and list on a piece of paper the names of clients to whom I can present one or more of the ideas that may have come from the day's reading. I try to present the few thoughts to these people in order to develop a possible sale. I would say that the only set pattern that I follow is to study a lot and try to put the ideas I learn into practice." Sandy's business objective is to install and service more than one hundred pension plans with an annual production of over two million.

Sandy advises other young men, "In the life insurance business, your earnings depend on you and on no one else. If you work a little harder you will do a little better. Your production record will reflect if you are the kind of fellow that follows along for the ride. If you are willing to work, see prospects, learn your product and about human nature, life insurance is the greatest business in the world." Sandy sees as a problem to the new man in life insurance "the possibility of being discouraged on one or more occasions. Slumps and the loss of business to competition should be taken in stride just like any other setback."

Sandy recalls as his most discouraging experience a situation in which this happened to him:

Very shortly after returning home from the service, Sandy had a referred lead to a dentist in one of the suburban communities. The dentist had already applied for a life insurance policy through another company, although he had not as yet received the policy or paid the premium. Sandy asked him not to accept the policy until they met again, which the dentist agreed to do. At that first meeting, Sandy was able to convince the dentist to go through the complete process of reviewing his life insurance policies, and Sandy did a simple program for him. After doing a lot more work for the dentist, preparing a lot of figures and making a lot of recommendations, Sandy believed the man appreciated the job done for him.

One of the recommendations was to buy a different type of life insurance policy than he had applied for. He had young children; he had a nominal amount of life insurance; and he had a minimum amount of money that he could use for the purchase of life insurance. The policy for which he applied with the other company was a Twenty Payment Life for $10,000. Sandy suggested rather than apply for $10,000 Twenty Pay Life that he use the same premium and purchase roughly $16,000 to $17,000 Whole Life. He would increase his family's protection quite substantially during the first 20 year period. His dollar outlay would not be more than it would have been for the Twenty Pay Life. Yet, at the end of the 20 years, if he felt that he wanted to stop paying premiums, he could take reduced paid-up insurance in the amount of approximately $9,300. For the possible loss of $700 of paid-up insurance, sometime in the future, he would be doing the wiser thing by giving his family additional protection in these early years. Sandy also explained to the dentist that it was possible when the 20 year period was over, he might need more insurance than the $10,000 Paid-up Life would give him under the Twenty Pay Life Plan. And, if he were to purchase more insurance at that time, he would have to show evidence of insurability and pay premiums based on his advanced age. If he purchased the Whole Life, he would merely continue to pay premiums on the original policy. The dentist thought this was a tremendous idea, and he and Sandy spent a lot of time discussing it and deciding on details. The dentist then advised Sandy that he was going to do what had been worked out, but not with Sandy. He was going to do it with the man from the other company, because this other man lived in the town in which he was practicing dentistry and could possibly become his patient in the future.

As Sandy recalled this discouraging experience he could still see the bright side. "It taught me that, if I should have a discouraging time with a client or prospect, I would just have to forget about him and go to the next person. There were probably many more discouraging experiences in my short career, but I honestly can't remember them, and I am very happy that I can't. This first experience taught me a lesson. It taught me to forget any bad experience or discouraging experience and go on to do the job for the next fellow and to do it right."

"If you overcome and forget discouraging setbacks, and if you work hard at prospecting, study, etc.," says Sandy, "I don't believe that you can really miss making a good living in the life insurance business, while doing a true service to your local community by providing the values of life insurance to its inhabitants."

In thinking of the man who is now in a job that he doesn't enjoy and is considering a career in life insurance, Sandy points out that he has the advantage of business experience and maturity. He can often see the businessman's problems and help him in solving them. Too, the man with past experience is usually older than the man just out of college, and he knows more people, and thereby has a natural entree to more prospects. Sandy believes that if this man learns the products and the by-products of this business, he can be successful a lot faster than the man coming straight out of college.

As far as sales training is concerned, Sandy says go to work for a dynamic agency, particularly one in which you know few people. "I made a mistake originally, although I don't think it has hurt me too much, by going to work for my father's agency. I would have been able to accept training and criticisms from strangers a lot more easily, than I was able to accept it from people I had known for many years. The agency I would have picked, if I had known then what I know now, would have been one with a dynamic general agent, one with ideas and one who had built successful men in the life insurance business. An agency that specialized in advanced underwriting type of sales—primarily pension trusts, estate planning, etc.—would have been ideal for me."

Sandy's advice to any agent, whether he is a new agent, or one who has had experience, is to continually study, to learn more and more about his product and about the side effects of his product. By side effects he means court decisions and treasury regulations such as the parts of Internal Revenue Code which apply to estate planning, pension planning, and life insurance in general. Sandy believes that no matter how good a salesman you may be, you owe it to your client to be an expert on life insurance and to know as much as possible, just as the other professional advisors, such as the C.P.A., the attorney, and the trust officer are experts in their fields. "You are being paid quite handsomely for the job you do; therefore, it is your obligation to do it right, and in order to do it right, you have to know an awful lot besides what is shown in the rate book."

And what makes all of this worthwhile for Sandy? "I like my work, but it is the means to an end. The end is to provide for my family. I want to provide a comfortable, happy home for my family, to be able to give them whatever they need and most of the things they want. I want to be able to take vacations and take time for travel after the children are on their own and self-sufficient." At the rate Sandy is going he'll be traveling around the world several times!

CHAPTER 21

JOHN S. HART, C.L.U.

SEVEN HUNDRED POLICYHOLDERS in seven years of selling in a city where he originally knew no one! That's the record of John Hart, million dollar agent for the John Hancock in New Haven, Connecticut.

John has an uncommonly strong commitment to life insurance from a personal standpoint, in that for some years now, he has committed 20% of his income to its purchase, and from the standpoint that it performs an invaluable function as the cornerstone of his estate. John strongly conveys this thinking to his prospects and policyholders—that they have a duty and responsibility to purchase life insurance in adequate amounts for family or business protection. If they don't buy this philosophy, then these prospects never become his policyholders, for his entire life insurance operation simply consists of meeting new people and converting them and their thinking to building a sound financial plan for their families. And John accomplishes this by getting them to trust and like him. "There is something in my makeup that requires that people like me and trust me which transcends the more technical aspect of what I have to present," explains John. And that in simple terms explains why John has 700 policyholders, one hundred each year beginning his very first year with his first hundred.

Although John's father has always successfully worked in the life insurance business, John didn't think of becoming a life underwriter until he was overseas in the service, married and with one child, when "all of a sudden it dawned on me that I had to support this young family." Meanwhile, John's father had taken the John Hancock general agency in Connecticut after ten years with the Berkshire Life Insurance Co. as a company officer; and, since John's wife and family were in New Haven, he returned there and entered the life insurance business.

John's immediate goal was "to keep from starving to death, which I almost did in the first three months I was in the business." But his desire to make money, to be a top producer, and to be able to associate with those he admired in life insurance, kept him going and constantly upgrading his method of presentation.

Selling in the beginning was pretty much a matter of being fairly hard-nosed about seeing as many people as he could, and he was not very particular as to who they were. Looking back, John believes that this approach had both advantages and disadvantages; the disadvantage was that most of his clients had no future except for the twenty med students then studying at Yale whom John had known at Amherst. But the advantage was the hundred cases he wrote that first year in cold territory which he says did more for me than anything else at my stage of immaturity.

Hiram S. Hart, John's father, inspired him in those early months and years and gave him much of his early training—"and my father is recognized as a successful management man." Learning the business from your father, traditionally considered a dangerous thing to do, worked out well, benefiting not only both of the Harts but also their relationships in the community, "although we did lock the door a few times and went at it," John admits.

Another man who has inspired John is Albert Schmerge, General Agent for the Mutual Benefit in New York, whom he met at the first MDRT meeting he attended. Says John, "I really buy the psychological approach to selling life insurance and the whole concept of the proper mental attitude—which has sometimes been a weak point with me. I have also seen the strong impact of the men who simply take action and get things done. Al Schmerge has these qualities, and he has inspired me to try and adopt them in my procedure."

Specifically, John applies psychology to develop a proper give and take in his first interviews. Basically, John attempts to do two things at this time: He wants to control his prospect both from the standpoint of selling himself to the prospect as a person who can do things for him—"I want to sell myself and control him from a personality standpoint." And secondly, he wants the prospect to commit himself not only to a sound review of his financial planning, but also to the fact that life insurance is the only way to accomplish some of his objectives.

To do this John moves immediately in the first interview to get the ground rules established. "If I don't, then I never see the prospect again, unless he calls us." This is one reason why most of John's selling interviews result in sales, and the reason for his high percentage of sales to policyholders at a relatively early stage of his career. Believing that "it is encumbent upon us to develop the facts as fully as we can, so that these can be as complete as we want them to be," he adds that "for the most part my fact-finding does not involve great detail and estate planning techniques." In this first interview John also finds out how much this man earns from all sources, and if possible where his earned income goes.

John has found that life insurance underwriters serve as the only financial advisor to most people, and he uses this trust to help a family budget their particular requirements and build a sound financial plan. Since he has bought a considerable amount of life insurance himself and has attempted to master his own financial planning in other areas, he has become a great deal more effective in dealing with his prospects.

John also relies on psychology to bring out the strong motive of most men to develop an estate that is permanent in its nature. If a man has enough resources available, there is the possibility John can usually show him how he can develop an estate which will yield enough income from interest to meet minimum family requirements and have enough left over to set up a trust for his future generations. If we can show a man how to do this, we have helped him create a monument and have helped future generations develop a sense of independence from Federal or State or charitable assistance.

Based on these guidelines then, John initially sold almost all of his personal life insurance on a package basis. With more knowledge and experience, he began selling with programming, first using company forms and more lately using just blank pieces of paper on which he gathers information to present a solution in a subsequent interview.

Many of John's clients are young doctors whose basic problem is a matter of creating an estate that they can afford. Therefore, much of John's work revolves around finding the necessary money, and John uses a simple transfer theory, getting the money from other sources.

Although selling is still the major aspect of John's life insurance career, he is now the Associate General Agent and is doing some recruiting and considerable initial training with new men in the business. He has been responsible for bringing five men into the life insurance business who are still in it. John uses his record to effectively demonstrate to new agents that without previous contacts either family or otherwise, with no family market whatsoever, no association with any group of people who have directed business his way, no wholesale development of minimum deposit insurance or bank loan insurance, and with no military market, a business worth a considerable amount of money was built. It was done purely by prospecting, by trial and error methods of direct mail, etc., but mainly through the strong endless chain method of developing referred leads, John got his 700 policyholders over a seven year period and has maintained a persistency rate of some 96% on all of this business. This represents a large amount of volume and premium gotten by using sound service techniques which are not new but, if applied consistently, produce good results.

John says that he discusses the above with every prospective agent, adding that "I am not afraid to mention income figures or anything of that nature that they may ask me. My situation is not a far-out one in terms of a big income, yet my record is usually a very meaningful one and a practical one for new men or prospective men to look at."

John is careful in his selection of new agents not to entice into the life insurance business men who don't belong and who would be better off seeking their career somewhere else. The problem, of course, is recognizing that indefinable quality that makes a man succeed in this business, for the life insurance business offers so much to the right person. And a few of the things it offers is being in business for one's self without initial capital investment, the freedom and flexibility of the work, the opportunity to market your own name, and the opportunity to do business with only those you wish to work.

And where does John place emphasis in training new agents? He believes that a high school graduate entering life insurance needs to write as many people as he possibly can, to get maximum exposure in as short a period of time as possible, so that he can build a large clientele. He should also continue his education.

A college graduate can do best by immediately trying to build a young clientele of college people his age. He needs to get as much knowledge of the life insurance business as possible and to proceed as quickly into C.L.U. study, so that he can overcome his age disadvantage with knowledge.

A major recommendation John makes to all new agents is to seek out help from others in areas in which he is not yet qualified, or in areas that don't fit his temperament or personality.

To older agents who seem to have reached a stalemate, John emphasizes self-evaluation—"Where have I been? What have I accomplished?" And "What are my objectives, both long and short range?"—these questions the man must ask himself, for being at a standstill is objectively part of his own making and corrective measures must be undertaken by himself, believes John. Some help though can be obtained from men more experienced than the agent in question, if he will ask for it.

In summary, John knows that "no one sales idea as such is going to determine the future success of any agent. Rather a sound method of operation built on self-discipline and individual commitment to and faith in the strength and services of our product, the ability to know ourselves and what our limitations are, where we have strengths and where we have weaknesses, and to glean from others who possibly may be a great deal more creative in their thinking. All of these factors and more should be considered when developing a method of operation. And, when applied to the kind of prospect you want to develop, this method should yield satisfactory results and a long and prosperous business career in the sale and service of life insurance."

And for John, his wife Patricia, and children Laurie, Scott, and Robert, it certainly has.

CHAPTER 22

RALPH HESTER, JR., C.L.U.

RALPH HESTER, JR., M.D.R.T. member, and Co-General Agent for Pan-American Life grew up in Jackson, Mississippi, where he was literally raised in the insurance business. Both his father and two of his uncles were successful general agents and personal producers with Pan-American. His father, Ralph Hester, C.L.U., and his late uncle, W. C. Hester, C.L.U., were partners and co-general agents for Mississippi, until W. C.'s death in the fall of 1960. Both men served as president of the local and state Underwriters Associations, and Ralph was the 1964-65 President of his local Association. At present, Ralph and his father are one of the few father-son teams qualifying for the Million Dollar Round Table, and his father and uncle were previously one of the few brother teams in the Round Table. Both his Dad and Mother are listed in *Who's Who in the South and Southwest,* and his wife, Sally, has continued a family tradition of civic work by teaching part time in the X-ray departments of the local hospitals without pay. She has done this since giving up her career as an X-ray technician to look after Ralph and their three children, all under six years of age.

Ralph's entry into the life insurance business came after a four-year hitch as a Naval Officer in Korea, Japan, and on the Pacific Fleet. His only previous business experience had been a disastrous pre-college summer as a Fuller Brush man. And only after a Baylor University course enabled him to realize that his opinion of himself was far more important than what others thought of him did he have the confidence to enter upon a life insurance partnership with his father.

"Most people have a well-known opinion about the sons of successful men, and in many cases I am sure that the opinion is well justified. I cannot be satisfied, however, with being known only as the son of a very prominent and successful life insurance man. For years this feeling prevented me from even considering the possibility of entering the life insurance profession myself. It was only during the latter part of my service with the Navy, that I finally realized my opinion of myself was far more important than what others thought of me. This decision was to a large extent the result of what I had learned in Professor Paul Baker's class at Baylor University. The course, 'Integration of Abilities,' had a manifold intent: to break the habit of thinking and creating in a stereotyped manner; to encourage creativity in everything that we do; to encourage curiosity and interest, particularly in unfamiliar subjects; to stimulate a desire to exceed and surpass self-imposed limitations. An unusual mishmash of philosophy, applied psychology, and seemingly lunatic activity, the course made a profound impression not only on basket-weaving majors, but also on football players and serious scholars as well. Because of what I learned there, I was able to enter the Agency operated by my father and uncle without feeling that I would be competing against them. I accepted the fact that my real competition would be with myself and that my own self-respect would give me my greatest incentive."

"If a person's main objective is to achieve his own self-respect, he can become successful only by refusing to be satisfied with mediocre goals, standards, and performances. The success of Dad and my uncle gave me the incentive to raise my personal goals to a higher level, and the instruction I had received from Professor Baker gave me the extra self-confidence to attempt what I previously would not have considered."

Ralph says that he has never been a full time agent for when he started out in 1957, Ralph was on a salary in the office of the State Agency of Pan-American Life. He wrote personal production only in off hours. Since his appointment as general agent in 1961, Ralph has been able to devote a great deal more time to personal production. Yet even now 50% of his time is devoted to agency administration and to servicing policies written years before he entered the business. He has in fact never been a full time personal producer, yet his personal production in each of the three full years before being appointed general agent was between $200,000 and $300,000. It is now well over a million.

In 1961, 1963, and 1964 Ralph and his father tied for first place in personal production with Pan-American based on ordinary premiums. In 1962 they tied for second place.

The Hesters' partnership is a rather unusual operation which specializes in group, pension, and profit-sharing plans. Ralph's father and his late uncle, W. C. Hester, started work in this market about 17 years ago, and "it just grew." About 50% of their new clients are referred leads and about 50% are the result of cold calls.

Ralph says that in their work they first of all try to develop interest in the client for establishing a pension plan. During the initial discussion, Ralph shows samples of the descriptive booklets about their plans or a list of their clients in the area. Based on the payroll data of the employer, they present figures on suggested plans, sometimes with as many as 15 or 20 variations in formula, funding medium, etc. On group insurance plans, they present the Company proposals. On pension and profit-sharing plans, they present proposals on their own forms.

After selling the client on a particular plan and obtaining the agreement of his C.P.A. and attorney on the merits of the plan, they assist the client, his attorney, and his accountant in putting the plan into effect and in submitting it to the Internal Revenue Service for approval. They conduct annual audits to bring in newly eligible employees and to adjust benefits for participants who have changes in salary. They assist the client and his accountant in the preparation of any necessary reports for the Internal Revenue Service and Labor Department, and they even assist some corporate trustees in preparing their accounts and reports.

In the organization of Hester and Hester, there is an Associate General Agent, an Agency Supervisor, and two secretaries who assist in the administration of the General Agency. The Associate General Agent works primarily in recruiting, training and assisting the agents; he also takes care of many administrative duties and directs the activity of the new Supervisor. The Supervisor has recently been hired to develop a new unit of agents. They have one male Pension Administrator and three secretaries to handle the administration and service of the Retirement Plans. One other secretary assists on special projects and in the administration of their group plans.

Ralph inherited his secretary, Mrs. Frank Sills, from Mr. W. C. Hester after his death in 1960. She notes that "although I am some 25 years his senior in age, I have found Ralph, Jr. to be a most delightful person with whom to work. He is even-tempered, considerate, and is never too busy to be courteous. Although we do much of our work under pressure, he never expects more than is possible for me to do; and, if I have any problems, he is always quick to come to my aid. He is very systematic, orderly, and a clear thinker. He has a very keen mind and studies constantly to keep always abreast of changes in things pertaining to the insurance business."

Hester and Hester have enjoyed an exceptionally high persistency. Only one of their pension plans has been converted or diverted into other methods of funding, and very few of their plans have been terminated except as a result of corporate liquidation, merger, or reorganization. Ralph believes this may be true, because Hester and Hester try to make themselves as indispensable as possible and stress the continuous service rendered by their organization.

The greater part of Ralph, Jr.'s time is devoted to the sale and administration of pension and profit-sharing plans, and the greater part of his father's time is devoted to the sale and service of personal policyholders and group insurance plans.

Ralph's goal when he entered the life insurance business was to achieve personal happiness and earn a reasonable income. The life insurance profession enabled him to attain his goal far earlier than he had expected. His present goal, which is an extension of his original goal, is to become as efficient and capable as possible in the practice of his profession, thereby rendering the greatest possible service to his clients. Ralph believes that this should result in far greater happiness for himself, but may not necessarily result in greater income. "I have long been convinced that the best and most beneficial results are attained by conscientiously attempting to do the best job possible for your client. His interest, desires, and welfare are paramount, and any success which I might attain is only a reflection of the degree to which I implement this belief."

Ralph believes that to have a reasonable goal, but one that will require you to extend yourself to your greatest limit is important for continued success in a life insurance career. To a young man who wants to be more successful, Ralph advises, "Turn every effort toward the accomplishment of your set goal and do not quit trying until you have reached it. When you reach it, you should set another goal and repeat the process. If you cannot obtain your goal, evaluate to find the cause. If you really haven't worked hard enough to achieve your goal, then you probably don't have the right incentive and you should re-examine your reasons for setting that goal. If you have worked hard and still haven't reached it, then you have probably set your goal too high to be reasonably attained within the time that has elapsed."

Ralph believes that the main danger for a young insurance man is the fact that he is his own boss. Obviously, this is also one of the greatest advantages in an insurance career, but if it is not handled with a great deal of self-control, a man will find himself very quickly out of the business. "An insurance agent must be imbued with the spirit that he is performing as real and vital a service to his clients as do their ministers and physicians," Ralph maintains.

"If a man's only concern is for the personal gain which he can derive from insurance sales, then he will never be happy in the business, he cannot become a good insurance man, and he probably won't last very long. He should never stop trying to improve his knowledge of the business and should continually try to improve himself as an agent, or he will find himself in the rear echelon, eating the dust of those who study and learn through the years. His insurance education should never be considered finished, even when he attains his C.L.U. designation. By all means, he should become active in his Life Underwriters Association, because of the many and varied benefits which he will derive from it. If an insurance man is not interested in trying to improve his profession and to improve himself as an agent, then he is in the wrong business."

Ralph adds: "Work like the devil, and don't worry about impressing other people. If you have the right motivation and incentive in your work, they will be impressed. Try to help yourself by serving others through your profession."

And this is exactly what Ralph is doing.

CHAPTER 23

DAVID H. HILTON, C.L.U.

QUIETLY AND INTELLIGENTLY, David H. Hilton, C.L.U. is becoming one of the Northwestern Mutual Life's most sophisticated agents. Although it took him nine weeks and 259 calls to make his first sale, he now regularly writes over two million, and in the agent's year of 1966 reached four million. Today he is well known for his outstanding intellect, his organizational ability, and his perseverance.

Dave Hilton and his wife, Ginny, live with their son, David, and daughter, Linda, in Evanston, Illinois. Ginny, primarily interested in her home, in music, and in charitable work, is also able to be of specific help to Dave in three significant areas: She maintains an efficient household filled with love; she picks Dave up when he becomes discouraged; and she also helps him in preparing life insurance talks.

Dave is a special agent in the O. Alfred Granum Agency of the Northwestern Mutual Life Insurance Company. He received his A.B. Degree from Dartmouth College in 1951 and his M.B.A. in 1952 majoring in accounting. This background has been very helpful to Dave in his present work.

In the community Dave has been active in college alumni affairs; he has served on the Board of Family Service, and he is a member of the Union League Club of Chicago. His primary interest, however, is in the church where he has served on the vestry at St. Matthew's Episcopal Church. For two years he was warden of the parish.

Dave says that two words describe his low-pressure method of selling—organization and dedication. He creates his image primarily through satisfied clients. He uses only two mailings, a personalized monthly calendar, which goes to each person in his active file, and a birthday card.

To get an interview with a prospect, Dave uses the referral

method. He asks the referrer to call the prospect to tell him the type of work Dave does. Generally, when he is referred to a new person he will use the two-interview system. On the first interview, Dave attempts to get all the factual information concerning the man and his family, plus his thinking on life insurance and annuities. When he starts the interview, he tells the client how they are going to proceed and shows him a completed audit folder of his own as an example of what he has done for other clients. Dave uses the regular Northwestern Mutual audit folder.

On the second interview, Dave uses a programming procedure called the Northwestern Mutual Planned Incomes service. Whenever it is possible, Dave tries once a year to review the client's situation with him, either on the client's birthday, or on his age change. At this time the client brings Dave up to date on any new factors; and, if appropriate, Dave will try to sell him additional life insurance on himself, his wife, or his children.

Dave's method of selling is direct, and he stresses the living benefits in life insurance. He emphasizes that a man must save money in any event and that the investment which a man makes in the death benefit portion is only about $1\frac{1}{2}$ to 2% of the interest on his money. The remainder is a tax free build-up.

The following sources gave Dave his four million plus production for 1966: New clients—$1,300,000; Repeat business—$1,700,000; Wives and children—$1,000,000; Year's total—$4,000,000.

One-half of Dave's business comes from attorneys and accountants, and the other half comes from all types of businessmen, but mainly from junior executives between the ages of 25 and 40.

Dave chose the life insurance business, because as a professional life insurance agent you can run your own life and be your own boss; you can help people to create order out of their financial situations; you can acquire many friends; and you have an unlimited income.

Dave gives credit to John Jamison, Al Granum, and Pauline Jefferies, for showing him how to use his time, for teaching him how to motivate himself with a plan of prospecting, and for surrounding him with a "success" atmosphere. Dave also maintains that outstanding underwriters do the things that many people do not wish to do.

Dave's basic objective is compellingly simple; it is an elaboration of his present successful work system. He would acquire fifty new clients each year for twenty years; this would make 1,000 clients. If the first sale to each was $20,000 that would be $20,000,000. If one-half never bought again, but the other half increased their purchase to $100,000, that would make an additional $40,000,000. If wives, children, business insurance and gift situations were added, he could hope to acquire $100,000,000 total production.

To a young man thinking of life insurance as a career, Dave would stress organization and dedication as absolute musts. He would emphasize the value of life insurance as a living benefit. "If an agent does not or will not believe this, he should not be in the life insurance business. I believe it to the extent of a $6,000 annual premium, and this makes me much stronger when I am discussing it with a prospect or client," states Dave. "I would particularly advise the young man entering the life insurance business of the emotional ups and downs, and to be prepared for negative reactions."

In summary, Dave emphasizes that life insurance is a positive thing; a man should not buy life insurance just because he might die too soon, but rather because he might live too long. In effect, a man must save so that he will have money when times are difficult. Dave believes that there are basically four financial catastrophies that could occur to the men he generally deals with: early death, disability, economic depression, and not saving enough money. Dave presents life insurance as being a hedge against all four catastrophies, not just the first. For statistics show that the chances of one of these four catastrophies occurring between now and age 65 are very great. Most men either do not realize this or do not want to realize this. Dave knows that if one of these four things do happen, life insurance is the best property to own. If none of them happen, he's gotten back about 2% interest compounded annually, which is probably better than he would have done himself, if he had not bought life insurance. Dave also believes that a man should keep in mind that life insurance cash values accumulate tax free and offer favorable settlement options. He concludes, "I don't believe a man can find a better investment."

O. Alfred Granum, C.L.U., and Pauline B. Jefferies, who have worked closely with Dave since he came into the business say this about him:

To begin with, he is very superior intellectually. In addition, he is highly accurate in all of his activities and not the least bit given to guessing when uncertain. He reaches decisions promptly after careful analysis of whatever problems are involved.

He always has been and continues to be eager to improve himself and to attain new goals. He seems to require new challenges and a diversified life.

In his dealings with people he is frank and sincere and develops enduring friendships with those who learn to know him. He is not the high-pressure type of salesman, but is most effective where he has the opportunity of living with people over a period of time. This, of course, gives him a tremendous advantage in building the solid career of lifetime counselor to between 500 and 1000 of the outstanding young men in our area.

We feel that one of his great strengths is an unusual ability to hew to a program of action once he has decided upon it. Nothing gets Dave Hilton off the track.

Also, from the personal standpoint we feel that he is an all around swell guy who lifts everyone with whom he comes into contact. He participates in, and makes excellent contributions to, all of our agency groups. As you know, he has contributed generously to the industry and a number of his speeches and articles have already been published.

And in our opinion and in theirs Dave has unlimited potential for future growth. He will be a giant in the industry.

CHAPTER 24

EMORY L. JENKS, JR., C.L.U.

THE DIVERSIFIED RENAISSANCE MAN had nothing on Emory Jenks of Atlanta, Georgia, who balances business interests, civic activities, and the life of a father to four with equal aplomb. He had already begun acquiring this knack when, during his high school years, he served as President of the student body, basketball Captain, and Salutatorian, and was the winner of the *Atlanta Journal* Cup for the best all-around student. He also lettered in basketball and football. In 1950 Emory entered Georgia Tech. He dropped out in 1951-53 for Army service in Korea, where he was praised by the Commanding General for his work in psychological warfare.

Emory re-entered Georgia Tech and joined Pacific Mutual at the same time. Upon graduation in 1956 with a B.S. Degree in Industrial Management, he was accorded highest honors and membership in Phi Kappa Phi, the honorary scholastic fraternity. Emory also finished his C.L.U. exams one month after his graduation.

"My main activity during college years," says Emory, "was entering the life insurance business on a part-time basis, liking it, and then arranging my college courses to provide maximum benefits to me as a career underwriter."

Emory was already the father of two little girls and a member of his father's Pacific Mutual General Agency in Atlanta, when he graduated from Georgia Tech. While a part-time agent, he had become sold on the life insurance business, after handling a death claim on an orphan policyholder.

Emory proudly points out that his wife, Moppy, was willing to stand these first low income years to allow him to become established, while at the same time she was competent and confident enough to go ahead with having and rearing their four children. Today they enjoy four or five vacations a year—

two long trips of two weeks each and two or three long weekends. Their suburban yard houses a regulation size trampoline and numerous children's athletic devices. Moppy helps Emory in entertaining clients and in interviewing wives of prospective new agents, for Emory is now Agency Manager as well as a member of the Million Dollar Round Table.

Emory has served on the Board of Directors of both the Atlanta Life Underwriters Association and the Atlanta Chapter of C.L.U.; he also served three years on the Content and Technique National Committee for the LUTC Health Course.

Without variety in his work, Emory tends to go stale, therefore, he develops a new approach every 12 to 18 months. These come from an adaptation of another's idea, or revitalizing an old technique or using a new tax insurance law, or a law change. Emory then develops one basic approach from this, and contacts all his prospects about it, including policyholders. After the initial contact using the basic approach, information is often developed which leads to sales ranging all the way through juvenile, accident and sickness, up to estate plans or business insurance. Some of these ideas have been the addition of the disability provision to government life insurance (or of purchasing the same type of plan for non-veterans); programing of disability insurance in conjunction with Social Security benefits; eliminating income taxes on dividend accumulation interest by using them to purchase additional new insurance; programming cash value accumulations; life insurance as a capital venture vehicle, etc.

For the idea on Social Security integration with insurance, Emory received wide recognition. When Social Security benefits were changed, he developed a significant method of integrating these changes with the financial plans of his clients. This method was incorporated into an article which won the Pacific Mutual Best Story Award and was reprinted in *The National Underwriter*.

Another idea, selling level term riders instead of accidental death, has generated many additional sales for Emory.

And the idea of adding a disability rider to GI insurance yielded over 85% of Emory's business in a six month span. Emory has only one complaint: "It worked so well that I've just about quit using it." He simply checks with policyholders and referrals about adding this disability rider to their GI insurance. "While that's all there is to it, the results have amazed me," admits Emory. A $100 lifetime accident and sickness rider costs $9.50 per year. Knowing this was a good buy, Emory called a few policyholders to tell them. None of them knew about the provisions of the GI insurance, and the original five prospects that Emory contacted added the rider. They, in turn, referred him to twelve more people and this method just kept snowballing. "For the first time since I had been in the business, strangers began calling me to get information," notes Emory. "Since I couldn't make any money out of the arrangement, they appreciated it as pure service, much more than the elaborate programing I had done for many of them. Although I had no idea of selling additional insurance, all five of the original people contacted bought more insurance."

Another unique prospecting idea Emory uses is related to his owning a real estate subdivision. Emory asks a contractor for the name of his best subcontractor, saying that he wants to know because the contractor has done his subcontractor a favor. In explaining this, Emory points out that one business can suffer when another business is tied up. "But, with my client-contractor's arrangement the subcontractor doesn't have to worry about the many terrible things that could otherwise occur. I don't mention it, but it is plain that the other side of the coin is the problem of what would happen to the client-contractor's business if his subcontractor's business were to be tied up." Generally, Emory then finds it easy to get his client-contractor to introduce him to the subcontractor and to tell him a little about the type work Emory does so that the subcontractor can check things out, if need be.

Once a policyholder starts going along with this, a lot of leads can develop. The best case of results started with a sale to a paving firm. In turn, business plans were worked out with the asphalt firm who was supplying the paver, with another paver who was using the asphalt firm, with the trucking firm carrying the asphalt, with the land developers and bulldozers using the paver, with the curbing firm used by the developer, and with the plumber used by the builder. This amounted to $675,000 of life insurance and $19,045 in premiums!

In selling, Emory often uses a flow chart. He also has a

detailed brochure which contains visuals and explains how you can use life insurance as a means to build up large liquid funds for business or other uses, if desired.

Normally, Emory puts a new prospect on his mailing list for several months, before he telephones for an appointment. When he does telephone, Emory tells the prospect he has an idea which should be of interest to him, etc.

"I've had better success in asking for names to put on my mailing list rather than for people to call on immediately," notes Emory. "The monthly memo calendar, or whatever you send your policyholders is generally well received; so there is every reason a client should think his associates would find one useful too."

To make a success of a life insurance career, Emory recommends joining the company's "application a week" club as a minimum requirement. "Only through having a large number of clients can you normally succeed." Emory adds, "You must also believe that nothing can take the place of life insurance—both for living and dying."

These are the things he emphasizes when he serves as Chairman and Instructor in the Life Underwriters Training Council (A&S) Program. Emory also points out that a life insurance agent can be his own master and as self-reliant as it is possible to be in our society, with both his financial and physical rewards limited only by his own desires and efforts.

Emory strongly believes in what he calls his five-point magic circle of work:

(1) The harder you work, the more new work there is to do.
(2) The more things you have to do, the less time you have for details, worry, and unproductive work.
(3) And the better job you do for your clients and yourself.
(4) And the better job you do, the more you enjoy it.
(5) And the more you enjoy your work and feel it's important, the harder you work.

This circle worked to make him a member of the Million Dollar Round Table, and he is now using it to achieve an agency production goal of $250,000 new life premiums each year and personal production of $50,000 in new life premiums. For the year ending May 31, 1965, he was Number Two salesman for his Company with $90,000 in paid premiums.

Emory sells disability and hospitalization insurance as well as life insurance, and his premiums have averaged $15,000 annually from disability income sales and approximately $500 from hospitalization sales.

In 1957 Emory had his first opportunity at a big case. He sold a deferred compensation case on three executives for a $60,000 annual premium. "This not only compensated me financially at the time, but enabled me to ask people for $5,000 premiums thereafter without fainting."

Emory Jenks by his various activities and approaches to the life insurance business is one of the most creative thinkers and motivators in the business today. He has so many good ideas it's even possible to conceive a time when he could see each of his policyholders every day of the year, and still introduce them to a new idea worth hearing about!

CHAPTER 25

W. DONALD JORDAN, C.L.U.

DON JORDAN is phenomenally successful, both as a father—eight children, and as an insurance man—a Life and Qualifying Member of the Million Dollar Round Table. And what lies behind this record? Don gives his wife much of the credit: "Marie makes the family schedule and her own requirements conform to my business schedule—whatever it may be. Many a wife can and often does kill whatever desire may be within an individual to become successful by her lack of understanding. Fortunately for me, my wife's attitude has been such that she is willing to do whatever is necessary to enable me to attain the objectives I have set for myself and the family. Especially was this so in my early days in the business, when I had to work just about every night during the week." And today one of the things that continually drives Don toward success is the size of his family and his desire to earn an income sufficient to provide them with the better things of life.

But Don's drive alone could not have achieved such a record, unless it had had a solid foundation. Although he entered the life insurance business almost by accident, Don had graduated from the Wharton School of Finance. How he graduated from Wharton is in itself a lesson in drive and determination.

After high school, where he earned eleven letters in football, basketball, and baseball, Don spent a time at Fort Dix before enrolling at the University of Pennsylvania in the Wharton School of Finance for a business education. His education was interrupted after a year and a half, however, when he was recalled to active duty and spent ten months in Korea doing administrative work. Since Don had already utilized all of the G. I. Bill to which he was entitled at Pennsylvania, he went to work as an accountant for an import-export firm in New York City while living in North Plainfield, New Jersey, although he commuted back and forth to New York City every day. He also attended Columbia Night School for a year and a half, picking up elective credits that would be transferable to the University of Pennsylvania. When the Korean G. I. Bill was passed, Don went back to Wharton and graduated 1954.

He has continued his studies by attending the Advanced Life Underwriting School at the University of Connecticut in 1959. And in 1960 he completed four years of study and successfully passed the last of the five four hour exams to receive his C.L.U. designation. These studies have given a firm foundation and direction to Don's drive.

But even more basic than his education was the influence of his father. Don's father had taught at Columbia and was a noted tax authority who, before his death, was secretary of the Chemical Bank New York Trust Company. With this type of career in the back of his mind, Don started work, while still in college as a clerk-typist in an insurance office. Very soon Don found that, with his background, he was enjoying doing the programs for agents. Then, almost before he knew it, he was selling.

Don liked life insurance as a career, because of the opportunity to reap the entire benefits of his efforts, and because of the financial opportunities available to adequately compensate for the hard work expended. Don's immediate goal was an income of at least $10,000 by the fifth year; he reached this goal by the third year. He first made the Million Dollar Round Table in 1957, and he has qualified every year since that time except in 1961, when, as he recalled with a grimace recently, he decided to become a pension specialist. "I am now the most knowledgeable pension specialist outside the pension field!"

Don credits two men with big contributions to his success during those years: William G. Pierce, C.L.U., his first General Agent and former Vice-President of Fidelity Mutual, and Robert J. Kistler, C.L.U., his present General Agent and the man who brought him into the business. Both of these men have proven superior in their abilities to build and maintain the outstanding Fidelity Mutual agency in Philadelphia.

But Don has never buried himself completely in work. An active member of the Sigma Chi Club of Philadelphia, Don has held all the positions on the board, including that of president.

For recreation, he plays basketball once a week, relaxes with his family, reads trade magazines, and watches television. Don and his family take ten day vacations two or three times a year. Every year and a half Don and his wife have a two week vacation which coincides with the four day Company Convention. Also, at least twice a year, they like to get away for a weekend, leaving the children at home. Depending on the scheduled arrival of their next child, Don tries to get away for the Round Table Convention. In addition, the last week of the year is vacation time with very little business activity.

Don's full schedule requires superb management. Thus to get organized, Don lists the prospects he expects to see during the month, marking the ones he thinks are most likely to result in a sale, and he tries to see all of them or as many as possible. "Not seeing enough people," Don maintains, "is where many agents, including myself, have their shortcomings."

Don's one and only method for obtaining appointments is by telephoning leads referred to him by one of his clients. Don adds that he never seeks a referred lead from people he has not sold.

The greatest per cent of his new business comes from his old clients—70%. The majority of his new clients come from the medical market. Don tells how he gradually worked into this market six years ago, after getting a list of referred leads from an individual whose name had come to him through the use of his Company's lead letter service. These referred leads led him to other prospects, and Don is still using the endless chain they have formed.

For he used these early leads to develop nests of clients. When one of his medical clients changes hospital affiliation, Don calls and asks him to send a list of interns and residents, checking off the names of those with whom he is friendly and indicating whether each one is married or single. In this way he builds nests of clients in which he has prestige.

In a speech entitled "My Partner, the Telephone" which he delivered to the Life Underwriters Association of the City of New York, Don explained the gist of his telephone approach to get an appointment. After identifying himself, Don begins: "I specialize in estate analysis for physicians and have many of your associates as clients. Our mutual friends, Ed Jones and

Bill White, have told me that you have the potential of a very successful physician, and they feel that you should have the opportunity of seeing the type of work I have done for them. Will it be convenient for you to see me at my office Thursday afternoon at three, or would you prefer that I see you at your residence Wednesday night about 7:30?"

Although Don may vary his words slightly from call to call, they are never hurried, for Don wants the prospect to get a lot out of the sentences. Don stresses his name, that he is a specialist, that many of the prospect's friends are his clients, that the prospect's friends told Don to call, that perhaps he has something to show the prospect, and that Don wants to see the prospect either at his office or his home.

In the approach the prospect has only one decision to make —which time and place is more convenient for the appointment. About 25% of the time Don says he has no problem in getting the interview. He gets objections 75% of the time, ones with which we are all familiar.

Don counters all objections with questions designed to disturb the prospect's complacency. To illustrate: "Dr. Smith, has your present financial advisor pointed out how you and your wife can have more than $12,000 a year tax-free income at retirement? Dr. Smith, has your present financial advisor guaranteed that your children will receive 100% of your life insurance estate if you and your wife die? Dr. Smith, has your present financial advisor pointed out the disability income benefit of your life insurance?"

After each attempt, Don restates the appointment choices, and he doesn't stop until he either has the appointment or is convinced that the prospect has a closed mind. "I know I can get an appointment with two out of three referrals and sell 80% of these contacts," adds Don.

"As soon as I have made an appointment with a new prospect," Don says "I send him a resume which outlines my complete background and experience. In this way, he knows something about me when we get together."

Just before the interview, Don again uses the telephone as a time and energy saver: "Bill, this is Don Jordan. I am just calling to mentioned that I may be five minutes late for our 7:30 appointment tonight. That's okay, isn't it?" Of course, the real purpose in calling is just to be sure that the prospect is at home. As a result of doing this, Don has been stood up only twice this year on appointments, and these were to be held at his office.

"My sales procedure is necessarily long—an average of two and a half hours with the prospect. If I find resistance during the interview, I will often suggest that the prospect phone the man who referred him to me, if I find that the prospect hasn't had any contact with him since the appointment was set up. Eighty per cent of my sales are made on this first interview."

"When my clients plan to move, I remind them that a collect phone call will place me at their disposal should they want to see me before time for our next scheduled review. This offer to accept charges on long distance calls has paid off tremendously. Each year I can trace at least $200,000 of my business to long distance calls to or from clients from my immediate area. My classic example is a $23.60 call from Alaska for a $50,000 conversion."

Who could ever beat Don with the telephone, a wife, and eight children for partners?

CHAPTER 26

ALLEN R. KORBEL, C.L.U.

"YOU DON'T HAVE TO BE the popular stereotype of the born sales-man and like everyone to be a successful life insurance agent. Like anything else, skills are acquired, whether they are mechanical or mental. And if a person wants to do something strongly enough, he can and will do it. The whole world puts the price on you that you put on yourself, and if you think you can, or if you think you can't, you are right." This is the philosophy of Allen R. Korbel, C.L.U., who qualified for the M.D.R.T. his first full year in the business, and is a Life and Qualifying member at age 33. He knows what he believes and how to achieve his objectives. He single-mindedly goes about selling life insurance, now at the $3,000,000 a year mark in just nine years.

Allen's entry into the life insurance business was an accident. In December of 1950, Allen enlisted in the U.S. Air Force for four years. Although his father was a general agent with Central Life, Allen had never thought of going into the business, at least not until April, 1952 when he was at home on leave. At that time, one of his father's associates asked him why he didn't sell life insurance. The agent proceeded to give Allen a five minute savings presentation, and then asked him if he could repeat it.

Says Allen, "I hadn't thought that I possessed the ability to sell insurance, but after the agent did some explaining about saving money, I was impressed and thought that I certainly could repeat the same presentation. I went to my father, asked him how to read a rate book, and requested that his secretary type out a sales talk for me. The one page savings sales talk, plus the rate book and some applications went back with me to the Air Force Base, where I sold one of my friends a $10,000 policy. Writing out that application was one of the biggest thrills of my life. The amount of money that I earned from that sale in comparison to what I was making in the Air Force seemed so

125

big and so fantastic! I will always remember it as showing me the way to make money!"

Upon his discharge, Allen returned to the University of Wisconsin, majored in life insurance, served as president of the University Insurance Society, and was given the award for being the outstanding senior insurance student. While at the University, Allen sold life insurance part-time and passed all his C.L.U. exams in two years. He was also president of a corporation which was formed by the students in the dormitories to sell school materials and miscellaneous dry goods. While he was president, the store made more money than it had made in its entire fifteen year history. Allen believes that these college activities helped him in his understanding of the business world.

And on top of all this, Allen was married during his senior year at school. His wife, Grace, is a medical technologist, a graduate of the University of Wisconsin. They and their two young daughters now live in a home with a swimming pool, an extensive stereo-hi fi system, and three cars—one a Sting Ray and "strictly for play," notes Allen. "Complete relaxation has escaped me for quite a while, but it is something I am learning. My hobbies of stereo music and doing mechanical work on cars bring me closest to relaxation. Skiing, swimming, and yearly vacations are additional relaxing diversions."

Allen's favorite work organizer is a layout of the week, with the things he wants accomplished preplanned. His office personnel, two secretaries, are "partners in my business," states Allen. His office layout consists of his own 12 x 18 room, and an adjoining room for his secretaries.

Allen's first full calendar year in the life insurance business was 1958, when he wrote $1,450,000. During his first eight years, he has averaged over $2,000,000 a year.

One of Allen's earliest convictions helped him achieve these substantial amounts. Allen decided his first year in the business that if you want to get ahead, the best way is to go out and work, not join organizations to make friends so you might be able to sell them insurance. While you're joining and wasting time and money, you could be going out and sincerely making friends by actually showing and giving them the benefits of life insurance. This philosophy generates about 200 life insurance policies every year or one application every day that Allen is working.

Allen initially introduces himself with a pamphlet which gives his complete background and is designed to build prestige with people so they will listen to him. He also uses *Query* for mailing. But Allen has found the best method of getting business is to go out and knock on the prospect's door. He does know the names in advance and has gotten them either as a reference or else they have been qualified from some list or occupation, before he calls on them.

Allen begins the initial interview by telling the prospects he has some ideas that might be profitable to them, and that he would like to have their opinions. He always tries for a close in the first interview. During his first few years, his basic approach was savings. Now he is more flexible, and he listens to the prospect to find out what he wants. He does use the M.D.R.T. "Round Table Story" to help create his image as a successful life insurance man. Most of his interviews are done with a pencil and paper. He uses an 8″ x 12″ pad of graph paper upon which he draws diagrams. The majority of his policyholders receive audits of their policies and graphs which give the clients visual pictures of the incomes they will receive at retirement, and the incomes their families would get in the event of death.

To keep up with his policyholders, Allen reviews their master card once a year on the husband's age change date. Then Allen contacts these people, if he thinks it is necessary. Last year 65% of Allen's business was with old policyholders or members of their families.

In Allen's first four years in the business, he spent six and a half days a week in active work and study. He now leaves his house by 8:00 in the morning and returns to eat dinner. Then he sees people in the evening at their homes. Allen has always worked nights. At first he worked many Friday and Saturday nights, as well as the usual Monday through Thursday nights, with and without appointments. In the past year many lunch hours have been used profitably by lunching with policyholders and prospects.

Allen says that he gets most of his ideas from other successful agents. He had always read all the industry's magazines religiously until last year. He became more selective then, because he had already mastered many of the ideas and his time was at a premium. He has filed the best ideas into logical categories, and he reviews them periodically to master them and pull them out when the right situation arises.

Crediting his father with having given him the greatest inspiration to be successful, Allen says, "He showed me how things should be done and had me do them rather than do them for me." Allen also finds the members of the Million Dollar Round Table very inspiring men. "If they can do it, so can I," he says.

Allen's suggestion to young men entering the life insurance business with no business experience is for them to get a list of every classmate and go through every list of every organization in which they have been active—then go out and see all of these people with an idea for saving money.

As a result of his experience, Allen strongly believes that the best position in the life insurance business is that of an agent, or a personally producing general agent. "Here you have no problems and no entanglements with other than what you yourself create. I feel very strongly about this. There is no promotion from that of agent!"

Allen's secretary describes him as having an "I can and I will" attitude. "Each year he sets new goals for himself, and has always made it."

"He lives and breathes life insurance almost to the exclusion of anything else. That is, he is able to strive toward his goals to the exclusion of unnecessary things. He has the energy, and he doesn't waste it. Allen has KASH—Knowledge, Ability, Skill, and Habit!"

CHAPTER 27

BUDDY LEAKE

ANY FAN WATCHING BUDDY LEAKE spur the Winnipeg Blue Bombers to victory at the football games of 1956 could not have guessed that within three years Buddy would be a full time life insurance agent and on his way to Life and Qualifying membership in the Million Dollar Round Table. Even Buddy himself admits that "a life insurance agent was the last thing I wanted to be, when W. F. Hughes, General Agent for the Mass. Mutual, called me." Although Buddy already owned $55,000 of life insurance when he graduated from college, he knew almost nothing about its uses except for death benefits.

When Buddy did accept an appointment to meet with Mr. Hughes, he intended to say hello and leave, for Mr. Hughes was a friend of the family. However, Buddy found himself talking for over four hours about the life insurance business, why people buy insurance, and the benefits they derive. Although under contract to both the Winnipeg Blue Bombers and the St. Louis Cardinal's Baseball Organization, Buddy signed a part-time contract to sell life insurance. For three years he combined football with selling life insurance before signing a full time agent's contract.

In 1956 Buddy worked four months selling life insurance for a volume of $280,000 and commissions of $2,000. In 1957 he worked six months, produced $336,000 and made $2,400. In 1958 he worked nine months with production of $700,000 and earnings of $7,500. The next year Buddy became a full time agent and earned over $10,000.

Simplicity in his operation and conscientiousness at his work have helped Buddy qualify for the Million Dollar Round Table every year since 1962. Buddy now spends 75% of his time selling and 25% as a unit manager. He wants to find out whether he likes management and whether his ability lies in this area, believing that "it would not be v.ise to accept any of the many offers that come along without first getting a little experience in dealing with other agents and their problems."

Asked why he chose life insurance as a career, Buddy replied that "after three or four years I began to realize how great this business really is and that as far as I was concerned there was no other selling like it. But, at first, I had the same apprehensions that everybody has, when they are asked if they would like to sell life insurance."

As Buddy learned more and more, he realized that for any ambitious man who wants to control his own destiny and be his own boss without any substantial investment in a business, life insurance offers the greatest opportunity. "You also gain the satisfaction of doing work that you honestly know is helping others more than it is helping you." Buddy believes that the satisfaction one gets from selling life insurance exceeds the personal satisfaction a person gets from selling any other product.

Buddy went into selling very cautiously, but settling a death claim on his first client made him an insurance man for good. He had called on a medical intern at 12:30 one night in the hospital. The next day Buddy was successful in selling him a good size policy. Exactly two years and nine days after he had bought the policy, Buddy picked up the paper and saw where the intern had been killed in a plane crash while in the service. His widow was expecting their second child. "This experience gave me an insight into our business, that I don't believe an agent can get, until he has settled his first death claim," Buddy recalls. "I now felt that I could look anybody in the eye and tell him that, if he wants to provide for his family whether he is here or not, the only way he can do it on a guaranteed basis must include life insurance."

The competitive spirit, generally regarded as of prime importance for success in selling, came quite naturally to Buddy. The second oldest child in a family of six children (his own family today also has six children) Buddy remembers competing in organized sports from the time he was in the seventh grade. "Even before, there was always a lot of activity going on around our house. My brothers and I were always involved with either football, baseball, basketball or track."

His prowess in sports earned Buddy a football scholarship

to the University of Oklahoma, where his coach was the immortal Bud Wilkinson. There his competitive spirit was honed to a fine edge, while he piled up over 240 points to win the career scoring record at the University of Oklahoma—a record that has never been surpassed. Buddy remembers vividly some of Wilkinson's advice: "Everyone needs someone to make them do what they can do." Buddy tries in the life insurance business, to be that someone to himself. Buddy adds, "I have always found that one of the hardest battles that we have is to overcome ourselves. If we can achieve this, then we won't have any trouble with anyone or anything else."

College and professional football also gave Buddy a great deal of publicity which has helped him get interviews with many prospects under favorable conditions.

Each month he also mails out a publication with his name and address. And he announces his membership in the Million Dollar Round Table in newspaper ads. Buddy has found that attaining membership in the Million Dollar Round Table has helped, in more ways than he can possibly enumerate, to create an image for him in his business. And as he often tells newer men, nothing can contribute to their success in life insurance more than striving to become a Million Dollar Round Table member. In addition to the newspaper ads and monthly mailings, Buddy has found that the most effective advertisement in creating an image is the recommendation of your policyholders and people that you do work for and call on. Buddy has found that, if you do a good job for a man, he will tell on the average twenty people of your work.

To get the interview, Buddy uses Hank McCamish's method. Buddy sends the approach letter back to his center of influence with a post card enclosed. He indicates in his letter to the propect that he is sending the letter to the mutual friend and asking him to write any comment on the letter that he wishes. When the center of influence writes a note on the bottom of the approach letter, he mails the letter on to the prospect and mails the post card back to Buddy at the same time. In this way Buddy knows the letter has been received, before he telephones the prospect for an appointment. Adds Buddy, "This approach has always been successful for me."

Buddy believes that a life insurance agent should be seen

and not heard, at least not until he is sure he knows what his prospect wants to accomplish. On his first interview, Buddy makes sure that the prospect does most of the talking. Most salesmen, and Buddy includes himself in this group, tend to forget to keep quiet and ask only provocative questions to stimulate the prospect's mind, so he can communicate what he really would like to do.

Buddy's work organization pattern is set up on a monthly basis. At the beginning of each month he lists all the people he has reason to see that month. He then reworks this list, listing the prospects in order of importance. As he sells or contacts each person, he checks them off and records the amount of production that came out of the interview. In some cases it is necessary to transfer the prospect to a later month. To make this system work, it is necessary to continually ask for and receive new qualified prospects from the people with whom you are currently working.

The greatest per cent of Buddy's business today comes from the small, closely held business market. Several years ago Buddy decided that, if he was going into the business market, he would have to call on businessmen and strike out a few times to learn the market. After much work making himself call on businessmen, especially those 45 years and older, Buddy realized that he knew twice as much about insurance as they did. Therefore, there was absolutely no reason for him to fear calling on them!

The idea which has been most beneficial to Buddy has to do with the business market and came from an article written by Ben Feldman in the Retail Credit Report publication. Primarily an approach to people of substantial means, it begins: "Mr. Jones, in spite of today's high taxes and increasing costs, you have done a beautiful job in building a fine estate. It has been my experience that when a man dies after spending a lifetime building an estate, it is not long thereafter until that estate begins to fall apart. Let me show you what I mean." Buddy then takes out his estate booklet and starts discussing some of the cases illustrated there. This approach resulted in a number of life insurance sales to solve the problems that were brought to light. In fact, using this idea Buddy insured two people each for over a million dollars of Ordinary Life.

But even with this record, Buddy still has an occasional

slump in production. "These have occurred from time to time and even now still occur. But the experienced salesman has less trouble getting out of these slump periods in that he knows what he has to do to get moving again. Comparing a slump in selling to a slump in batting might help the younger man. It would be hard to believe that any great baseball player would think of giving up baseball, because he goes 30 times without a hit. What he does is go back to work, and take a lot of extra hitting practice, until he gets the base hits dropping again. I believe the same is true in the insurance business, but the younger agent needs to be counseled and shown the way in the early years." Another suggestion a newer agent might use to overcome a slump is to enroll in L.U.T.C., if he hasn't already done so. Still another way is to seek help either through his general agent or some other successful life insurance man in his area. Buddy is quick to point out that he does not mean that the new agent should expect this other producer to take him under his wing, but Buddy knows that most any good life insurance man would have lunch, etc. with a newer agent who is at a standstill.

Buddy believes that every young agent should be warned, so that he can develop a thick skin in the beginning while he is acquiring the skill and knowledge of his product and services. "I have seen many young agents fail because they have taken the 'no's' too personally. Once the agent obtains skill and knowledge, he will not get nearly so many rejections of his ideas."

Another of Buddy's suggestions for the new agent is to find a few ideas that he can sell, and then look for prospects who fit those situations. Buddy is strongly convinced that, if for example a man understands package selling, he should then look for people who are prospects for this idea. Doing this will keep the new agent producing and earning an income, and he can gradually work into different areas and try new ideas. Buddy believes and practices the idea of never spending more than 20% of his time trying something new. "A new man should try to sell the things he knows most about," Buddy points out. "If he will dedicate himself for the first five years to doing whatever is necessary, whether he likes it or not, then the life insurance business can offer him a most rewarding career, both financially and spiritually. The one ingredient that must always be present to overcome slumps is the willingness of the agent to go out and work to get the ball rolling again, even though he doesn't like it."

And Buddy has taken his own advice so that many a new agent starting into a life insurance career has looked at Buddy and been inspired to work harder to progress and take advantage of the opportunities in a life insurance career.

CHAPTER 28

WILLIAM J. MACKENBACH

JUST THE PLAIN ENJOYMENT of doing his work motivates Bill Mackenbach to sell $2,750,000 a year. With his desire for perfection, recognition, and accomplishment taught him by a father who encouraged him to be best at whatever he did, Bill has been a million dollar producer from his very first year. Highly motivated, Bill has channeled his drive into one market, and today he is considered an outstanding expert by the people in this market. He is a six times qualifier for the M.D.R.T., and long range he wants "to be one of the best in my specific market, and to sell ten to twenty million of life insurance a year."

Working exclusively in the medical market, Bill gets his first interview over the telephone from referred leads or from a list of senior students in medicine, dentistry, or veterinary medicine.

Bill spends this first interview pointing out how he specializes, working strictly with professional people, and how he continues to give them service as they move around the United States. He also shows them a proposal or a sample of one. Bill uses forms he has developed, and after making the sale he is careful to keep in touch with the client through letters, telephone calls, and a complete follow-up system.

This is the strong point of Bill's method—a good follow-up system. "So many people are flattered when you call them again," Bill notes. "Far too many agents forget a person once he has been sold a policy." Bill also sends out newsletters to classmates and on occasion calls them long distance. All of his work with doctors is connected with tax saving ideas that affect them, and Bill believes that selling these ideas is what he does best.

All of his married clients who own or buy $25,000 of life insurance are automatically audited. Bill explains to the client the importance of his knowing where he stands if he lives, and what would happen to his family should he die at a premature age. After Bill gets this information, he and his secretary meticulously complete the audit so that it is perfection itself.

Bill's secretary then makes an appointment for Bill to deliver the audit. Bill deliberately has his secretary call for the appointment so that the client will know that Bill is a progressive business man, willing to invest money in his work, and is the type of person that the client can with confidence do business for the rest of his life. "I pay my secretary well and consider prestige a part of her job," Bill emphasizes.

When he delivers the audit, Bill makes it clear to his client that he is happy to have had his secretary spend the ten to twelve hours it took to complete the audit. "I want him to know how enthused I am to be on his estate planning team. I want to be number one on the team, so I have to give the best service. As the attorney, trust officer, etc. see my work they feel they have to do the best job also. This is great because with everyone trying to do their very best, the results for the client are superb," Bill points out.

Bill believes that it is a must to invest—this does not mean spend—money in your business. Pointing out that most professional people must invest years and years in preparation for the income and reputation they earn, Bill says we should expect to expend time for insurance courses, to put money into our business operation, and to work hard.

We can never think pessimistically; we must always be looking ahead. This doesn't mean to forget about tying up the loose ends, the details of the insurance sale, and getting on with the next sale before we give the best service to our client. It means we have to hire people to do the details for us.

Everyone goes through periods of thinking that no one can do a job as well as they can. This is insecurity. Only after you realize that many people are trained to do jobs better than you are can you begin to be really successful.

Try to limit the work you do to only the things you enjoy doing. We only have sixty to seventy years to live on this marvelous, beautiful paradise, so why in the world do we want to do the things we dislike doing. It only upsets the motivation and enthusiasm we generated by doing the thing we enjoyed. Hire someone who enjoys doing the things you don't like doing. The result—her motivation and your motivation produced from two happy individuals working together toward a common goal will help generate more business.

It took Bill eight to ten hours of work a day for a year to sell his first $1,050,000 for an income of around $10,000. But Bill says that he really became successful as a life underwriter, when he realized he had abilities "to do more than sell just a million, if I set a goal." Last year Bill sold almost $3,000,000 working only four to five hours a day. But he stepped up his night work from the two or three nights he had gone out his first year in the business, to the four or five nights a week he goes out now.

Of his "almost $3,000,000," Bill says, "Not acquiring that $3,000,000 of sales in 1964, because I didn't discipline my time better is my most discouraging experience. I got to $2,751,500 and just couldn't do it. It was hard to take!" But the advice he would give anyone who seems to reach a standstill, Bill quickly applied to himself—evaluate, read inspirational books, consider new directions and better organization, and think how important a life insurance career is to the happiness of thousands of people. And they put him back to work!

Bill is very much interested in seeing young men succeed. In fact, just working with them as President of the Alumni Association of Delta Tau Delta Fraternity gives Bill enthusiasm. Bill is especially happy to see young, self-motivated men considering a career in life insurance. "Selling life insurance gives a man a sense of belonging and feeling of accomplishment. In this career you are richly rewarded in many ways." "But," Bill cautions, "the potential agent must know why he is entering this business and then go and do it. Good organization and direction are also vitally important; there are ups and downs, but you have to be willing to work around them. Be aggressive, not high pressure. Be respectful of other people and have real concern for their well being. I wish that I could give all talented men enthusiasm in their life's work of selling insurance and show them how they can do as well or better than I am doing. It is so simple, if you have a plan!"

In talks that he has made at various John Hancock conventions, at the 1964 Baltimore, Maryland, Underwriters meeting, and at the Ohio State Life Underwriters meeting in 1965, Bill has reiterated this enthusiasm for selling life insurance. Speaking to these groups, and working in the Columbus Life Underwriters Association are Bill's way of putting something back into the life insurance industry, which he knows is giving him so much.

For Bill gratefully remembers the inspiration he received from his successful cousin, E. J. Mackenbach, and from Dr. Bickley of Ohio State University, who encouraged him to enter the life insurance field, and the help and encouragement his John Hancock General Agent, William B. Hoyer, and his own wife, Gretchen, gave him, once he became an agent.

For Bill believes that the debt he owes to his fraternity, his college, and his profession can only be paid back by helping others. The things that he might have done during college days that would have smoothed his path in selling life insurance, he now encourages others to do: Take accounting courses and pass the C.P.A. exams; take the law courses and pass the bar exams. Bill, himself, is now working on his C.L.U., which he considers of greatest importance.

Bill is generous in giving out his new ideas, the latest—hiring a secretary and devoting the time saved to prospecting. Another unique time saver is dictating letters to clients and instructions to his secretary on his way to and from their lake lodge while Gretchen drives the car! (We aren't sure just what he has two year old son Eric doing! But we do know that Gretchen "never nags about my long hours and entertains graciously for weekend client-guests at our lodge on Grand Lake St. Mary, Ohio.")

Bill has come a long way since working as a gas station attendent in high school and selling storm windows during college. In a way he has come full circle, for his hobbies today are plumbing, woodworking, boating, and electrical work, with his major work, of course, life insurance.

And what does Bill believe finally separates the men from the boys in all of life's jobs?

The extent we will go to undo the things we know we do wrong. Realizing our mistakes and then being willing to give up something for a time to correct these errors is a sacrifice that won't last long. We all have to give up something to get something. But once we have done it, the joy of accomplishing this weakness is the most delightful experience one can have. The Lord has given everyone of us many things, but even the most successful men can tell you the Lord has also omitted something from them. The challenge is, can we take the few weaknesses and deal with them? Can we overcome them? The successful people can and have, and the unsuccessful people can't or won't—they don't have the conviction to change. And —until they do, they won't succeed!

CHAPTER 29

JERRY I. MATUSOFF

JERRY IS A YOUNG MAN IN A HURRY! He wants to see as many potential prospects as possible every day and to take care of their insurance needs as completely as possible.

Now General Agent for the Franklin Life Insurance Company in Dayton, Ohio, Jerry has tried to make every moment count ever since he entered the life insurance business in 1950. In 1956, he joined the Franklin Life as a General Agent. In 1960, 1961, 1962, 1963 ,1964, 1965, and 1966, he qualified for the Million Dollar Round Table and has consistently earned the National Quality Award. Charles Becker, Jr., First Vice President of the Franklin Life Insurance Company, tells us that Jerry qualified for the Franklin Million Dollar Conference last year with a volume of $2,395,200 and he is a life member of the Franklin Million Dollar Conference.

Jerry attended Ohio State University and Carnegie Institute of Technology, and at one time he was intensely interested in dramatics and considered a career in the theater. This talent has helped him to achieve poise and to become a persuasive salesman, always in command of the interview.

And to get those needed interviews fast, Jerry uses the telephone. An article he wrote for *Life Insurance Selling* in September, 1960, called "Consistent Prospecting: Use of the Telephone Are Keys to My Production" details how the telephone has been the tool that helped him reach the goal he set for himself at the very beginning of his career—membership in the Million Dollar Round Table.

His philosophy revolves around this statement: "To obtain a worthwhile interview the prospective client must be expecting me and be able to give me the time I feel is necessary to discuss his insurance needs."

His favorite sales approach, when meeting with young business or professional men is, to suggest to them that they purchase a large amount of term insurance, in most cases $100,000 as a minimum, to take care of their many immediate needs—general family protection, mortgage, personal, business equipment, etc. Then he strongly impresses upon them the idea of systematic conversion of this term insurance into permanent insurance. This approach has provided Jerry with many immediate clients. Jerry then gives these individuals continuous service, thus allowing him to stay in close touch with them. He steadily converts the term insurance they have purchased within a short period of time. It is estimated that one-third of Jerry's production each year is the result of these term conversions.

Jerry secures most of his new prospects through referred leads, the majority of which come from his many yearly calls on his term policyholders. In addition, he does the following: He watches for birth notices relating to his clients and prospects and other people he knows, and then he makes it a habit to call on these people. Secondly, he watches for marriage announcements, and, if he knows either the bride or the groom or some relative, he calls the newlyweds. Third, Jerry follows up business notices which appear in the daily press. And, he contacts newcomers to the community. Jerry's ideas are simple, yet how many of us consistently take advantage of situations that are open to us through newcomers, marriages, promotions, etc.

Jerry has also secured many clients through community work. In the City of Dayton, Jerry has been very active in his Temple and his Jewish Community Council; he is also past president of Dayton's B'nai B'rith. Like so many other young insurance men, Jerry has met many community leaders as they have worked together in various community activities, and often these people have later become Jerry's clients.

Like many other professional life underwriters, Jerry believes in preparing a survey analysis for his clients which includes an inventory section showing the record of all personal, business, and family life insurance; it also includes a policy analysis section, a distribution section, a retirement section including Social Security benefits where applicable, a miscellaneous section, and, of course, a premium calendar. He uses a handsome leather binder with the client's name embossed in gold. Then he keeps in touch with his client through a yearly review of the client's survey book, by contacting the client at age-change time, and by calling the client, if his name appears in a newspaper.

Of course, he calls the client at dividend time and delivers to him the Franklin Life's famous dividend check. Jerry feels that these methods have stimulated many new sales, and they are avenues that all agents who sell participating contracts could take advantage of—that of calling the client at dividend time, telling him about his additional money, and suggesting that he use the dividend for additions to his present program. Many times Jerry also uses as an appointment-getter the projector and film telling of Franklin's President's Protective Investment Plan.

Jerry's secretary, Roberta Kugel, describes him as a perfectionist when it comes to planning a client's life insurance program. She states, "Jerry works very hard to see that everything is done in the client's best interest. He is always in touch with his clients and keeps up to date on what is happening to them. He is a friend as well as an insurance advisor."

His secretary's opinion of him is borne out by a letter I received from his client and policyholder, Vic Green of Western Iron and Steel Company in Dayton. He states, "The service he (Jerry) offered in the beginning and the way it was maintained over the years has proven to be invaluable to me. The little extras, probably not necessary but very noticeable, make his service stand out in comparison with most of his competitors." And this service keeps Jerry's clients coming back for more and more and more.

CHAPTER 30

HENRY L. "HANK" McCAMISH, C.L.U.

IN MAY, 1956, a new face entered the production ranks of the Massachusetts Mutual. Since that time, his paid-for business has amounted to $31,738,857, none of it from pension or profit sharing plans. In nine and one-half years, this young man has averaged 3.3 million per year in production, and he was company volume leader in 1963 and 1965.

How did he do this? How did he have time to produce $7,576,000 for 1965 and also head the leading unit of his company in the United States with $11,925,837? How has he had the time to make significant contributions to the life insurance industry and the Million Dollar Round Table, for he has served as Vice-Chairman of the 1966 Million Dollar Round Table Program Committee and is repeating as Vice Chairman of the 1967 Program Committee; such a repeat is a "first" in the MDRT organization.

Hank has also been the editor of Unit IV of the Manual of Personal and Office Efficiency published by the Million Dollar Round Table in 1965. This unit detailed office procedure and forms that he gathered from leading life underwriters throughout the country plus his own streamlined methods. These can serve as a guideline for any new man entering the life insurance business or an experienced man who wishes to streamline his operations.

The key point of Hank's entire operation is his ability to organize. He gives much of the credit for his success to the three girls associated with him in his office. He would be the first to admit that he could not do the work that he does both for his clients and for the industry as a whole without their totally unselfish approach and willingness to give their all, especially when the going gets rough. Hank's office is situated on the 21st floor of the Fulton National Bank Building, and he does his work in Suite 2106—a beautifully furnished gold-carpeted walnut-paneled office.

It is obvious that to accomplish this much production, Hank must plan, and he starts his yearly operation by marking out the final week in December and the first week in January exclusively for planning; during this time he makes no appointments. He reviews as objectively as possible every case which he has worked on during the previous year, and he sets his goals for the coming year. Hank says that setting his goals has been largely responsible for the success he has achieved to date. For example, in 1963 his personal production goal was $4,200,000, and he paid for a little over $4,300,000. He states that "I am convinced that if I had set my goal to write $3,700,000, I would have only paid for a very little over $3,700,0000." In 1964, his goal was $5,000,000; he paid for $5,421,250. In 1965, his goal was $6,000,000; he paid for $7,576,000. He feels it is impossible to reach any destination, unless you decide precisely where you want to go. It's just that simple. He makes a goal, and he plans a year in advance how to achieve that goal. He feels that any agent faces impossible odds in an attempt to reach any destination, unless he decides exactly where to go and how to get there.

Hank has stated that "When I came out of the service I wanted to stay in Atlanta, because I had attended Georgia Tech. I went to work for the R. L. Siegel Company of Atlanta selling floor covering on a straight commission. For a while I worked for Siegel in Savannah and then returned to Atlanta. Finally I decided to enter the life insurance business. I did so primarily because I wanted to be in a field where I was talking to the individual who had the final decision to make. Life insurance is the one business where my success would not be dependent upon another individual selling my merchandise. In the floor covering business I could do the job by selling the dealer my product, but he could not reorder, unless his salesmen moved my product. When I reached the decision to go into the life insurance business, I knew that my success or failure would hinge upon my own ability. I would be compensated entirely on my ability and willingness to work."

Hank McCamish may be termed a general agent's dream. When he first walked into the office of his future general agent John Humphries, he was told that he could not be financed.

Hank replied that if he could not finance himself this was the wrong business for him, adding, "All I want is an office." The general agent assigned him to a small office without a window and did not see him for thirty days, during which time he was studying the Mass Mutual's way of doing business. In the next thirty day period he was paid $2,600 in first year commissions. John Humphries says, "Hank is beyond a doubt the finest organized man it has ever been my privilege to know in this or any other endeavor. And because he has mastered his time, his continued growth in the life insurance business is assured." Hank, in turn, believes he was fortunate in his selection of a general agent: "John has given me an opportunity to run as fast as I can run and has never in any way discouraged me from trying to do something which may have been a little out of the ordinary. I honestly feel that it would have been impossible to have achieved as much happiness and success in another agency. The climate and overall atmosphere created by John has contributed greatly to whatever success I have achieved to date."

The dental market, especially dental school seniors, developed over the years into Hank's prime source of clients. Although he did not confine himself to this market in the beginning, most of his follow-up business came from referrals by men he wrote as dental seniors and on whom he later expanded coverage. In the last three years or so, however, there has been a shift in emphasis to the business insurance market, and today the majority of his volume comes from outside the dental profession.

What exactly is Hank's system and how does it operate? First and foremost, he uses the referred lead. This involves Hank's sending his pre-approach letter through a client or referral, by asking them to make a notation at the bottom of his letter, mail it to the prospect, and then send Hank a postcard which he has prepared. This postcard then lets Hank know his letter has been mailed and gives him the go-ahead to telephone the prospect for an appointment. At this first meeting Hank sells himself and aims for the complete fact-finding interview. He has developed his own questionnaire, which he uses to gather information concerning the individual. Returning afterward to the office, he dictates what has transpired during the interview into a form which he calls Financial Planning Notes. When he goes back for his case presentation interview, Hank opens the interview by telling his client that before he goes into any of the details of his estate plan, would he please check over the Financial Planning Notes and this Financial Planning Inventory to be sure that they are correct. He states that the notes are his (Hank's) understanding of the information the client gave during the first meeting. Then Hank lets him read the notes, making any necessary corrections. This information, which in essence is a financial x-ray of the prospect's personal estate and of his objective, forms the foundation of all their subsequent discussions.

After getting agreement from the client on his notes, he moves into what he calls Financial Planning Ideas. This is an outline that he has his secretary prepare, listing every idea that he intends to discuss with his prospect. Some of these ideas might be disability income, systematic accumulation of capital, a self-pension plan, the creation of an adequate net income producing estate for the family, trusts, and a formula $(2/3 + 1/3 + C + E + E + 1/2)$ to help the client pinpoint exactly what his family will need in case of his premature death. He goes over each idea in detail and asks questions, because he wants the client's acceptance or rejection of each basic concept before proceeding to the next idea. When this has been accomplished, he simply checks off the first idea and moves to the second.

He does not bring out the specifics of his recommendations during the discussion of the Financial Planning Ideas because he wants his prospect to understand the total basic concepts. He is attempting to present these before offering him solutions to the problems which he hopes will be brought into focus through discussing the Financial Planning Ideas. This has helped Hank in closing the client, because the premium is never mentioned while he is trying to get across the basic underlying concepts. To save time he has developed standard illustrations which he uses to explain that life insurance can solve the individual's problems and accomplish his objectives for him. He explains that the program which he has recommended solves the particular client's problems and shows how they are woven together into one composite estate plan. Then he asks his prospect to go back and tear apart each of the ideas that he has presented and to tell him what is wrong with them. If he has done an adequate job of preparation, the close is automatic. This is Hank Mc-

Camish's closing secret which led to 7½ million last year.

As a final follow through, each one of Hank's clients is furnished with an individual policy analysis which is prepared by the Insurance Data Corporation of Atlanta. From these the client can ascertain very quickly the values that his permanent life insurance program is building up and learns to appreciate the real value of this reserve. Each year Hank sends the client a yearly progress report. It is a summary of the values within his permanent life insurance program, whether it be one policy or fifteen, all in one company or seven or eight different ones. All this is handled by the Insurance Data Corporation; and Hank, in his fine talk at the Million Dollar Round Table in 1964, presented this step by step, becoming one of the first, if not the first man in the country, to make available to his clients the benefits of electronic data processing as far as up-to-date yearly records are concerned.

Is there any other basis for Hank's fantastic selling success other than his tremendous organization? Perhaps it can be analyzed by simply this. He has sold more insurance by asking questions than with statements. He has concentrated on attempting to become an expert in asking questions. And, just as important as asking questions, he has developed the ability to listen in every sense of the word. He has complete empathy with his clients, and he makes them feel appreciated and tries to understand them as human beings. Though he goes through the same formalities as most other agents in the fact-finding interview, he is more concerned about understanding the person as an individual than in finding a need for life insurance.

Even as successful as Hank is, he has paid and is still paying, the price for success by hard work and organization. And he has this to say to the young agent: "I have used the analogy that a man, if he is really going to be successful, must be willing to give the life insurance business basically what an individual going into the medical profession is willing to give to become a physician. In the early years it is going to require a tremendous amount of concentrated effort and study, long hours, night work, virtually a six day week. There are a lot of disappointments along the way, but if a potential for greatness is there—and it is in the life insurance business—then success is worth the early sacrifices. To potential agents I have said many times, if you aren't willing to pay the price, then stay out. If the life underwriter is not completely dedicated, if he fails to give of himself, it is the meanest business in the world. The man who does the job half way will soon find that job is tearing him to pieces. I have run into many disappointments and discouragements; I have managed to overcome this by praying. All I do each day is to ask God for strength to do that day's job to the best of my ability. At the end of the day, I thank God for that day and forget it. I have absolutely no control over what happened yesterday, and at this time I can't control what may happen tomorrow."

Dr. G. Hugh Russell, a management psychologist at Georgia State College, a professor who knows Hank well, is quoted in the Atlanta Magazine as saying, "There is one word for him and that is excellence. I know him professionally as well as personally, and I can tell you his empathy is remarkable, and it is genuine. You figure most of these four, five and six million dollar producers are going to be hard to get along with, but Hank still has the time to be a person."

Hank's life has shown that success is achieved by a willingness to pay the price, the ability to organize, and a strong desire to serve his fellow man and God. For Hank's long range objectives from the very beginning, other than his personal production and the building of his unit, has been simply this one—to live daily a Christ controlled life. This he practices each day. And each day seems to bring him a fuller and richer life.

CHAPTER 31

GORDON R. MEISNER, L.L.B.

MILLION DOLLAR PRODUCER GORDON MEISNER began his fast moving career as a lawyer. Today he is the General Agent in Detroit for the Indianapolis Life Insurance Company. He entered the business in 1951 and became general agent for his Company in 1958. He graduated cum laude with an L.L.B. Degree from Detroit College of Law, and during World War II served in the United States Marine Corps as a Japanese language interpreter. In Detroit he has been active in his country club and his Masonic Lodge; he is a trustee of his Temple and has taken a very active part in Cub Scouting.

Gordon obtains his prospects almost exclusively from referrals, and he telephones for all interview appointments. In his initial interview he asks questions concerning the individual and records these answers on a scratch pad. From the answers given in this initial interview, he programs on a worksheet, sometimes in front of the prospect. This worksheet, put out by his Company, is called "Your Financial Independence Plan Worksheet," and for those of you who do one-interview programming sales and are interested in perfecting your skill in this area, I suggest you write to Gordon or the Indianapolis Life for a copy. They would be very glad to send you a copy of this sheet. It is a most interesting way to do one interview work in front of a prospect and a useful calculating device in programming.

The majority of Gordon's sales are made on the first interview, after he has received a definite commitment on the amount of money to be invested. If a second interview is necessary, the real purpose is to give both the prospect and Gordon a chance to go further into the program already proposed.

Gordon's law background has proved most helpful in building up a clientele for whom he specializes in estate planning and insurance for tax purposes. He does much follow through work with trust companies and attorneys to set up estate plans. His principal market at this time is business and professional men from 30 to 45 years of age.

He keeps up with his clients by sending birthday cards, age change cards, and a quarterly mailing piece entitled "You and Your Money" which is published by Indianapolis Life.

When we asked Gordon why he entered the life insurance business he told us that he became a life underwriter "because I was determined to make more money than I thought I could practicing law." In life insurance underwriting we have an unusual opportunity that attorneys do not have. We can solicit business and still give professional help to a man in planning his estate and financial situation through our knowledge of taxes, estates, etc.

In discussing the problems of the young life insurance agent, Gordon made two points: "Work hard and develop as many clients as possible, because this is the foundation from which success springs. The number of clients one has by the age of 35 will practically determine how successful a man will be in the years to come. He can spend the rest of his days selling and servicing these old policyholders and obtaining from them adequate referrals to consistently produce a million a year."

Gordon's second point dealt with avoiding high pressure and unpleasant persistence. "One of the errors I made in my early years in the business was pushing too hard too often. Unfortunately, one of the errors I find in our business is that of making young agents overzealous in their attempts to spread the benefits of life insurance. I thoroughly believe in the benefits of life insurance and own a substantial quantity myself, but an agent must learn the art of pleasant persistence, and in training agents I have sought to impress upon them the need to act in this way."

You may wonder how this young million-dollar producer has been able to make so many sales on the estate planning programing approach in just one interview. For one thing, Gordon is as thorough and considerate of someone who buys a $2,000 policy as he is of one who buys a $100,000 policy. After all the same man who buys the $2,000 policy today may someday buy a $100,000 policy! In addition to this sincere consideration for all men, Gordon has assiduously cultivated the art of conveying ideas by means of the spoken language. Gordon's clients buy from him because he has been able to simplify his presentation; they understand what Gordon is trying to explain—the fact that life insurance can and will fill certain of their financial needs.

We have in Gordon Meisner a young man who wrote $600,000 in his first year and has continuously built up his production to a volume in excess of a million, while at the same time handling a general agency for his Company in Detroit.

Gordon's approach to the insurance business shows us how one can build an agency and still produce a million each year. Gordon sold enough people early in his career so that by growing each year with this clientele, he is able to write well over a million.

CHAPTER 32

GALEN J. MEYERS

GALEN J. MEYERS, of Topeka, Kansas, became a million dollar producer in 1960, his first full year in the business. He has made the Round Table every year since that time. Galen says that his Agency Manager, Mr. Otto Schnellbacher, and his Supervisor, Mr. Thomas M. Gregg, committed him to that first million dollars of production. "I was told that this was what I should shoot for, and I did. My goal hasn't changed."

Galen's wife, Carolyn, readily accepted the idea that Galen would have to be gone for long irregular hours and for many nights each week. "Without her initial support at the time I entered this business, my home life would have been hellish. Every life insurance man knows how important this is, and I am grateful to my wife for understanding."

Galen discussed the place of social, civic, and business activities with Mr. Schnellbacher and Mr. Gregg, and they decided that participation in these activities should come only after Galen was well grounded in the fundamentals of life insurance and was making a decent living at it.

Galen's desire to be recognized as an outstanding life insurance man makes any desire for money a secondary goal, and he very early realized the price attached to such a goal. "When I started, I had no personal image. I just worked as hard as I could and saw as many people each week as possible, and I began to make a few sales here and there. With these people I did simple programming, all the while trying to do the best possible job for the buyer or prospect. As a result of this hard work, it has been my good fortune to have more referred leads than I can use. I think this is the image of our Agency as well as myself personally. My Supervisor and Agency Manager taught me this attitude, and it has worked for me. I have always tried to keep the welfare of my clients uppermost in my mind and have paid little attention to any remuneration that I might receive from any one sale or combination of sales." Galen was told when he came into this business that, if he would think of his clients first, his pocketbook would take care of itself. Galen adds, "This is simply the way it has worked out. I don't worry about money anymore. I do the best possible job I can for my people, and it seems that I always have enough to spend at the end of each month."

Galen even sends out thank you letters after a closing interview, whether or not the sale was made. He also sends out birthday cards, and clips articles out of the paper to send to prospects and clients.

During his first year and a half in the business, Galen did everything on a cold call basis. He came into life insurance from the heating and air-conditioning business where he had been accustomed to parking his car on the street and walking four or five blocks down one side and up the other, knocking on every door. That is what he continued to do when he came into the life insurance business. With the policyholders he got in this way, he built his image; but in the last year and a half 90% of all his new calls have been a result of referred leads. He made these calls either in person or by phone and has had fabulous success with them."

Galen's initial interview with a referred lead is conducted on a simple programming basis. He goes through a series of steps: First, he uses a Confidential Preinterview. From this, he gets a dollar commitment and puts it in big letters on the table in front of him. He also indicates on a piece of paper in big letters any additional money the prospect now saves or can save.

After this has been determined, he begins to motivate his prospect, using a Success or Failure sheet. This section of the presentation deals with the part that ability, opportunity, and time play in financial success. Galen then goes directly into the Save and Create, and Create and Save illustration. Since Galen has already determined whether the prospect is saving money, and if he is saving at a bank or a savings and loan association, Galen can now use this information in his illustration. He continues the interview by asking the prospect where he would feel best about saving his money. The prospect usually agrees with Galen that the Create and Save method is the best. Thus, Galen gets another commitment.

He then shows the type of plan he recommends and uses the simple programming device called a Security Chart to illustrate his recommendation. Galen sells mostly ordinary life and usually adds term.

The final step in Galen's interview prepares the way for his next sale. He reminds his young prospect, now a policyholder, that he will be buying life insurance through the years, until he has acquired somewhere between five and ten life insurance policies. Galen explains to him why and what he intends to sell him in the future. "At this time he knows I am coming back, and that I will expect him to buy again from me in the years to come."

When Galen delivers the policy he also delivers a green notebook which has the policies broken down in chronological order.

Galen then sees his clients regularly, every month or so. Topeka is a small town, and Galen can go from one side to the other in fifteen minutes. Hence, it is fairly easy to keep in contact with his clients. "If I didn't someone else would, and I don't intend to have this happen," declares Galen.

Galen now makes six calls a day; he works five nights a week from 5:00 to 10:00 P.M. "These are my golden hours, and the hours when I have the best success in seeing my people and selling my product." In his first year in the business he worked these same hours.

Galen spends his mornings in the office. The Schnellbacher Agency operates out of a new two-story office building in a suburban area of Topeka; it was built on one of the old golf courses, which is now beautifully landscaped. Galen has a private office which was given to him, when he became a million dollar producer. During the mornings he does a tremendous amount of detail work. He has 900 policies in force on approximately 700 lives. He and his full time secretary do the necessary service work to keep all clients' records up to date. He makes calls in the afternoon, as well as doing outside detail work in the field. Galen goes home at 4:00 P.M., eats dinner with Carolyn and their four children, and goes out again between 5:00 and 5:30 P.M.

Galen's market is young men. "I started cold canvassing in a young market; these people became clients of mine, and from them I get the referred leads that keep me going today." He adds, "I wish I knew of a way to make it easier to get started in life insurance, but I don't. I just made a lot of cold calls and wrote enough business that the referred leads now come from my many policyholders and clients."

Galen believes that a good secretary is a necessity to success. "When I have to sit in my office and do detail work, I go wild. I have now worked out a routine with my secretary which accomplishes this task fairly well. The work load gets so heavy in this business that a writing agent must have somebody helping him all the time."

Galen's secretary says that he is an easy man to work for and with. "I have never heard him say a cross word or ever known him to fly off the handle. If I make a mistake—and there have been some lulus—he never gets angry. He takes the blame himself, and begins immediately to straighten things out." She continues, "Mr. Meyers is sincere; he never tries to oversell a client, and he always has a helping hand and an understanding ear for all of his people who are in financial trouble. It is a matter of conscience to him that every man who cares about his family has adequate protection. He contacts countless policyholders each month to remind them of their premiums and to keep their insurance programs up to date. As a result, he has won the favor of his many clients and kept a high persistency."

Galen credits Mr. Schnellbacher and Mr. Gregg with training and motivating him. But Galen adds, "It gets to the place where education and motivation are pretty much an individual thing, although we continue to take study courses and to motivate each other." Frank Sullivan, C.L.U., of South Bend, Indiana, has also been a tremendous inspiration to Galen.

To continue his education Galen has found insurance meetings helpful. He told us that he has never attended a meeting of the M.D.R.T. or a sales congress at which he didn't get one or more ideas which help him in his work. He has taken four parts of the American United Career Course, both parts of the LUTC, and the R&R Tax Course, and he has attended the American United Home Office Training school. He has received the National Quality Award for the five years he has been eligible, and he is a qualifying member of the M.D.R.T.

For the policyholders' issue of the *Weekly Underwriter*, Galen wrote an article entitled "How to Write a Million in the First Year." This article emphasized that a positive attitude, the proper training, plus good personal organization and perseverance helped Galen reach the "magic goal" in his first year as a life underwriter. After completing the pre-induction course, Galen set his objectives, organized a time schedule, saw that he had continuous contact with prospects and clients, made sure that he had the prospect's undivided attention during the interview, set about creating a desire, got referred leads, and laid the ground work to make the prospects into lasting clients.

Galen would encourage a young man to make life insurance his career, if the man has a basic belief in life insurance and the desire to be successful, especially the willingness to sacrifice and put in the long hours that this business requires. He would encourage him, because life insurance is the only business in the world where you can own your own shop and, without specific college or university training and without a big name or family backing, pave your road as you wish it to be.

By working hard and diligently, and by trying to do the best job he can for each client, Galen is paving his million dollar road to lifetime satisfaction and security.

CHAPTER 33

GEORGE NICK MICHALE

WHEN WE ASKED GEORGE NICK MICHALE to be in this book about "young Turks under 35," he quickly set the record straight: "I must confess that I am presently a young Greek not yet 30. If you can make room for a few of those, I will be happy to comply with your wishes." And indeed we could make room for a $2,700,000 producer whose parents came directly from Greece.

George Michale is a special agent in Kansas City, Missouri for the Provident Mutual Life Insurance Company and President of the Life Underwriters Association of Kansas City. He works with professional men and businessmen. In 1964, $1,700,000 of his production came from the medical market and $1,000,000 from the business insurance market.

Since the largest percentage of George's business comes from the medical market, we will concentrate on this phase of his operation. His sales presentation is based around an idea called "The Triangles of Financial Security." In his presentation, George uses two pyramids on triangles—one made up of fixed values of life insurance, and the other made up of fluctuating stocks, real estate, and other investments. George shows these triangles balanced on a seesaw, and he explains to the prospect what value each triangle would have in case of death, disability, or a need for cash. After he has discussed these "Triangles" with the medical student or doctor, all future material George sends to the prospect contains the "Triangle" symbols. For example, a key chain that George gives to medical clients has the "Triangles" attaining balance on it. George also makes available playing cards which have the "Triangle" symbol on them for the use of medical students, interns, and residents.

In the Student Union Barber Shop at the Kansas University Medical Center where nearly all of the doctors and medical students (totaling approximately 900) get their hair cut, George has been allowed to place his calendar which gives his telephone number and reads, "George N. Michale—Estate Planning for Physicians." George has never received a phone call because of the calendar, but twenty-four people a day see his name. George has also installed in the barber shop a General Electric Stereo set which provides music for the entertainment of these people when they go to the barber shop for their haircut. "The barber was nice enough," says George, "to have a small sign engraved, reading 'George N. Michale—Estate Planning for Physicians' placed next to the set." For his newsletter, George uses a quarterly letter called the "Medi Gram" which he sends to over five hundred medical people. George encloses information concerning Estate Planning and, in addition, adds a page called "Who's News Bitz" which has to do with the whereabouts of classmates, where they are practicing, where they are continuing their training, who's had children, etc. "Naturally, this type of information is received with delight by our clients," adds George.

During Christmas time, George and his wife, Marsha, hold an open house and invite many of their clients in the area; this is George's way to say a gracious thank you for their business.

Sixty per cent of George's sales come from the medical market, 30% from the business insurance market, and 10% from accountants, attorneys and individual sales to people in all types of work. After completing each sale in the medical market, George then asks his client to address a referred lead letter. This is a letter which George has devised and which the client addresses to one of his friends. In the letter, the client asks his friend to see George. George then takes this letter around to classmates of these satisfied policyholders to use as an introduction. This system has kept mushrooming until George can now meet on a favorable basis the majority of the people in each medical class of 100 seniors at the Kansas University Medical Center.

The method George uses to get an interview involves several steps. First, he sends a direct mail letter which the Provident Mutual Home Office has devised to advertise the Estate Planning for Physicians pamphlet. George will often receive a 10% reply requesting the pamphlet. He then takes the pamphlet, supplied to him from the Home Office, and delivers it to the individual's home himself. He does not tell the prospect he is coming; he simply meets him at the door, delivers the pamphlet, and asks for an interview in the future. "If he balks at this point, I ask him to have a cup of coffee with me at the Medical Center, which he usually consents to," continues George. "I call this our warming up interview. I get to know my prospect, and he gets to know me. At this point, I again try to sell him on a future interview to discuss the importance of estate planning for the physician." After these coffee interviews, George obtains eight yes's out of ten interviews.

George carries an easel on his selling interviews as the result of an idea given him by Charlie McCaffrey of the Provident Mutual Advanced Underwriting Department. Charlie would always carry a blackboard to the wealthy estate owner's office to discuss the problems the man might be concerned with. "If Charlie McCaffrey—as important as he is—was not too proud to carry a blackboard with him, then I shouldn't feel badly about doing the same thing," George decided. "I worked up my presentation on an easel and have carried this with me since that time." In his easel presentation, George again refers to his Estate Planning and Triangles of Financial Security. George sets up the interview, which usually takes an hour and a half, for an evening when the man's wife will be present.

At this interview George sets forth the problem—why it is necessary for a young doctor to look to life insurance for the answer to many of the problems he will be facing in the future.

George also offers his solution at this time. "I often recommend as much as $100,000 of life insurance as the initial step, if it seems warranted. The average policy usually ends up being approximately $40,000."

After George has completed his easel presentation, fixing the problem and offering the solution, he ordinarily tries for a medical close. He is usually able to have the person consent to being examined, before they arrive at a definite amount of life insurance. In the meantime, George obtains the prospect's other policies and takes them with him to use in working up an estate survey. George does an audit of the policies, works up a program booklet, and then goes back to the prospect with recommendations written out on the final two pages of the program.

The amount George recommends depends upon how much life insurance the individual presently has. George takes the amount the prospect presently has, subtracts it from $120,000, and this amount is the figure he recommends the prospect buy. The significance of this $120,000 figure is that this amount invested in a Trust Fund yielding 4% after expenses and taxes each year would produce an income of approximately $400 per month for a widow and children. This, George believes, is a basic minimum, without which the wife could not get by, and the prospect usually agrees to this. Then, George comes back with the recommended steps and a C.O.D. policy of anywhere from $100,000 down to $10,000, depending upon how much life insurance the prospect presently has.

George keeps in very close touch with his clients each year after they buy a policy. He sends them a letter two months prior to their age change with a form asking them to name any definite changes that may have taken place which would require getting together and updating their estate plans. "We emphasize that, if we do not keep in touch with them each year, we are letting them down. This puts them in the frame of mind of expecting to hear from us each year, whether or not they purchase any life insurance."

Even when his clients move out of town, George keeps in close contact with them. George recently completed a trip through Texas, during which time he had ten selling interviews; these resulted in six sales for a total of $280,000 of permanent life insurance. "Frankly, I am most concerned at this point with indicating as best I can to my doctor clients, that I can keep in as close touch with them as anyone else can. For this reason, I am not too concerned with what amount of life insurance they purchase on these trips, when I visit them just after they have started in practice. The important thing is that I have kept my promise to keep in close touch with them so that they know they can count on me in the future."

In brief, then, George's work organization is based on having one interview every evening, four evenings a week, in addition to making eight other contacts each day—either face to face or by phone with other prospects or clients. This is an increase over the interviews he had his first year. In his first year he made approximately five calls a day, now he makes approximately ten calls a day. He uses direct mail, delivery of the Estate Planning pamphlet, a coffee or lunch interview for fact-finding information and qualifying a prospect, initial sales presentation, and finally, the closing interview. "Depending upon the outcome of the coffee interview, I know either I have a good prospect or I eliminate him. I would eliminate someone at this point only if he has a closed mind toward insurance. I will set up a selling interview with a man as long as he has an open mind and is willing to look into the importance of estate planning at this stage of his career." Once George is able to come back for the final interview, he closes eight out of ten cases.

"I have a deep dedication to this business. I meet many people each day, each week, each month, each year, who need and want what life insurance has to offer. However, they don't know that life insurance is the answer to what they are looking for. It is up to me and others in our business to tell and show these people how life insurance is the answer to what they are looking for. I feel this deep dedication in helping these people solve their problems. It keeps me going and carries me through business slumps and allows me not to be easily discouraged by the numerous objections we encounter in this business day in and day out."

CHAPTER 34

ALBERT S. MORIARTY, JR.

AL MORIARTY has sold over eleven million dollars of life insurance to the student market of just one college. His extraordinary methods are so well thought of that he was recently asked by the Mercantile Security Life Insurance Company to serve on their advisory board entrusted with the job of designing a complete college program.

How did Al get into this college market work? It all began with his own college years. While attending the Oceanside, New York, public schools, he won a football scholarship to California State Polytechnic College. He played four years of varsity football, lettering each year. In 1957, he graduated with honors and was listed in *Who's Who in American Colleges and Universities*. In March of 1957 he was persuaded by Bill Ulrich of Lincoln National to enter the life insurance business. This decision became the turning point of his life. In his very first year he had a volume in excess of a million dollars, and an income in excess of $11,000. Each year since then he has made the Million Dollar Round Table, working exclusively in the college market at California Polytechnic. Last year his production was $1,250,000 on 118 lives.

Al has always been athletic and his whole family is interested in sports. They have a full size basketball court in their backyard, and all the family—Alicia his wife and their two sons and a daughter—enjoy this sport, together with other athletics.

Al has also found time to serve as both assistant football coach and head basketball coach at the local Catholic High School for the past six years. He is also past president of the Central Coast Life Underwriters Association, and is chapter supervisor of his fraternity, Delta Sigma Phi, at California Poly.

Because of Al's interest in athletics and his love of California Poly, it was natural that he should choose the college market for life insurance selling.

His first letterhead read "Albert S. Moriarty, Jr.–The Lincoln College Plan" which described exactly what he is doing–selling a college plan to college students. He approaches these students through direct mailings and unique ideas of his own. In the approach letters, which he sends out to graduating seniors in the fall, he states that he knows he will be unable to personally contact all of the seniors. But before they talk to any other life insurance man, Al suggests that it would be to their advantage to call him first. And, believe it or not, this boy has such a reputation at California Poly that the seniors do just this!

Another unusual promotion idea which Al uses is the spread sheet. Each year he gets out this sheet, very expertly designed with pictures of the graduating seniors he has insured in the previous years. As an entree and an interest getter this spread sheet is unexcelled. And it's just another reason why Al has been able to write a million every year for the past nine years in the college market.

Al approaches these seniors by direct mail, approach letters, and cold calls. In his initial contact he explains the uses and the types of insurance and gives the college senior an education in exactly what insurance does and the different types and kinds that are available to them. He closes with a simple programming approach pointing out tax advantages, etc.

Al told us that when college seniors cannot pay their premiums, he finances the first year's premium and gives them a year and a half to pay it back. He does this through a note, if necessary.

Al told us that when these young men leave his area, he sends their files to Company agents in the other parts of the country where they are going. What an unselfish young man Al Moriarty is!

Al originally had his office in his own home, and when his young college clients came to this office to discuss life insurance, the informality seemed to put them at ease. However, now that he is a personally producing general agent with four men, he has moved his office downtown.

Working with so many young men has given Al some very definite ideas on the type of person who can grasp the opportunities of a life insurance career: "If a young man has the initiative to do hard work, there is no other business left, where you don't have to invest anything other than time, perseverance, and intestinal fortitude to be successful."

At age 32 Al Moriarty has already developed and used new ideas to point up the importance of the college market. We wish him success, for his innovations can benefit every one! In fact his ideas had become so well known and were so unique that he was hired by the Mercantile Security to design their college policies. He continues to grow in his business, building up first year commissions and a substantial renewal account.

His parting advice to other young men and to all of us is: "Have some place to go, and then go. Don't hesitate or be fearful of the situation. Keep in full command of yourself at all times, be steadfast, and you will fulfill your goals, and then your dreams."

CHAPTER 35

H. A. PAULEY

HAP PAULEY'S CALENDAR for the year may read like that of a fun-loving playboy: Winter holidays in Florida and summers in their country home on Lake Massawippi for the entire Pauley family—Hap, Mary, June Mary, Brent Stephen, and Gail Ann. But don't be deceived. Hap Pauley of Montreal, Canada, is a Qualifying and Life member of the Million Dollar Round Table whose production in 1964 was $3,810,800. "I believe in vacations," says Hap. "They keep you from going stale or climbing walls. I set production goals for four or five weeks. Providing I meet my self-imposed quotas, I take a week or two off. Altogether, if my production is up, I should be off twelve weeks in the year." Hap also lives in a large split-level which abuts a golf course, permitting him to jump the fence and practice his iron shots. The Pauleys belong to two golf and country clubs, two curling clubs, and a business club.

But things have not always been so. When Hap was fourteen he got a job to help his family, and he felt pride in doing this. His education up to that point reached the end of the eighth grade, and he managed the ninth and tenth grades at night. In seven years of public school Hap ranked first in his class for four years and second the other three. He was in the Navy for two years during the war. At the age of 24, he joined The Imperial Life Assurance Company of Canada and is still with them. He has no college degrees, although he did take night courses at McGill University in Income and Death Taxes, Business Law, etc. after he came into the life insurance business.

"Dad's philosophy is now my philosophy, at least in regard to myself and my own accomplishments. When my career is over, I want the self-satisfaction of knowing I did the very best job, not that I was capable of, but the best job that anyone was capable of. I may still be naive, but I don't know of any reason why I can't accomplish that."

In order to get an interview with a prospect (who is usually the owner of a business), Hap will often write a brief but persuasive note on his business card and mail it to the prospect. Hap's philosophy gives him his approach to the initial interview.

Hap knows that his prospect is usually a busy man with little chance to spend any time at all on his personal affairs, except to write checks once a month to pay the bills. (He often doesn't even know where all the money went!) Therefore, Hap points out to him that his corporation hires a firm of auditors to look after its accounting, a firm of lawyers to look after its legal problems, and a large number of employees—superintendents, department heads, officers, executives, directors, etc.—to oversee specific areas of the corporation's business. They use one, two, or more banks to handle their cash and to arrange financing. They use the services of one or more general insurance firms to be responsible for adequate and efficient general insurance coverage, etc. All of these things are done because the smallest detail is vitally important to the progress, well-being, and security of this corporation. Hap continues by asking the prospect if equally efficient attention to his estate and personal affairs are not at least as important to him, his wife, and his children. Hap then points out to him that he can render these services in conjunction with the prospect's trust officer, lawyer, and accountant. "The difference in my work and theirs," Hap tells him "is that my services are yours for life and free."

If Hap has difficulty getting past a secretary to talk to her boss, he will put the man's name and number in a diary and take it with him when he goes on a trip. At his destination he places a long distance person-to-person call to the prospect. Somehow when that operator says, "Mr. Pauley is calling Mr. Doe from Hamilton, Bermuda. Will you put Mr. Doe on," Mr. Doe always gets put on. After telling Mr. Doe that he has had an opportunity to do some serious thinking about Mr. Doe and his corporation, Hap tells him that he will be back in Montreal on such and such a day, and he would like to come right down and spend twenty minutes with him. Like most simple things, this works.

Each of Hap's clients gets a highly individualized report. Sometimes this report takes weeks or even months. At any rate, when the report is ready, it is not discussed with the prospect. It is gone over thoroughly with the prospect's advisors first; and, either their concurrence is obtained, or the report is rewritten to incorporate their views. If Hap cannot reach an agreement with the prospect's lawyer or other advisors, he merely advises the prospect and the case is over. "I don't have time to fight those in whom the prospect has confidence, and I'll make no recommendations I don't believe in. I see my client again only when I have the added recommendations and concurrence of his advisors, and usually one or more of them will accompany me. I think you'll agree that this makes the close rather easy."

Hap reviews each of his clients' files every two years. Before anyone becomes one of Hap's clients, he is told of and agrees to this two-year diary and review system.

Hap's unique method for gaining new insurance ideas, and one he likes to employ as often as possible is to "just sit and think, not about any one case, just about me and the work I am doing. Some of my best ideas and some of my biggest cases have come from this rather obvious method."

These think sessions help Hap reach his goals. He works as many nights as necessary to make sure of reaching his objectives. During his waking hours, when he is not on one of his vacations, he is in the business of selling life insurance and looking after his clients. Hap says that his only pattern is a minimum goal of $1,000 per week of new, first year commissions paid. This goes on for four or five weeks, and then he lets up and rests.

Hap has already surpassed his early specific goals, and he is now aiming for $60,000 new first year commissions per year in 40 weeks. Out of this, Hap can save enough to be financially independent within a relatively few years.

Hap says the biggest secret about success in this business is to set big worthwhile goals, stick to them, and not to accept failure. "Every man is master of his own destiny, if only he would realize it," Hap maintains. "It's easy to rationalize failure, but it's even easier to accept success."

Hap believes that the percentage of all men who cannot make a rewarding career of this business is insignificantly small, but the man's attitude has to be positive. "Nobody ever entered the life insurance business and fell into a fortune. Everyone had to adapt himself, had to learn, had to put what he learned into practice over and over again. Everyone had to fail a little, before he could begin to succeed. But the man who fails completely in this business will most likely fail in any business."

Hap says that the real turning point came a long time ago when he set out to make a cold call on the vice-president of a fairly large corporation. It was one of Hap's first calls of this type on a high-grade prospect.

"I took the elevator up to the sixth floor of his building and walked down the corridor, and suddenly I was in front of a glazed door that was terrifyingly inscribed with, not only his name, but also his title—Vice President. Then I knew what a cold sweat was. I did the only sensible thing to do; I turned around and walked down the corridor and took the elevator down and left the building. But—boom—I stopped myself on the sidewalk and gave myself a dressing down. I told myself that there were now only two things I could do. One was to immediately return to the office and resign, because I certainly wasn't going to achieve any measure of success, if I couldn't get up enough courage to go and call on a vice-president. The other thing I could do was to immediately go back up to that sixth floor and go in and see that man. That was part of the price I had to pay. I wanted success, so I paid for it. I wish I could put the perfect ending to this little story and tell you I sold the man. I didn't, but I did have an amazingly fine interview with him, and found out he had false teeth and couldn't bite hard anyway. That didn't vanquish fear for all time, but it did prove it could be overcome and even put to work for me, because when you're just a little awed by someone, you're also enthusiastic. For, as any fine actor knows, a few butterflies in the stomach assure one of giving a fine performance."

Hap says he has received added support from his manager, Bern Kane, who "honestly believes I can do the things I want to do." Hap tells of joining Bern's agency after his was dissolved. Hap was already a Million Dollar Round Table man. His problem was to fit into this new agency and be accepted as one of the boys. Bern took the bull by the horns and told Hap to write on the huge blackboard in the agency room that he would cover anyone's bet that he could bring in $4,000 of new premiums in the short month of December. "I couldn't quite follow his reasoning," admits Hap, "but, when you accept a guy as manager and counselor you don't question him, so I did as he suggested." Twenty or thirty dollars were covered, but Hap didn't really expect to win just before Christmas. Hap, however, found himself getting caught up in "this ridiculous thing and darned if I didn't pass the goal." With the money he won, he threw a party at his home for the other men and their wives. "I think this got me accepted in the agency as a regular guy, and I think too that Bern knew tough goals were good for me."

Bern Kane knows even more about Hap now. "It is almost impossible for me to be objective about a person that I like, and I like Hap Pauley," Bern begins. "He is the kind of fellow I respect and admire. He is a self-made man. He has been quite prepared to take a calculated risk and to be different, particularly in the early years of his career. He has a high selling skill and good interviewing techniques."

In his first year, Hap established a Company record for the number of sales made by a new man. In accomplishing this, Hap used a simple package of the old Twenty Pay Endowment at Sixty Chassis Plan.

Within about two years after becoming a life underwriter, Hap began to see that there was a much wider scope and a more important contribution that he could make and set about to increase his knowledge and skill in the fields of estate analysis, survey work, and business insurance. In order to do this, he quickly mastered all the material which his Company has available on these subjects. Following that, he enrolled at McGill University in Montreal, taking a night course in Business Law and Business Tax. As his knowledge broadened, his marketing technique widened to encompass his new knowledge. But the big reason why he has arrived at the point where he is today is, not so much because of this extra knowledge—other salesmen have been able to go that far—as it is due to the fact that he is still an extremely skillful, competent salesman in an interview. This competence allied with the new knowledge he has achieved, makes him an outstanding professional salesman.

He is professional in his attitude toward his clients; he is professional in his attitude towards fellow underwriters, and the institution of life insurance as a whole.

After adding his knowledge to his selling skill, Hap began to share his thoughts with others. He became an editor of his own column in a financial paper published in Montreal known as the *Financial Times*. He did his own research and for a number of years devoted a great deal of time to the publication of articles. He recently gave up this column with regret, because of the increasing pressure of time required by his clients.

Hap also became active in the affairs of the Life Underwriters Association. He is past president of the Montreal Life Underwriters Association, which, I understand, is the biggest bilingual association of life underwriters in North America.

Hap's sales record is, as we know, impressive. Hap has been a National Quality Award winner eleven times. He has been continuously a member of his company's senior Production Club, from 1953 to 1966 inclusive. In 1963 Hap's record of earnings entitled him to qualify as President of the senior Production Club because he was highest in earnings of all agents of The Imperial Life in 1963. He was also highest in volume and new premiums. At the end of 1963, Hap had over eight million dollars of life insurance in force. He has qualified for every convention in every year since he first became eligible in 1952.

One would wonder with his record, whether everything had been sacrificed to achieve his goal. These are the facts. Today, Hap owns his two homes, one in the finest residential area of Montreal. He has three small children and is a very devoted father. He takes an active part in the local Parent-Teacher Association. He has indeed lived a well-balanced personal life.

Up to now, it almost sounds easy and that Hap was one of the lucky ones who did it the easy way. This is not the truth. Anyone who achieves the success he did, does it only by paying the price that success itself demands. To be as conscientious as he is about the affairs of his clients, no matter how complex they may be, has extracted its physical penalty. Hap is tense, when working on a case. He is inclined to be short-tempered, demanding, and overbearing, until he has found the solution. People who don't know him might think these outward traits are the true personality, but they are not. He works under pressure and is not satisfied to make any recommendations, unless he is absolutely sure of his grounds.

Hap recently spoke to the Estate Planning Council of Montreal, of which he is a director, and he was introduced as one of the top life insurance men in the Tax Analysis field in Montreal. This statement is thoroughly true and is a real tribute to him, because Montreal is the most competitive sales area in Canada. It is roughly equal to the selling atmosphere in New York.

Hap is a very dedicated life insurance salesman. He is extremely well organized and has the ability to minimize personal distraction, which makes the difference between the professionals and the amateurs.

"But what is Hap?" Bern Kane asks and answers the crucial question: "He is a man who believes that he is able to achieve anything that his mind can conceive." Bern adds that he has valid proofs to confirm the truth of this belief:

Not so long ago on the last day of the month, I was short one application and $500 worth of premium to meet a branch objective for the month. I went to Hap and asked him to get me the business that day. He looked at me and said, "I haven't got a prospect, I have been working on a big case. I haven't got the time to go out and find the business for you." Knowing Hap, I didn't argue with him or plead either. I simply said to him, "Hap, I need the business, and I need it today. I'll wait until you bring the case in, but I need it today." Hap left the office at 10 o'clock and at 5 o'clock he was back with an application on someone he had never called on before with a premium of $500. His record is phenomenal. He has had the courage to be different. He has paid the price where it had to be paid because he is dedicated to his profession. He earned his success and the respect he has today from his clients, from his fellow associates in the Imperial Life, from members of the Montreal and Canadian Life Insurance Fraternity.

And what does Hap Pauley think of life insurance as a career?

Where else can you earn really big money doing tremendously important work to help people help themselves? Where else can you really be your own boss? Where else can you be in a position to meet so many different people? Where else can you get such a complete sense of job satisfaction? Where else can you get such a variety of different jobs to specialize in, if you wish to specialize? Where else can every day be so different and free from monotony? Where else can you get a job where the toughest competitors bend over backwards to help you succeed by passing on their sales methods, etc. to you? Where else can you get such a large opportunity to bring peace of mind to entire families? I suppose you can get these things in other jobs or professions, but where else can you get them all?

Hap encourages the new man to "at first make each week a whole career and don't quit—don't be soft on yourself—next week will be easier because you are more experienced."

For Hap believes that "anyone can be a success who wants to badly enough to be willing to pay whatever the price is. And, heavens, it isn't that expensive!"

And enormously successful Hap Pauley should know.

CHAPTER 36

JACK PECKINPAUGH

JACK PECKINPAUGH's civic interests in Muncie, Indiana, read like a biography from *Who's Who in America*. Jack is on the Muncie School Board, the Muncie YMCA Board of Directors, the National Council of the Sigma Tau Gamma Fraternity; he has served as Co-Chairman of his United Fund Business Division, Membership Chairman of the YMCA, president of the Ball State University Alumni Association, Chairman of the Wills and Bequest Committee of Ball State University, Chairman of the Alumni Division of the Community College Auditorium Campaign in 1960, Prairie Creek Reservoir Advisory Committee, Executive Committee of the Batholomew Planning Commission, former Member of the Delaware County Boy Scout Council, Member of the Elks Club, Charter Member of the Delaware Kiwanis Club, Member of a number of Masonic bodies; he served three years as deacon, three years as trustee, and six years as Sunday School teacher of the Walnut Street Baptist Church. In fact he has been engaged in so many more activities that it would take another full page to enumerate them. The summation of all the good Jack has accomplished in these organizations came when he was selected by the Muncie Junior Chamber of Commerce for their Distinguished Service Award.

In addition to all of this, Jack has been a speaker in the Iowa Leaders Round Table, the Tennessee State Sales Caravan, and the Ohio State Association Underwriters Sales Congress. He has spoken to the Columbus, Cleveland, and Middletown, Ohio associations, the Detroit Association of Life Underwriters, the Oklahoma Sales Congress, the Annual Meeting of the Indiana State Association, the Louisville Association of Underwriters, and he has spoken at least once to every local association in the State of Indiana. In 1965 he appeared on the Million Dollar Round Table program. In addition to all of these speaking engagements and local civic activities, he has served as president of the East Central Indiana Association of Life Underwriters, president of the Indiana State Association of Life Underwriters, and he has served on two committees for the National Association of Life Underwriters.

I am sure you are wondering, if Jack ever sells life insurance. Indeed he does. He has qualified for the Million Dollar Round Table for eleven years, and the National Quality Award for nine years. He wrote $1,100,000 his first year as an agent, and earned over $12,000!

With all of these civic activities and this much life insurance production he still finds time for recreation. During the winter, he plays handball three or four days a week at the local YMCA and attends all of the high school and college sporting events in the City. In the summertime he leaves on Friday afternoons with his family—wife Thelma Ann and daughters Beth, Ann, and Jane Ellen—for the Lakes where they have a cottage in North Webster, ninety miles from Muncie.

Jack says the real turning point in his career came during his first year as an agent when he went to the 1955 National Association of Life Underwriters meeting in St. Louis. This was the year he met Nate Kaufman and other members of the Million Dollar Round Table who, recognizing his ability, told him he could qualify for the M.D.R.T., if he would work hard enough. He went home determined to become a Million Dollar Round Table member, and he did it that very year.

And Jack's greatest thrill in the life insurance business came this first year, too. Writing over a million dollars worth of business, Jack found himself neck and neck with another young man in his Company, for the "New Man of the Year" award. At the end of the year Jack had $8,000 more business in force than the other agent, so it was a terrific thrill when he received the "New Man of the Year" award in 1955.

When asked how other men might have early success in selling life insurance, Jack's advice was to grasp the concept and purpose of the life insurance business, so he would never hesitate to ask someone to buy if they needed insurance. "You have a great service to offer your clients."

Getting down to specifics, Jack lists as musts for the beginner at least twenty new calls a week and an accurate set of records.

"A new agent must understand that there will be a lot of nights he will have to work and will not be at home with his wife. I would also make it a point to explain these things to his wife. This is the way I have patterned my own career, and I don't know of any other business in the world where you can be of as much service to your fellowman and still make a good living while doing it."

Jack became General Agent for his Company, the Indianapolis Life, in February of 1957; and his determination to make the MDRT year after year has kept him a constant leader in volume with his Company.

Jack, in singling out the person who has helped him most in his life insurance career, named his wife. "Constantly, she has stood beside me and has always given me encouragement when the going was tough. She does not have a defeatist attitude, nor does she ever let me know that she doesn't have belief or faith in my ability to get the job done."

Now, let's get at this man's sales patterns and see how he actually operates. The dynamic Jack has the good fortune to be at his best when he is selling a prospect face to face. Using a clear explanation of life insurance, Jack has from the very beginning used a savings plan approach and is still using it to the advantage, of not only the prospect, but to his already existing clientele. He resells them year after year on the uses and benefits of life insurance.

Denying that he has any unique methods for getting interviews, Jack sends a pre-approach letter, if it is a referred lead, and simply states, "Your name was given to me by Bill Jones who appreciated the work I did recently on his life insurance program. He suggested that I see you." Or, if he has an idea applicable to a prospect, he simply goes to see the person and tells him about the idea. Jack uses very few prepared proposals. He prefers to work out solutions by sitting in the man's office or living room discussing his particular situation with him and by writing things on paper that come into Jack's mind which would be interesting to the prospect. Jack still uses the Insured Savings Plan Sales Talk, but not always the pictures. "I do develop the ideas that start out with the Insured Savings Plan Sales Talk based on the individual case I am working with. I still find that people are interested in saving money, and that it is one of the easiest ways to get immediate action." When Jack begins discussing the specific contract to be purchased, he usually breaks it down into the cash value and the paid up insurance.

Jack keeps up with his policyholders by sending a Cal-O-Minder to them once a month. In addition, he sends wedding anniversary cards and birthday cards, and everybody is called at least every two years and sometimes more often.

Jack's market is varied. He sells to farmers, school teachers, college students, general office workers, and to small factory and corporation owners.

Jack Peckinpaugh is a real general practitioner in the life insurance business, doing a splendid job in his career and in his community.

CHAPTER 37

FERDINAND PHILLIPS, JR., C.L.U.

"IF A MAN is basically sincere and honest, particularly with himself, has that unknown quality that won't allow him to do a poor job, and goes to work for a manager who gets him started in a market where he can get off the ground relatively early, that man will do well," writes M.D.R.T. member, Ferdinand Phillips, Jr. And he should know. Phil wrote $500,000 in 1954, his first year in the business, and three years later became a member of the Million Dollar Round Table. That membership has continued to the present.

Until his transfer to Miami as the Equitable Life's District Manager in January, 1964, Phil had lived in Norfolk, Virginia, where he was born. He graduated from Washington and Lee in 1951 with a B.S. Degree in Commerce, and served as an Infantry Second Lieutenant during the Korean War. He worked in an advertising firm in New York City from January, 1954, to March, 1954, and at the same time he took the Equitable Life's Training Course at their Home Office.

Phil married in 1954, and he and his wife, Barbara, now have two daughters, Jane and Margaret. Phil says, "I place my family ahead of my business, and I have tried to cut down on activities which prevent me from spending my limited leisure time with my family." As an example of this, he gave up golf about two years ago.

Phil found living and working in Norfolk quite different from working in most cities. Since the economy of that area is inextricably tied to the government, Phil's market was unique in that it consisted mainly of Naval officers, although he had several sizeable pension, group, and business insurance cases.

Phil has a well-organized approach. He uses the telephone extensively to get most interviews, but when he thinks that it is more applicable, he has cold calls. He relies on the telephone to qualify prospects when at all possible. Notes Phil, "Since I relied on this method in a mass market, I believed that I should attempt to get an interview only with the people who have a need for life insurance, not those who just want to talk."

At the initial interview, Phil attempts to show the man something specific as soon as possible. "You may talk and talk, but you cannot know your prospect's real thoughts until you give him some figures or ideas to approve or dispute." Phil does everything possible to get an application on the first interview. About 75% of his business is written initially unbound. He sells the policy at the time he allows inspection of it by the prospect. It is a terrific approach that nearly always works for Phil. When a policy is issued, he will generally do a very simple programming job. He sends all of his clients birthday cards and Christmas calendars. He attempts to take care of their service requests as quickly as possible, and he gives them more and better service than is actually required.

What keeps Phil on the selling track? "I keep a hefty backlog of prospects, and I know that I could be on the telephone 24 hours a day, if it were humanly possible. I have always been a good prospector, and I am convinced that this has resulted in my sales, more so than my ability as a salesman. I have developed a philosophy of calling a large number of people, eliminating the tough nuts and attempting to get to the man who is close to buying. This has worked so successfully for me that I hesitate to change."

In Virginia, Phil was a part of the leading Equitable District within the leading Equitable Agency. This heady atmosphere encouraged Phil to keep his goals high and his production over the million mark for the eight years he was there. Phil believes that having been in a well-organized agency run by dynamic and interested district manager, Stan Watts (who is on the Executive Committee of the M.D.R.T.) made the difference between outstanding success and mediocrity.

Phil decided early not to let minor discouragements affect his day to day production. "When I came into the business," Phil admits, "my feelings were very easily hurt by the wise guys, but now I feel sorry for them. I am so convinced that the next yes is just around the corner that I welcome the no's, since they mean that I am just getting closer to that corner."

Although he was the president of the local Washington and Lee Alumni Association and treasurer of the United Cerebral Palsy organization while in Norfolk, Phil says this did not help his business. "You can write many more policies by being at work rather than spending the time socializing or just joining and attending meetings of a large number of organizations." Thus he carefully chose to join only those groups that were of personal interest to him, and not for business reasons.

Although Phil still personally produces since moving to Miami, his primary job as district manager is recruiting. In the last full year, prior to Phil's becoming District Manager in Miami, this district had first year commissions of $68,546. During Phil's first year, 1964, this figure rose to $91,971, up to $110,000 in 1965 and is expected to reach $150,000 in 1966.

"It took me nine and a half years to realize that management was for me, but the decision was the wisest I've ever made. When I find a prospective agent that I'm convinced has the essentials necessary for success in our business, I can sell him with my heart and soul, because I know I'm offering him the most wonderful opportunity he'll ever have. Unlimited individual achievement is life insurance selling's most appealing aspect. I am a firm believer in free enterprise," maintains Phil, "and today, unless your father owns the store, life insurance selling is one of the few avenues for success in the Horatio Alger style. It is all well and good to sell a prospective agent on the wonderful things that he can do for others, but if he is to be successful, he must have that elusive trait called 'desire.'"

Phil has often noted that many new agents either attempt to sell the big case too soon or refuse to change their method of doing business, after it has long ceased to be productive.

"I strongly believe that the key to an underwriter's success isn't his knowledge of several sales ideas. It is his overall selling philosophy that will make him aware and desirous of using the sales ideas that do come to his attention."

Phil explains his driving force as "a desire to never do less than I did the previous year, and a conscience that bothers me, if I do. Money is not my prime driving force. It is, rather, that I don't want to violate a trust that has been given me."

For Phil never forgets that of a man to whom many talents are given, much is required.

CHAPTER 38

ROBERT G. REBER

"I was a one-third equal stockholder in an office equipment company, operating on extremely limited capital in a highly competitive market. It was quite apparent that the business could not grow. In fact, the manufacturer really held a club over our head, because he could cancel your exclusive franchise within thirty days. On two different occasions I had seen men work for a number of years establishing customers—then within a thirty day period be out of business. I didn't want this to happen to me, so in 1957 I began looking for a new career," reminisced Bob Reber.

Bob made a list of what he wanted:

1. The opportunity to render my customers or clients a service so valuable it would reward me with excellent compensation; where I could build a clientele who would depend on me, thereby buying Reber and guaranteeing me a secure business future; a career where I could grow—to an income of $50,000 or more.

2. A production that would not be bought strictly on a price or bid basis—one that would be quality merchandise.

3. A business of my own to operate and manage according to my judgment—not that of a manufacturer 500 miles away. The business could not require any substantial capital investment.

After extensive investigation and upon reading Frank Bettger's book, Bob chose a life insurance career in Cincinnati with the William T. Earls Agency of Mutual Benefit Life. Today he credits Bill Earls, Al Schmerge, Francis Merritt, and Ted Hawes with having the greatest influence on his career.

Although his start was not particularly spectacular—he entered the business in 1957 and made the M.D.R.T. for the first time in 1960—once he hit his stride nothing could stop him. An unusual creativeness, a strong desire to do the best job possible and to be the best life insurance agent—all these and more made him 1963, 1964, and 1965 leader in the Earls' Agency (which is the largest and the number one agency in the Mutual Benefit). Bob is now a Life and Qualifying Member of the M.D.R.T.— he has made it every year since 1960—as well as a winner of the National Quality Award since 1960. He has been a member of National Associates, Mutual Benefit's organization of its twenty-five leading agents since 1963.

To continue in top production Bob knew he had to keep learning, thus he made it a point to attend an advanced life underwriting school one month out of each year. Among those he attended are the Purdue University Life Insurance Marketing Institute and the Mutual Benefit's Analagraph School (Estate Planning).

He has also been very active in civic affairs. In 1957 he served as Vice-Chairman of the United Appeal Fund and has since worked on the drive each year. In 1958 he was voted the most outstanding Board Member of his local Junior Chamber of Commerce. And when he served as President of the "Jaycees" in 1960, he was honored as one of the three most outstanding Presidents in the State of Ohio. He also serves on the Board of Directors of several corporations and a charitable foundation.

Bob has been very generous in sharing his ideas with others by giving speeches throughout the United States. He spoke at the New York Underwriters Association Sales Congress in 1962, at the Cincinnati Life Underwriters Sales Congress in 1963, at the Million Dollar Round Table in 1964, to the Nashville Life Underwriters in 1965, and to innumerable company meetings.

Bob is also a member of the Executive Committee and a past Vice-Chairman of the Professionals' Planning Associates, a group of Mutual Benefit agents who do business with professional men.

However, the most unique group that he belongs to, in fact instigated, is SAGGA, Selected Agents Growth Group Association. He has served on the board of directors and as treasurer; he was the charter president and is currently serving again as president of these men. Bill Earls got the idea for SAGGA from Willard H. Griffin, General Agent for Northwestern Mutual Life in Hartford, who wrote about it in a 1960 edition of *Manager's Magazine*. The concept was that a select group of agents within an agency could on their own begin a series of meetings for their individual upgrading. At these meetings the agents themselves would compare records, compare work habits, compare production results, and compare procedures during the morning session. The afternoon part of the program was a guest speaker from outside of Cincinnati who was extremely prominent in the life insurance industry or related fields. Bill Earls knew that comparison of efforts and results by the agents themselves could have a far greater motivating effect than a meeting planned by the general agent for them. Thus Bill put the bug in Bob's ear, and Bob took it from there.

The initial group of SAGGA was comprised primarily of men who were well established in the business, who had a strong desire to improve their selling methods and their efficiency—men who were ambitious and wanted to move ahead fast. The group met once a month at an attractive club, hotel, etc., away from the agency, and they limited their membership to ten.

Each man kept records and his organization and achievements were analyzed by the group. Bob remembers that in the beginning there were many hurt feelings, because they were so ruthlessly critical of each other. But this paid off. All the members of SAGGA are million-dollar producers with the exception of one, and he has been told to raise his sights or get out. Bob credits SAGGA with helping him to write over two million instead of one.

But all of the inspiration in the world cannot sell insurance. It still takes plain hard work, and Bob's case is no exception. His first year he worked six days a week, twelve to fourteen hours a day for five to seven interviews each day. He also worked four to five nights a week—"anytime I could find someone to listen, I was there," he told us. Today with ever increasing production, he still finds time to take a new idea to each one of his clients every year. And this works to give him even more sales.

One of Bob's growth patterns for production is based on this client building idea which originated with Alden H. Smith, C.L.U., who said:

"This is my best single piece of advice to a young man. Let the young man pick out 200 other young men within ten years of his age, educate them, sell and service them, stay with them, and in the normal course of time, they and their contacts or referrals will buy more than a million a year."

Bob uses an easel board, a scratch pad, and a felt pen to make his presentations, during which he lists the client's financial problems and gives the solution in simple language. Bob rarely permits himself to become involved in detailed discussions of illustrations, net cost, and so forth. He prefers to discuss the solutions with his clients using analogies and concepts for better communication. He knows people will not buy what they do not understand. His most unusual presentation is the one which he uses for corporate owners which is entitled "The Corporate Cow." On a printed sheet of paper, 14" by 17", which shows a cow consuming dollar bills, he develops tax saving ideas for corporations using a felt tip pen.

He also listed his "sweat questions"—questions he uses to probe, disturb, and quiz (or PDQ as John Todd, who originated the idea, put it). These are a few of the ones Bob has developed for himself:

How are you planning to redeem the substantial increase in your income tax resulting from your wife's death?
How do you intend to prevent your wife's second husband from becoming the heir to your estate instead of your children?
Will your family receive the maximum benefit from your life insurance estate, or will they be short-changed ten to twenty percent of its *real value?*
We have taken a survey over the last three years and found that eight out of every ten people we called upon have considerable "frictional waste" in the premium dollars they are spending for life insurance. The "frictional waste" ranges anywhere from fifteen to fifty-five percent. Do you know how much "frictional waste" you have in your premium dollars?

To help him in his tremendous amount of work, Bob has three associates, and he hastens to add that they are associates in the true sense of the word. His Executive Assistant is Mrs. Alberta Rand; and she has a secretary to help her. Some of Mrs. Rand's duties include doing the computations and other detail work in order to put Bob's presentations, especially his easel presentation, together. She takes clients to the doctor for examinations, picks up the medicals, and goes on interviews and conferences with Bob. She is very adept in handling people, and she makes many of Bob's appointments by phone. Bob also employs a man to handle the bookkeeping and to pay all bills, both personal and business. Thus Bob has freed himself to concentrate on the things he does best.

And in summary what does Bob Reber do best?

As a young man with the will to win and a desire to be the best both for himself and for his wife and two children, as a man blessed with the ability to communicate with his clients by using simple presentations to solve their business and personal financial problems, as a man who has earned membership in the Million Dollar Round Table every year since 1960, who had a $1,129,500 month in November, 1964, all whole life, and as a man who has an expected production of three million for 1966, it is very easy to clearly see exactly what Bob does best—sell life insurance!

CHAPTER 39

RICHARD B. RIPLEY, C.L.U.

RICHARD RIPLEY, C.L.U., is a member of Lambert M. Huppeler Company, 400 Park Avenue, New York, an agent for the New England Mutual Life Insurance Company and a life member of their Hall of Fame. He is also a Life and Qualifying Member of the Million Dollar Round Table. Over 90% of his business is from pension, profit sharing, and business insurance sales; and at the present time, Dick has 20 profit sharing and 75 pension plans in force.

The son of a physician, he graduated from Upsala College and did advance work at Columbia and Pennsylvania. After Army service he became a professional football coach and teacher, but his marriage and expanding family, which now consists of five children, sent Dick looking for a new career, one he could believe in, and one akin to teaching.

He found what he was looking for in life insurance. He became an agent in 1953, and set his goal as M.D.R.T. membership. That first year he wrote $500,000 for an income of approximately $6,000, and in 1956 he qualified for the Million Dollar Round Table. He has qualified every year since that time. He is also a ten year qualifier for the National Quality Award.

Dick finds organization his most difficult problem, and frankly says his most discouraging moments have occurred in personal financial management. This liability has been all but voided by his major assets of effective prospecting and closing so that he wrote $2,575,000 in 1962, and his production for both 1963 and 1964 was $2,500,000 plus, and over $3,000,000 in 1965. You don't have to be perfect to succeed!

To achieve his goals, Dick prospects continually for six times the volume of premium he wants to write, primarily through others. For, practically all of Dick's prospects are acquired through a second party, usually a C.P.A., lawyer, or another

185

agent. He uses the telephone to contact some semi-referrals.

Dick uses no special mailing pieces, depending only on his ability to talk with men on their own terms as his approach.

Dick also believes in an ultra simplified method of selling life insurance; he encourages the prospect to talk of his problems. Dick listens and isolates the key desires before showing him how certain types of insurance can solve his problem. Dick then keeps reiterating how insurance is the solution, until the interview comes to a close.

As to the actual mechanics of his work, Dick explains at the initial interview what he does, shows a list of firms he has done work for, and offers the prospect a similar service. Not using a formal proposal, Dick amplifies his solution verbally and gives any necessary supporting figures in pencil or on accounting paper. "Any material I use is on the back of old envelopes," admits Dick, "except standard R&R, Home Office material, etc."

The sales presentation that Dick has found most effective begins:

Mr. Prospect, my solution to your problem (retirement income, estate liquidity, family income, or whatever the need may be) is provided by a program whose maximum cost is less than the minimum cost of any other solution.

Let us examine the other possibilities. Basically, the solution of every problem is in providing the proper amount of cash at the proper time.

How else can we raise cash?

Invest? (Add tax cost + uncertainty.)

Borrow? (Add tax cost + uncertainty + interest.)

Steal?

Life insurance and adjuncts (annuities, etc.) provide cash when needed, without uncertainty and with preferred tax treatment.

You can't pay more than 100¢ on a dollar for delivered life insurance.

Yet every other method costs 100¢ or more on a dollar.

Another idea that has helped Dick to explain and sell pension profit sharing plans is to compare its tax advantages as something for the client and his family paid for by Uncle Sam.

In the August 1965 issue of *Life Association News*, Dick gives in detail in "A Corporate Cornucopia" exactly how he shows executives that a pension and/or profit sharing plan can enable them to get more tax free profits out of their firms, and how he overcomes objections such as: "A pension plan is too expensive." "We are too new." "We're too small and have too many older employees." "Anyway, most of our employees are organized and are covered under their own plan." Dick's approach generally follows this outline.

There have been many changes recently in both the general approach to this area and in the tax laws that make it very attractive in spite of (prospect's objection). But let's face it. We have found that with most successful businessmen like yourself, the one thing that bothers them most is how to get more from the corporation for themselves and their families without hurting the business.

A really smart accountant friend of mine once said that there are only four legitimate ways a corporation owner can build for himself and his family from his business.

First, he can increase his salary or take a bonus (reasons against.)

Second, he can pay dividends (reasons against.)

Third, he can plow back his earnings into the business (reasons against.)

Fourth, he can adopt a qualified pension or profit-sharing plan. Any money the corporation may put into such a plan is a current expense, just like salaries or bonuses. But the participants are not subject to tax on their share now! Etc.

Dick then lists collateral advantages to this plan.

Next he asks: "Why don't I give you a rough idea now of how a plan might work for you? How many full time employees do you have? Etc."

Dick believes that at this point the agent should negotiate informally as many of the details of eligibility, etc., as possible.

The next step is to get into a general discussion of types of plans, ending with: "You have told me a lot about your company. I would like to take this information back to my office and think about it, and then come back with some proposals designed for your particular situation."

At this point the agent should build prestige for any expert he plans to bring in at their next meeting.

Finally, the agent should set up the next meeting with: "Could you have your fellow stockholders, your C.P.A., and anyone else you think might be helpful at a meeting in about two weeks? When we get together, I will have everything roughed out in the form of raw material, or building blocks, so that you can see exactly what you can do. Etc."

The agent should take his leave with: "If your bookkeeper is free now, I would like to get the information concerning your employees, dates of birth, etc.; and I will see you in two weeks or sooner, if I can. I will call you for a definite appointment."

This method of selling pension and profit-sharing plans has given Dick over a million of production for over five years.

Dick credits his General Agent, Lambert M. Huppeler, with giving him excellent ideas, and his first supervisor, John L. Bryden, with establishing his work habits. He has also attended L.U.T.C. Courses, New England Home Office schools, and Advanced Life Underwriter seminars. He passed his C.L.U. exams in 1957. Dick continually studies law and accounting, especially corporation law and finance.

The advice Dick would give to young men thinking of entering life insurance is, "Don't, unless you have had experience in human relations, or you have been successful in a prior business. And even then to become competent you will have to study for many hours. Only after extensive preparation will you have something of value to offer any client in almost every situation without being a know-it-all. Don't tell the prospect; listen to his problems, and only then suggest a solution, and in such a manner that the prospect will think he conceived it. *Why* is the most important question to ask. Keep studying and keep it simple."

When Dick isn't working, he, his wife Alice, and Richard, Warren, twins Ned and Katherine B., and Bruce vacation in Florida or take long weekends at the New England seashores and elsewhere. They sail, golf, and ski. Dick also counts among his recreational activities, participation in civic clubs and school. He has served as area Chairman of the Community Chest, Chairman of the Board of Trustees and Chairman of the Executive Committee of an independent School, a Director of a Child Guidance Center, and a Sunday school teacher.

Whether working or playing, Dick always seems to move to the forefront and a position of leadership.

CHAPTER 40

OWEN J. ROBERTS, C.L.U.

IN JUNE, 1960, at the age of 27 and with less than two years of life insurance experience, Owen Roberts passed all five C.L.U. examinations on his initial attempt. In calendar year 1965, his corporation, Capital Formation Counselors, Inc., was responsible for placing over $10,000,000 of Ordinary Life with paid, annual premiums exceeding $400,000. A Princetonian, a bachelor, and a Life Member of the Million Dollar Round Table, Owen Roberts is today making history in the life insurance industry.

He is President of Capital Formation Counselors, Inc., and with his associate, Edwin H. McMullen, Vice President, Owen works exclusively in the estate analysis market. They are primarily concerned with wealth perpetuation within the family group and preservation of business utility. Capital Formation Counselors, Inc. enjoys a nationwide reputation and numbers among its clients some of America's most prominent families and New York Stock Exchange Corporations. Owen and the CFC, Inc. staff are located in Clearwater, Florida, while Ed has his office in Lakeland, 60 miles inland.

Capital Formation Counselors, Inc. performs a financial service called Comprehensive Financial Estate Analysis, *i.e.*, the creation, the conservation and the ultimate distribution of after-tax purchasing power. Their procedure includes a complete marshaling of the facts, the isolation of the problem areas, the crystallization of objectives, the calculation of financial alternatives and the factual communication of the economic environment to the client. When an analysis and proposal are made by CFC, Inc.'s technical staff, it may include as many as 300 pages and may represent an investment of thousands of dollars. The purpose of the presentation itself is to reduce a given complex situation into a crisp, concise set of facts to allow a client to take prompt action to solve his problems and to achieve his objectives.

Their philosophy toward their clients is: "Any man whom we are given the privilege to serve shall have the sum total of all our energies, skills, and ideas applied in a diligent and concentrated manner to solve his financial problems and to achieve his economic objectives."

If, after a complete communication of the economic facts, the financial instrument of life insurance either solves financial problems and/or achieves economic objectives, they are paid—paid by the purchase of life insurance through their corporation for rendering this unique financial service. Their market includes any person or corporation that has the capacity to write a substantial check for needed life insurance.

They also have some unusual concepts—unusual by historical life insurance industry standards at any rate. For example, a majority of their production comes from a relatively few number of cases, possibly 10 or 12 a year, and they can be found working in Florida, Illinois, California, Boston or New York. Not only do they not take an "app a week," but sometimes not even one a month. Rarely do they take money with an application. They refer to everything in terms of paid first premium rather than in volume figures, yet in a very short number of years both Owen and Ed are multi-million dollar producers with a persistency level very close to 100%.

What are the results of these concepts? First, they close an average of one case every month; second, they insure on the average two lives in each case; third, their closing ratio has been 90%; fourth, just short of 80% of their total production of first year premium comes from situations which yield, on the average, $40,000 of paid first year premium per case; fifth, in this market the paid first year premium averages over $40 per $1,000, although their production includes essentially no short term paid contracts, endowment contracts, or annuity contracts; sixth, persistency, for all practical purposes, is 100%; seventh, the smallest amount of face volume sold in this market has been $400,000, the largest $4,000,000. Average size of volume per case is just short of $750,000.

On June 1, 1964, CFC, Inc.'s Associate Agent concept, which was responsible for these results, was formalized with the signing of a Corporate Consultant contract between the National Life Insurance Company, Montpelier, Vermont, and Capital

Formation Counselors, Inc.

By providing a Power Lead to the Dominant Personality in a Substantial Situation, members of the National Life agency force, if they so desire, may, as Associate Agents, call upon the unique services of CFC, Inc. to sell and service the estate needs of men and women of wealth, thereby availing these potential clients of a highly trained, experienced group of specialists.

A Power Lead is the ability on the part of the Associate Agent to have the prospective client set aside on a favorable basis an uninterrupted hour to meet with a CFC, Inc. representative to discuss in depth the advantage of a CFC, Inc. Comprehensive Financial Estate Analysis to him. The Dominant Personality must be the decision maker in a given financial structure. A Substantial Situation is any situation that can yield a $50,000 check per year for new, cash value life insurance. When the sale is completed, the Associate Agent is compensated for his efforts by receiving his share of the case. Although he has essentially no direct responsibility for the case after providing the Power Lead to the Dominant Personality, some of the monetary results to the Associate Agents have been staggering. In several instances the Associate Agent has received in first year and renewal commissions sums of money in excess of tens of thousands of dollars for introducing CFC, Inc. into a case.

Step by step, this is the way CFC, Inc., works.

Step #1. Case Initiation. The Associate Agent brings a given case to the attention of CFC, Inc.

Step #2. Case Acknowledgment. CFC, Inc., acknowledges by letter to the Associate Agent the receipt of his case inquiry.

Step #3. Case Evaluation-Preselection. CFC, Inc.'s Preselection Staff conducts an exclusive analysis of the case, drawing from the best of 182 sources of data. CFC, Inc. has over 12,000 financial statements on file.

Step #4. Opening Appointment Planning. The Associate Agent and the CFC, Inc. representative, usually Edwin H. McMullen, Vice President, absorb all the data developed on the case and study the estate owner and his advisors. Then, and only then, they decide on the most effective manner to approach the dominant personality.

Step #5. Setting of Case Opening Appointment. (Appointment Sale) The Associate Agent arranges to have the Dominant

Personality meet Ed McMullen on a favorable basis, setting aside an uninterrupted hour to hear the CFC, Inc. story.

Step #6. Appointment with the Dominant Personality. Ed meets with the Dominant Personality for at least an uninterrupted hour telling the CFC, Inc. story in detail, outlining the advantages of a Comprehensive Financial Estate Analysis to him and answering any questions he may have.

Step #7. Advisor Visit(s). Ed will often desire to meet in person all of the present advisors of the estate owner. CFC, Inc.'s insistence on making the client's attorney the number one advisor of its client, with CFC, Inc.'s role confined to "foot soldiering" the financial facts is well engrained in its concepts and operation.

Step #8. Estate Analysis Commitment (Document Sale). Ed now convinces the estate owner to proceed with a Comprehensive Financial Estate Analysis.

Step #9. Document Pickup. Ed gathers from the estate owner and his advisors, all the legal documents, personal and corporate tax records, financial statements, and family and business life insurance policies. This is often a difficult step, but an absolutely essential one. A quality analysis must be built upon a sound foundation. At this point Ed's responsibilities as case opener have been completed.

Step #10. Document Breakout. This raw data is then turned over to the Estate Analysis staff in Clearwater. A tremendous number of operating statements, balance sheets, tax returns, and policies must be broken down into digestable units and the information ordered in a manner that lends itself to analysis in depth. Over 100 forms have been created for this document breakdown phase; on these forms the staff marshalls all the cold, exacting financial facts surrounding any successful man.

Step #11. Data Session Planning. Owen now sits down with all the materials on the case gathered to date, starting with Ed's chronological, dictated notes. Owen must know all the "people facts" surrounding the estate owner and his family. Ed has gathered invaluable personal information on the case which helps put Owen on the right track. He then decides what is going to be said to the client, in what order it is going to be said, and why. Owen is now ready for the initial data session with the client.

Step #12. Initial Data Session. These data sessions may be held in one of CFC Inc.'s offices or in the client's office. The sessions may last only two to three hours, or they may last twelve to fourteen hours. It depends on the individual. During these sessions Owen asks a great number of questions then lets the client do almost all the talking. He listens. He is gathering the "people facts" and listening for the objectives of the client.

Step #13. Applications Taken (Medical Sale). Applications are taken on all potential insureds within the family group and within the business who are significant in the overall case.

Step #14. Medical Examinations. Medical examinations are completed on all the proposed insureds.

Step #15. Subsequent Data Sessions. There may be one or two possibly even ten more of these sessions. They may last only an hour or so, or may again run as long as ten or twelve hours each.

Step #16. Medical Underwriting. Final determination of the exact insurability status of all proposed insureds is completed.

Step #17. Case Financial Solution. The delicate financial balance between case problems and the capacity to solve these problems with the vehicle of life insurance must now be resolved.

Step #18. Final Case Development. These are the brutally difficult hours. This is when all factors must be integrated into one cohesive picture, which can be communicated crisply and clearly to the estate owner and his advisors.

Step #19. Case Presentation. The presentations rarely take less than eight hours, and some have run for five consecutive days. Because of the inherent nature of CFC Inc.'s work, it is a financial counselor of men, and as a financial counselor it must of necessity know the economic environment in which its clients perform. If CFC does not properly understand this environment and its impact on the economic decisions of its clients, then as a financial counselor of men, it can easily fail—fail its clients and fail itself. But it has not failed. It has succeeded.

Step #20. Consideration Rendered (Money Sale). Hopefully, the life insurance phase of the case solution is adopted and placed in force.

Step #21. Continuing Service. Continuing service with clients of this substance is an absolute must, and CFC, Inc. works very hard at it.

This is the story of Capital Formation Counselors, Inc. whose President is the almost unbelievably successful Owen J. Roberts. He is indeed one of the most creative young men in our business today with tremendous successes to back up every step he has taken, always forward in the right direction.

How did this fabulous young man enter the life insurance business? He answered a blind advertisement in a local newspaper while in the Air Force! At that time, he had no intention of ever entering the life insurance business.

Today, Owen has captured the imagination of life insurance men everywhere. But Owen was not always this multi-million dollar producer.

Until Harold Dillon reached down to me, I had investigated in detail the bottomless well of despair. The cold breath of failure in this life insurance business had chilled my heart and dulled my will. Over a period of eight long months, I had sold a total of five policies. My total paid first year premium per month was $185.60. In this prosperous era of a devaluated dollar, I was worth about $92.00 a month—not per week, but $92.00 per month. As mentally I calculated how I might enroll in law school with a minimum loss of face, hero badge slightly askew, and now burning to see justice done, a book was given to me—*Million Dollar Profiles* by Bill Earls. I read that book. No, more correctly, I devoured that book. Every morning by setting the alarm 30 minutes early, I could read and reread about the great men of the Million Dollar Round Table—Lou Behr, John Todd, Bob Burroughs, Grant Taggart, Paul Cook, Al Ostheimer—all the immense personalities of the life insurance business, and I learned that they too had encountered problems in the early years.

Thus, with renewed will, Owen went back to work.

How did Owen Roberts achieve this? "Harold T. Dillon, National Life's legendary General Agent, took me out of an 8 x 10 bedroom with one calculator—being paid for on time—and one filing cabinet, and gave me the office, equipment, and secretarial help to pursue my interest in marketing life insurance through the estate analysis process. I owe him a debt which I can never fully repay."

In his first year in the business, Owen averaged a sixteen hour day. It is now down to twelve. In his first year in the business, not only did he work seven days a week, but he worked every night. Now he works seven days a week but he quits at 9:00

p.m. This hard work is funneled toward the accomplishment of a definite goal.

His production in 1959, his first full calendar year in the life insurance business, was $2,290,000. His production has grown steadily to a point where he placed, early in 1965, six separate million dollar cash value policies in a 90 day period, all with annual premiums rendered.

When he first became a life insurance agent his original goal was simply to earn a living. That goal has now changed to building the financial estate analysis organization in America in order to provide the more dominant leaders of industry a service of unequalled excellence.

"Very early I learned two things about the life insurance business. First, it is a business of death; and second, little good is accomplished until the policy is in force. To be successful in our profession we need to possess or acquire the following traits: personal discipline, true humility, courage at the close, service through the years and a touch of showmanship. Only then can we place the policies in force, keep them in force, and thereby rob death of its final and absolute material victory."

Quite a philosophy for a young man!

CHAPTER 41

JOHN NORMAN FRANK ROBERTSON, C.L.U.

"A LITTLE EXTRA EFFORT will move you to the top!" says John Robertson, C.L.U., who by age 32 had already reached the top in two areas—he was a million dollar producer and a two-time member of the Canadian Olympic Sailing Team. John joined the Hamilton Agency of the Mutual Life of Canada in June of 1951. "Having been relatively successful in the sailing field, I was able to see that a little extra effort would move you to the top. Therefore, I wanted to get into a business where I would be my own boss and benefit from my own efforts. Fortunately, my present manager called on me when I was at McMaster University, and within five minutes I was sold on the value of life insurance. This is not an exaggeration, for I was looking for a job in the sales field. Since most of them appeared as strictly order-takers, life insurance had a great deal of appeal."

John Shea, C.L.U., the manager whom John gives much credit for his success says, "John N. F. Robertson brought with him two traits that he had developed in competitive sailing—a desire to win, and a recognition that to get the best results you must learn to do whatever you are doing in the most efficient manner, and keep on doing it that way."

On joining the Hamilton Agency, John accepted definite work habits and work objectives, and he has consistently met his objectives. Since 1951 John has never missed his monthly Agency Quota. He adopted the philosophy that he would follow the pattern established for him and not worry about the sales and appointments he failed to get. He was told that he would enjoy excellent results by following the pattern suggested. And, of course, John did.

As for his sailing activities, John helped organize the junior sailing section of the Royal Hamilton Yacht Club. Others have followed in his shoes and have built this into an organization that now gives training to sixty or seventy children each summer. At the present time John limits his sailing to racing on Saturdays in his fourteen foot International Dinghy. This is probably the fastest type boat in the world for its size. He also goes on a summer cruise for which the Robertsons and another couple rent a thirty-five foot yawl.

John and his beautiful wife, Edna Suzanne, have three daughters. Edna Suzanne was the head girl at McMaster University; she and the head boy ran all student functions at the University. She taught French and Physical Education before marriage, and her special outside interest is now the study of ways and means of bettering the educational system. In order to keep up on her French, she and several other women meet weekly and spend the evenings chatting in French. John states that the greatest thing Edna Suzanne does to assist him in his business is "to give me freedom to carry on this activity during the week. She realizes that our business is very time-consuming and does not demand any household chores from me during the business week. This is vitally important in my mind. You know as well as I do that many men are held back by their wives trying to interfere in their business or by asking them to do unnecessary errands. She realizes that we are in a difficult business and doesn't nag, if business is not going well. Having been brought up in a family where her father was in sales, she realizes the importance of creating a pleasant and happy home. She has that great facility of giving me confidence in a manner which is difficult to describe. No doubt, she is taking on greater responsibility in the home than most wives, but perhaps this is paying off for her in other ways."

John received his B.A. Degree in Political Economy from McMaster University in 1951. The training he received by being on his own and having to plan his own activities and work schedule required to graduate has helped him in the life insurance business. Only a person who has taken oral and written examinations at one time covering all four years of college work can appreciate what this means.

John says that the amount of business that he writes each year is the direct result of the amount of work he does. Ideally, John gets a new person's confidence quickly, and once this is obtained, it is usually smooth sailing. In most cases, he is able to point out that he is working for some of the prospect's friends and this enables John to get the information from the prospect more easily. If he is having difficulty in getting the data, he may point out how he can help the prospect co-ordinate his insurance with other estate assets or how he can make the man's present insurance more effective. John puts as much of this information as possible on graph paper, for he strives to make all proposals as brief as possible. If the situation is very complex, he makes use of the Estate Survey Department of his company.

John keeps in touch with his clients by simply phoning them and asking if they have any problems or questions; and, of course, the answer is usually negative. Then John changes the subject and chats with them for a while; in this way, he usually learns if they have had any new additions to their family, job promotions, etc., and he can soon determine whether their situation has changed sufficiently to warrant an interview. If this is the case, he asks for an appointment.

When John calls on his clients, he always remembers that the thing which usually makes them the happiest is seeing how much their cash value has grown during that particular year. John can usually show them a very attractive increase in their cash values, even if they have had the policy only a couple of years. John notes that "it is pretty difficult to suggest insurance, if they are not too happy with what they already own."

John has two interviews every day and one night interview a week. In his first year he had approximately four night interviews a week. Now he spends the other evenings in the week working on programs and contacting clients by phone. His work organization is geared to ten calls a week, and this usually involves eight interviews and two telephone interviews.

When John entered the life insurance business, his goal was simply not to fail. Then John Shea, his manager, began to set up goals, and John Robertson always reached them. "Basically, I placed myself in John Shea's hands in my first few years in the business," says John Robertson. "I have complete confidence in my manager and to this day will follow his suggestions pretty well to the letter. I try to work effectively each day and not to waste time. I also take the advice of my father-in-law, who told me, that, if you are willing to make the calls, the future will take care of itself."

John says of his manager, "He tends to be a friend and not to criticize you, even if you have not received a sale for several weeks, as long as you are working correctly. However, he has a tendency, when things are going well, to push you a little further."

John Robertson directs these comments to insurance men who seem to be in a slump:

"Unfortunately, most men work in spurts with the result that after a good period, they tend to ease up, which always creates a slump. During a period of slump, they become discouraged and find they probably make fewer calls than before. They seem to be looking for sales rather than opportunities to discuss with people their problems. If a young man would go over his past records and establish how many calls he must make to have a sale and so on, he can then set up a work week that is realistic and a goal that is possible to reach. Once he has established how many calls are required to do the job he wants to do, he should stick by this week after week. Consistent effort produces consistent production." In Hamilton John is sometimes known as "the machine," and he is proud of this nickname. It indicates that he is doing the things that most insurance men are not willing to do—making a consistent number of calls each and every week. "I have unfailing faith in my ten calls," says John.

To individuals entering the business from high school or college, John says what Mr. George Dunbar, Vice President in Charge of Sales for the Mutual Life of Canada, said to him at the time he entered the business—"follow to the letter whatever your manager recommends." John thought that this made good sense, "because it is pretty hard to analyze whether you are getting right information or not, when you know nothing about our business."

John also believes that new agents should get one sales idea and stick with it. The idea he used was a "Success Story" where one had to have, not only the ability and opportunities to be successful, but money as well to take full advantage of these opportunities. Here, John showed the value of the savings in insurance to build up this cash reserve for business opportunities.

Another point John stresses is the wisdom in a young man's

concentrating his efforts on people of approximately his same age. He says, "It is pretty difficult for a young man to call on older men, until he has proven his ability."

John lists five advantages of life insurance as a profession: In life insurance a man has freedom to develop his abilities without any restrictions from company policy. He can enter the business with no capital investment. He will be his own manager and have freedom of his own time. He is selling a product that everyone needs and that will do more for people than any other tangible product they can buy. He can earn a very good income that, in all probability, is better than he would earn in industry.

John firmly believes that men, who would be successful agents, must make a consistent number of calls each week. They must also do the things that unsuccessful underwriters do not wish to do, such as giving up coffee breaks, sending birthday cards, Christmas cards, etc. Men who would be successful must also remember that you have to give your efforts a little time to work. Nearly all large sales come from work done over a period of years rather than months. Hal Parsons, the great Travelers' agent, once said that he spent 60% of his time on future business and 40% on present business.

For John's plan of organization, he uses the Daily Diary and a monthly diary with an alphabetical section showing all phases of his life. In addition, there is a section in the book dealing with finances and general matters. This book is roughly 3″ x 4″ and John carries it in his jacket pocket. Thus, he is able to carry with him at all times the information he needs regarding his business appointments, holidays, etc.

Two original ideas from John that are worth remembering are: "It has always struck me that we should be having more interviews in our office as do the other professions." And, "I believe that you don't have to buy sales, but rather you obtain them through service. Thus, I do not wine and dine any of my prospects. I socialize with my clients after sales, not before."

Thus consistent and organized, John N. F. Robertson continues his outstanding work which in 1965 totaled $1,600,000 in volume.

CHAPTER 42

J. W. ROBINSON, JR.

A NATURALLY FRIENDLY PERSONALITY, unlimited energy, and an unusually perceptive wife are assets that make J. W. Robinson's hard work especially rewarding.

J. W. is a Texas MDRT member who says, "I have worked for as long as I can remember." His father owned a small town grocery store, and J. W. worked there after school and on weekends. Saturday mornings he sold newspapers. Later he drove butane trucks, operated grocery stores in the summer, and sold just about anything you could name in order to pay for his college education.

J. W. graduated from Texas A & M, having taken every insurance course offered. He knew he was going to make a career in life insurance. It was the only business a man could start in after graduation, be his own boss, earn while he learned, and make $3,000 to $5,000 the first year out of college. He received his B.S. Degree on Saturday, and began work for the Southland Life Insurance Company on the following Monday. Today he writes two to three million a year, and lives with his wife and son in a two-story brick with swimming pool set on four acres in Hereford, Texas. Hereford has a population of 10,652, and the County of Deaf Smith adds some 4,500 more to the territory that J. W. sells.

To arrange his interviews, J. W. will go to see a prospect and tell him that he has an idea he believes might be of interest, an idea that many successful men like himself have used to become even more successful. J. W. does not sell life insurance in the usual sense of the word, but prefers to help the prospect find out what he really needs and wants. J. W. knows that what benefits his sale of life insurance most is simply to see the people and ask them to buy.

To keep organized, J. W. keeps in front of him the names of

36 people he expects to close soon. When he sells one, he replaces it with another. His planner is a monthly one with each day printed on it.

J. W. uses three advertising slogans: "The right man for your insurance needs." "When you think of insurance, think of J. W.," and, "In appreciation, J. W. Robinson, Jr., your Southland Life Agent."

J. W. owns the Robinson Insurance Agency which handles both general insurance and life insurance, and he houses his Agency in a 4200 square foot building which he built and owns.

One tragic incident and six people have influenced J. W. significantly: Early in his career J. W. sold his twin sister, an R.N., a retirement income policy for savings and protection. It was the first death claim that he had to pay. She was killed in an automobile accident.

The people who have inspired and influenced him are his wife, Life Insurance Professor at Texas A & M—Sid Loveless, Herman Ford, Archie Castleberry, James Tanner, and Johnny Wright.

Herman Ford was J. W.'s high school principal; he is now the Assistant Vice President and Director of Sales Training of Southland Life, Dallas, Texas. Mr. Ford says that most of the same qualities that make J. W. a success in life insurance would make him a success in any business.

Of all the people I know, J. W. comes closest to being friendly with everyone. Even his competitors are his friends. When J. W. worked in his father's grocery store, it was the most popular place in Hereford. Everyone who came in had to stop and have a few words with J. W. His wife probably summed it up best by saying, 'J. W. thinks everybody just loves him.'

Another thing that contributes to his success in his boundless energy. He is never idle.

J. W. has a natural nose for prospects. Everywhere he goes, he is constantly sizing up each person he meets as a possible prospect. He almost always makes it pay off, too.

J. W. is a persistent individual. Once he has made up his mind about what he wants, he is almost sure to get it.

He has attained a very good knowledge of the business in which he is engaged. He does not sit down and study something for long periods of time, but learns from every transaction he makes, and he is very conscious of always trying to learn something by associating with successful people. He seeks out the leaders in any activity and spends his time with them.

J. W. is a very loyal individual. Being honest and sincere, he does not join in any activity that he cannot support with all his strength. He is loyal to his clients, his Company, himself, and his family.

His wife, Virginia, was a featured speaker at the 1962 meeting of Southland Life. These brief excerpts may give you some of the crucially important ways a wife can help a husband's life insurance career:

The W in wife should stand for willingness—willingness to take care of home repairs, odd jobs, errands, and yard work. If my son and I can't handle a job, we call someone to help us. I would rather pay a man to do yard work than to take valuable time from my husband. When he is at home, I want him to relax and study, if he wants to. I don't want him to come home from one job to have to take over another. After all, he won't be making many contacts with people behind that lawn mower.

The I in wife should stand for interest. Never ask if he sold. If he did, he will tell you; if he didn't, he certainly won't want to talk about it.

F stands for faith. Have the faith in him and his profession so that when he is down, you are up. I've seen it happen time and time again that, after making call after call and hearing no, no, no, the very next day he will hear yes, yes, yes.

Enthusiasm is the E in wife. Have enthusiasm for his profession; don't belittle or compare him to other men who make more money. Encourage him so that he can do as well as anyone else. A man needs his work, because it is the only way he has to fully express himself. Let him know that his work comes first, and be a good sport about that dinner that has to be kept warm on the stove because of his irregular hours.

I have found that it is important, especially in a salesman's life, to be in a good humor. That man of yours can't be in a good humor, if he has static at home. I truly believe that a wife sets the tempo of the home. If she is in tune, the whole family will be harmonious.

In comments which appeared in a trade journal, Virginia says:

J. W.'s greatest attribute is his true love for all mankind. He bends over backwards not to be a pushy salesman. People are his business, and he lets each person know that he likes him and wants to be of help in any way he can.

I belong to clubs and never pass up the opportunity to let women know how I appreciate life insurance, how it is the best way for a man to show his love for his wife and children. Often women say to me, "I wish J. W. would talk to my husband about life insurance," or, "I'm glad Joe bought that life insurance from J. W." Such remarks point up future prospects, and good ones, because the wife is sold on the idea.

It takes J. W. longer to get coffee at a ball game than any other man in town, because he has so much visiting to do on his way to and from the concession stand. He even has to visit with the policeman directing traffic after the game is finished.

Kenneth B. Skinner, Vice President and Agency Director of Southland Life Insurance Company of Dallas, Texas, sees J. W.'s most unique and outstanding characteristic as his power of understanding the viewpoint of others, his ability to see both sides of any question or situation. Since these characteristics make for a very pleasant business association in which J. W. can be most effective in his approach to any situation by establishing a relationship of complete faith and trust in his professional capacity, Mr. Skinner believes that herein lies the key to J. W.'s phenomenal success.

J. W.'s secretary points out another of his qualities: "After working about a year for J. W., we had a conference, and he told me at that time his gain would be my gain. Therefore, in working for him I worked for myself. The more I can do for him, the more time he will have to sell."

J. W. has written several articles for various trade journals. In "You Can Do Something About Objections," he explained how he answers the most common objections before they are brought up in "The Texas Close": "T . . . to whom payable: Whom do you want to be the beneficiary? E . . . Examination: Let's see if you can qualify for this plan? X . . . Extra Benefits: Some extra benefits on this plan that I failed to mention before, double indemnity, etc. A . . . Always pays: This plan always pays—to you if you are living, to your family in the event of your death. S . . . Start now: Wait several minutes and let the prospect do the thinking and talking. You have said all you need to say, and maybe more."

In "Going Around in Circles Can Be Profitable," J. W. showed that about 50% of his business comes from old policyowners. This is largely true, because J. W. never takes them for granted;

he is always letting them know that he sincerely appreciates their doing business with him. J. W. delivers his policies either in a policy wallet imprinted with the policyowner's name and his, or in a special insurance jacket. He also remembers them on their birthdays and at Christmas. J. W. lets everyone know, when he earns a convention trip or special prize. Invariably they ask, "Why, who do you sell all that insurance to?", and J. W. is off on a presentation with the reply, "To people just like you."

In "This Year's Goal—M.D.R.T." and "To Whom It May Concern. Re: M.D.R.T. Qualification," J. W. explained how his natural gregariousness needs the discipline of planning to keep it properly channeled toward achieving something worthwhile —"both for me and for those with whom I mingle." To do this, J. W. uses a monthly booklet called "The Southland Planner." In the front of each booklet J. W. writes down his paid business objective for the year, the business he has paid for to date, and the balance he lacks for that year's goal. On this same sheet he writes in his paid business quota for the current month. On the next two pages, he lists 36 of his best prospects (each of whom has already been qualified), showing beside each name the exact amount J. W. expects to sell him. On the following two pages, he lists about 60 prospects he plans to see and to qualify. J. W. goes over his library of Planners about twice a year. Frequently, in such reviews valuable names crop up— names of people who, for one reason or another, did not turn out to be real prospects when he originally approached them, but who have since become prospect material. "I lose no time in seeing these boys!" says J. W. The next two pages are numbered 1 through 31, one page for each day of the month. Every evening J. W. plans his activities for the morrow, making all relevant entries on the proper page of the Planner.

J. W. uses red and blue tags with his alphabetical file of policyowners. A red tag indicates a Term case—for eventual conversion to a permanent plan. A blue tag indicates the policyowner's need for wife insurance or insurance on a dependent not yet covered. Perhaps a breakdown of the 63 cases J. W. sold in 1964 (volume—$2,392,765; premiums—$26,993) will highlight the importance to him of the red and blue tags: 19% of the cases were Term conversions (each originating from a red tagged card in his alphabetical file); 37% of the cases were on old policy-owners or members of their families (each originating from a blue tagged card in the alphabetical file); 44% of the cases were on new clients.

In his article, "Sales Multiplication," J. W. comments on why men enter life insurance as a career:

1. To better themselves financially.
2. To feel wanted, needed and appreciated in their community; in other words, prestige.
3. To find real meaning in their life's work.

And J. W. has found all of these in his great success and happiness, as a life insurance agent and as a man—and it looks to us as if everybody just might love J. W.!

CHAPTER 43

MARSHALL SCLAROW, J.D.

IN A HUGE PINE FOREST, one thousand feet above Boulder, Colorado, Marshall Sclarow has found his thinking place. Here Marshall temporarily trades his office desk for a picnic table, the smell of the city for that of pine needles, and the view of glass and concrete for the Rocky Mountains. For seven years, this spot has been the inspiration for most of his new ideas, and it has sparked rare flashes of insight into his old problems. This place has often pushed him to a moment of truth, and has been his heaven and his hell from where he conceived the plans that made his first year income $11,300 with $1,016,000 production.

Marshall has always balanced work with regeneration from nature and travel. In 1962 this Million Dollar Round Table member spent six weeks in Europe, attended the Million Dollar Round Table meeting, and then took five additional weeks for vacations. In 1963 he spent three months in Europe.

When Marshall isn't traveling, however, he works exceptionally hard five days a week, but rarely on Saturdays.

Marshall graduated from Iowa University with a degree in Political Science in 1952; he received his Juris Doctor Degree from the University in 1955 and practiced law for a short time before becoming a life underwriter. Debating during his undergraduate days helps him now in life insurance, and his training in law, which taught him how to ask questions, has become the basis of the primary technique he now uses in his interviews.

Marshall works mainly in the college market. Although he did at first send lead letters to this market, he soon began to realize that the message in the lead letter didn't help get the interview, it just made him call. Recognizing that calling was the important thing, not the letter sent out ahead of time, Marshall discontinued all pre-approach material except for an ad placed in the University of Colorado newspaper entitled

"Central Life Thought for the Day."

Marshall either calls on referred leads or students whose names he has gotten from a list or student directory. Marshall makes 98% of his initial contacts by telephone. Something like this would be a standard approach: "Hello, Fred, this is Marshall Sclarow speaking. Do you know me?" The prospect will usually think for a minute and then probably answer, "No." Marshall would continue. "Well, Fred, I don't expect we have met. I have a life insurance office here in Boulder on the hill. The reason for my calling, Fred, is that Bill Jones has spoken to me about you and had some nice things to say about you. You sound like the kind of man I would like to meet. When would be a good time to make your acquaintance next week?"

This type of approach gives Marshall a lot of leeway in which to handle objections.

Marshall does little pre-interview work. His initial interview is generally his only interview, for he closes 80% of his business at this time. This works especially well in his market of college men. Marshall goes into a man's home with nothing in his hands. He has a little interview kit in his pocket. This consists of the application, two blank pieces of paper, and a simplified rate book. He uses the two pieces of paper to do a simplified program for most of his clients and then shows them the plan that would best solve their problem. He takes about 60% of his business on an unbound basis and sells college students with a presentation based on their projected earnings.

Marshall keeps in touch with policyholders that leave the area by long-distance calls and letters. As yet Marshall has done very little business insurance and no group insurance, mostly selling individual insurance to young married couples and single men on their way up. Marshall looks for prospects who are finishing college or have completed college. In the future he will most likely be drawn into more involved areas as his clients become older and have more financial responsibilities.

Marshall finds that making a consistent number of calls sets a work pattern for him. By a call, Marshall means any time he asks for an appointment, either on the phone or in person. He makes about 1,400 calls a year, and has about 344 interviews. In 1962 his calls dropped to 1,100 and his interviews to 325, with a consequent drop to only $894,000 of MDRT credits.

A closer look at Marshall's market reveals that currently 50% of his new business comes from policyholders, 25% from college seniors and graduate students, and another 25% from the general public, primarily engineers, physicists, chemists, and other college trained professionals. During Marshall's first year in the business, 95% of his sales came from college seniors and graduate students. Marshall ended his first year averaging 7.5 interviews a week and writing just over a million dollars of insurance from this college market. "Nothing happens until we make calls," emphasizes Marshall.

Since Marshall has kept an accurate record of his work since he became a life insurance agent, he can analyze his totals and make them work for him. In 1960 based on 46 weeks his work was as follows: Calls—1,408; interviews—344; Sales—104; Amount —$1,273,000; Average size case—$12,240; Closing ratio—1 in 3.31; Married purchasers—56; Single purchasers—48. He determined that his sources of cases were from the following: Policyowners— 11; Conversions—4; People Marshall knew personally—2; Referred leads—28; Published sources—18; Direct mail—34; and, People met cold—7. Marshall's average number of calls per week was 30.6; his average number of interviews per week was 7.5, and his average number of sales was 2.3. His first year lapses numbered 8, and his second year lapses numbered 6. Marshall qualified for the MDRT and the National Quality Award, and as of August 31, 1965, 74% of the above business was still in force. Marshall's biggest case is a $100,000 Ordinary Life which was delivered in August, 1965. Most of his cases are $5,000, $10,000, and $15,000, usually with term riders attached to them.

Four people have influenced Marshall. The remarks his wife, Davida, made at the Central Life Leaders Sales Meeting show why she has been an important factor in Marshall's success: "By far, my most important contribution is my sincere belief in my husband and in the life insurance business." Marshall also credits his general agent, Pat Bush, with "steady and sound influence," and G. Robert Matteson with "enthusiasm and willingness to share ideas." A trip to see Cleo Edwards, a four million dollar producer for the Central Life Assurance Company in Cedar Rapids, Iowa, was also extremely helpful in Marshall's career as a life underwriter: "I visited Cleo Edwards for a week in September of 1960 and just followed him around. Much of what I use today are ideas I picked up from him during that visit. The best four months of production in terms of closing ratio was the four month period following my visit. My closing ratio went from 1 out of 3.5 to 1 out of 2.5. It was not this good again, until the past two years."

Perhaps we can get our best insight into why Marshall is successful from comments made by one of his competitors in Boulder, Colorado—Harvey L. DeLoach of Fidelity Union:

"There is nothing complicated or mysterious about Marshall's success in the life insurance business. There are three areas in which he is superior to any life insurance man I know: His organization, his directness, and his desires to be of service to others and to himself.

"The first area is Marshall's ability to get organized for action and then stay that way. With Marshall, it's not only how hard you work, but how consistently you work as well. He sets the number of calls he will make for a given period and without procrastination makes them.

"The second area is Marshall's directness. Marshall makes honest, sincere, leveling remarks that really show the prospect why his reason for not buying is not valid. Some other insurance men feel that Marshall's directness is high pressure, and therefore harmful, but the prospects don't seem to mind; they keep on buying.

"The final area in which Marshall is superior is perhaps the most important. This area is desire. Marshall doesn't judge his work by what other men do, but he sets his own level of accomplishment. He has high standards and high ideals, and no one stands in his way, until he gets the job done."

Marshall's approach to organization, his directness, his desire to be of service, and that rare ability he has of recharging his batteries at nature's door mark Marshall Sclarow as a one of a kind Million Dollar Round Table member.

CHAPTER 44

BRUCE C. SHAW, C.L.U.

HAVE YOU EVER HEARD of an older brother following his younger brother into the life insurance business in a different town over a thousand miles away and becoming as his brother had done previously, one of the leading agents of the Connecticut Mutual and a member of the M.D.R.T.? This is the story of Bruce C. Shaw, the older brother of Howard C. (Chip) Shaw.

Bruce was born in 1929 and Chip in 1933; today Bruce Shaw is in Toledo and his brother is in Colorado Springs, and both are Million Dollar Round Table men and among their Company's leading agents.

Bruce Shaw entered the life insurance business in 1958 in Toledo as a total stranger to the area and qualified for the M.D.R.T. in 1960, 1961, 1962, 1963, 1964, 1965 and 1966. In his first year in business, his production was $1,150,000 and his earned income was approximately $10,000. He received his C.L.U. designation in 1963.

Floyd A. Rosenfelt, his former General Agent with the Connecticut Mutual in Toledo, calls Bruce a natural prospector. "Bruce gains the maximum benefits from his telephone technique, and his ratio of sales is proof of his inherent aptitude for closing. He enjoys an average size premium and the persistency of his business is 95% or better."

Robert A. Meeker, the General Agent in Toledo, says, "It was apparent from the very beginning of his career that Bruce Shaw was destined to be a tremendous asset to the life insurance industry. His dedication to reaching goals, his sincerity in sales presentations, and his ingenuity in uncovering needs have all played an important role in his success pattern. The other factors which Bruce shares with other successful men are his educational background, his desire to be his own boss, and his ability to set realistic goals both in terms of income, production, and activity. His enthusiasm has had a very advantageous effect upon both new men and veterans within the agency. It is demonstrated, not only verbally, but throughout his whole pattern of life."

The Shaws' father, Howard C. Shaw, Sr., has been in the life insurance business for 42 years. He has worked in Springfield, Massachusetts, and now is with the Connecticut Mutual in Colorado Springs.

Bruce attended the Wharton School of Finance where he majored in Insurance and received his degree as Bachelor of Science in Economics.

Bruce tells us, that the secret of whatever success he has is organization. He early learned from Floyd Rosenfelt a healthy respect for work units and their inevitable results. Bruce still keeps a daily record of his work units and knows exactly what he can expect from them in terms of business.

His work pattern is this: he telephones on Monday and makes ten appointments with new people. He knows that he must dial the phone about twenty-five times in order to reach twelve new people and make appointments with ten of them. In addition, on Monday he sets up appointments for closing interviews from the previous week's work; and he sets up appointments for fact-finding interviews on new people he has already met and qualified; and he arranges his service and prospecting calls. When he leaves the office on Monday afternoon, his work is completed in terms of appointments made.

The initial interview is simply a get-acquainted interview and rarely takes over fifteen minutes. In this interview Bruce attempts to qualify the prospect as to whether or not they like each other, whether he has the need for insurance, and whether he has the ability to purchase life insurance. If the prospect does qualify, Bruce arranges a luncheon interview if possible for the following week; this will serve as a fact-finding interview. Bruce uses no visual aids. In fact, he does not even carry a brief case to his meetings with new prospects, for he believes that the most important thing is that they "click" or like each other.

Bruce uses the mail a great deal, confirming all appointments with new people and sending follow-up letters with literature enclosed after each appointment with a new person. To Bruce "a letter is almost as good as a personal call, for it puts my name and my picture once again in front of the prospect."

Bruce uses simple programming and on the closing interview, he shows a color chart. The chart shows the prospect's existing Social Security, Veterans benefits, and other assets as well as the amounts he lacks to accomplish his objectives. After using this to establish the problem, Bruce then uses a Connecticut Mutual proposal to show the type of contract which he recommends for the solution of his problem. After solving the problem of additional insurance, he keeps in touch with the client by contacting him at least once a year. Bruce also puts him on his mailing list (eight hundred names receive a monthly mailing piece), and sends him a birthday card each year. And, for the most part, Bruce prospects with his policyholders.

It is obvious that this works for Bruce. In 1961 his ordinary production was $1,187,000 on 101 lives; in 1962, $1,320,000 on 93 lives; in 1963, $1,640,200 on 104 lives; and in 1964, $2,062,472 on 136 lives. Bruce thinks he gets results, because he has a consistent exposure to prospects and manages to keep going simultaneously the four phases of his operation: Prospecting, meeting new people, opening sales situations, and closing. If these are kept going, even when business is good, there is a snowballing effect in the business itself.

Bruce has used these methods from the beginning of his career, and Bruce gives his former General Agent much of the credit: "Floyd Rosenfelt is undoubtedly the man that has given me the most inspiration and help during the first five years in the life insurance business. When I started with the Toledo Agency, he told me that I was going to write a million during my first year, and he told me this so frequently and with such conviction that eventually he convinced me. He also told me what was necessary in terms of work units to reach this objective. Because I was new in the business and didn't know any better, I did exactly what he said, and the results were exactly what he said they would be. He has an excellent ability to motivate people. Mr. Rosenfelt also hired me from Springfield, Massachusetts, some 800 miles away from Toledo. He moved me to Toledo and loaned me the money to buy the home I wanted. Since he showed this degree of confidence in my future, I couldn't help but believe it was sincere confidence."

In an article written for "The Insurance Salesman" entitled

"Working by the Numbers," Bruce says that one part in his weekly work schedule is quite unpleasant for him, but most important. Each Monday he closes the door of his office, takes a stack of cards, and dials his telephone between twenty and forty times. By getting this out of the way on Monday, the rest of the week is not unpleasant, for he has done the thing that he likes least early in the week and can devote the remainder of the week to selling.

To control his operation, Bruce makes an outline at the beginning of each month of the things that must be accomplished that month. This is done on a large sheet of lined paper and there are on this sheet several columns of names. By far, the longest column is Prospects to Close. Normally, there are between thirty and forty names on this list. These are from age changes and transfers from the earlier months. Each of them is qualified in that Bruce has met them, and they have a need, the ability to pay, and are interested in discussing a specific proposal or at least willing to listen to a specific proposal.

Another column is headed Prospects to See. This is usually about twenty-five names. Bruce doesn't necessarily see all of these people. These are people that have asked Bruce to call them in this particular month, but for whom he has performed no service (there has been some service work done for all the people in the column headed Prospects to Close). Normally during the first week of the month these names are either scheduled for initial fact-finding interviews, transferred to a later month, or eliminated. This is done by telephone. They will not be transferred more than twice to another month.

The other columns on this sheet are shorter ones. One is a column of policy deliveries to be made. Another is a column of people who can be called on short notice for luncheon appointments. These columns are used for prospecting and are usually policyholders. A column is also provided for proposals and paper work to be done which is constantly changing throughout the month. And, finally, there is a column for closed cases.

This same method was described to the Connecticut Mutual field force in an article Bruce called, "How Work Units Stop Slumps." Here he conclusively proves that it is impossible for a slump to occur, as long as you are applying all the work units day in and day out.

This well-organized, determined young man would advise any man to become a life insurance agent, provided he is not reluctant to work hard and has a singleness of purpose toward achieving his own objectives. "There is absolutely no business or profession with the freedom of action and unlimited financial opportunities that the life insurance business possesses," Bruce states.

Bruce's own personal situation gives us another insight into a life insurance career. He says, "Having grown up in a life insurance atmosphere with my father, in the back of my mind I always knew that I would make this my life work. When I graduated from college, I was married and simply lacked the self-confidence to go into the cold, hard world of commission selling. During six years of industrial sales, I watched my younger brother doing very well in the life insurance business and felt as all big brothers do that if he could do it, so could I. Each year I waited it was more difficult to leave an increasingly attractive position. I have never regretted making the move into the life insurance business and feel that there is no business in existence today where with limited capital the future is as great. Particularly, I like the idea of being responsible only to myself and my clients."

"The Million Dollar Round Table has been a most important incentive to continue high production. In my first and second years in the business, membership in this organization was my single goal, and all my activity was channeled in the direction of obtaining this goal."

A well-organized, self-disciplined, determined young man has by the use of a simple work pattern and its constant application become one of the outstanding producers of his Company. His methods are certainly transferable and will produce a million a year anywhere in the country, if diligently followed.

CHAPTER 45

HOWARD C. SHAW, JR.

"THERE IS NO PROBLEM production won't solve—and the production problem is solved by the simple matter of constant and thorough exposure to many, many people." In 1964, Howard C. Shaw, Jr., wrote $1,348,972 on 133 lives; and his 1965 production was $1,738,092 on 140 lives—over 100 lives every year since 1958. He was leader in lives for his Company in 1959, and runner-up for the number of lives in 1961, and a Million Dollar Round Table member in 1960, 1961, 1962, 1963, 1964, 1965 and 1966. This is the record of the younger brother Howard C. (Chip) Shaw of the fantastic Shaw brothers.

Chip is supervisor and office manager of the Connecticut Mutual in Colorado Springs, Colorado. All of these lives and this tremendous production is in addition to the supervision of six full-time agents. You may well ask how he does both jobs so successfully. First of all, he has strong convictions; secondly, the will to do better; and thirdly, a firmly fixed goal. Chip Shaw says, "Live, die, quit, or become disabled, we have a product to sell, and we have a complete monopoly on it. No mutual fund, or stock, or oil well, or consumers good can compete with it. Furthermore, our Company has never run out of it, and it is a product every person we talk to should have either some of or more of. I believe with all my heart and soul in life insurance and the things it accomplishes for the people to whom we have sold it, and the people to whom we are going to sell it, today, tomorrow, and in the future."

Chip Shaw stressed these points in a speech entitled "Growthmanship" which he gave at a Connecticut Mutual Convention:

In business, goals are the starting point of all progress. All the advice and help we receive from our general agents, associates, and Home Office staff is designed to be helpful and to further our progress and lead us toward "Growthmanship." Our problem then as agents is not to accept and try all of it, but to utilize only what suits us best as individuals and to use that which suits us to the maximum. We hear lots of speakers and read lots of articles in our business. If we always bear in mind the importance of adapting the helpful ideas we receive, where they fit, instead of adopting them, we would all be in good shape. Always adapt, never adopt.

Chip has developed one basic method for securing prospects, one for securing interviews, one basic sales tract, one general closing pattern, and one manner of delivering policies.

We think his method of prospecting is worth studying in detail, for in 1960 Chip got the name of 369 prospects using it. After he has delivered a policy and has completely reviewed everything for his client, he will say something like this: "Naturally, you are pleased with what you have done here, both for yourself and your family. I hope you are also pleased with the service I rendered to you, the service which your friend, Bob Jones, felt would be of help to you. From each of my new clients, I ask only one thing, a minimum of three names of friends or acquaintances who they feel would appreciate having done for them the same service I did for you." Chip then takes out his pen and control book and waits. Sometimes he has to wait only a second. Other times, he says it seems like he waits for hours, but he waits, and he gets what he is after.

Chip also told in his speech to the Connecticut Mutual field force how the insurance he had sold to neighbors paid for most of his house. The approach he uses with the neighbors is this, especially if the neighbor lives closer than two blocks away:

You don't know me, but I am Chip Shaw, and I am a neighbor of yours over on Rose Drive, and what's more, I have an apology to make. Since living here, I have been doing, as time allowed, a little service for each of my neighbors. It consists of sitting down with them and putting on paper their complete Social Security Benefits, so they will know just how much money they could depend on from this source, when it was needed most. Being in the life insurance business, I am also able to help them with any questions that they might have along this line. I am a little embarrassed, because I have had your name for over a month now and have been constantly putting off seeing you, until I had more time available. I just wonder if tomorrow afternoon would be a good time for us to get together?

An associate, Thomas E. Parrish, says, "Chip is a very disarming sort of guy. I personally spent one Saturday with him while he made eight prearranged calls and secured six applications. In an interview, Chip is direct without losing warmth. He is factual without being statistical. I firmly believe that my being associated with Chip has definitely helped me in my early years in the life insurance business."

With Chip Shaw's ability to prospect, it is easy to understand why he has so many interviews and sells so many lives each year. Most of Chip's sales are made in the first interview. He does a Social Security review where applicable, together with a review of the client's present life insurance holdings using an on-the-spot package sales approach. Based on the insured's life insurance in force and the answers the prospect gives to certain specific questions, Chip looks for an educational, mortgage, retirement, or in some cases, business or estate conservation need; and, of course, his close depends on the situation.

This persistent and determined package salesman has always used a controlled work formula; that is 30 field hours, 30 calls, 20 progress contacts, 10 closing interviews, 20 new prospects, and 2 submitted lives each week. This plan has made him constantly maintain a momentum that has given him in excess of 100 lives per year for each year he has been in the life insurance business.

CHAPTER 46

WILLIAM M. SHELTON, C.L.U.

IF HOUSES HAVE FEELINGS, the California home that the legendary insurance giant Ron Stever built in 1930, must be chortling with joy. For its present occupant, like its builder is a Life and Qualifying Member of the Million Dollar Round Table. The present occupant, William M. Shelton, is an outstanding young life insurance man from Los Angeles with eleven years of M.D.R.T. membership behind him at age thirty-eight.

Bill was born in Seattle, Washington, but he moved to California in 1939. He attended Beverly Hills High School, graduated from U.C.L.A., and remained in California to become an agent for the New England Mutual Life Insurance Company.

"The one concept I think of significant value is the importance of getting a sales idea which will sell, putting it into a carefully designed sales tract, and then finding the type of person who is responsible and who will respond to either the protection of his family and future (if it is a personal sale) or the future of his business (if it is a business sale). Armed with the proper presentation and the conviction that no one will work harder than I in attempting to be of service to prospects and policyholders, I cannot possibly suffer a slump. For, if there are no sales, I know I am talking to people with defective personalities, and I never second guess myself or my ability to sell and service my policyholders."

Back in December of 1956, Bill Shelton, then in his second year of million dollar production, wrote an article for *Life Association News* entitled "I Give my Prospects an Education." Then and still today Bill uses his first interview to tell his prospects four things. First, he enumerates his services as a life underwriter and stresses the fact that he is primarily a salesman, and his income is dependent entirely upon the amount of money his clients put into life insurance premiums. Secondly, he tells his prospect that the average young client may get poor insurance, and that it is the client's fault rather than the fault of the life underwriter, if this happens. Pointedly saying that the only thing a life underwriter has to merchandise is his knowledge and his time, Bill emphasizes that a young man who cannot afford to put a lot of money into life insurance usually is unfortunately also a person who will not let the underwriter make good use of his time. Bill goes on to stress that only by forming the proper prospect-client relationship is the underwriter able to give his clients the proper service. Thirdly, he stresses that to get service the underwriter must be treated as a professional advisor. And fourthly, Bill lets the prospect know that he expects his policyowners to actively assist him in meeting other successful young men, who would appreciate the type of work he does.

Bill then goes on to tell his client what he will do for him, if this relationship is established. He will make an analysis of the client's life, disability, and hospitalization insurance policies to make sure they are in perfect order. He will show the income potential of the present insurance and other property in case of disability, retirement or premature death. He will project ideas on a realistic short term and long range insurance program. Over the years as the client's estate grows larger, Bill will work with the attorney and accountant to point out ways the client can reduce current income taxes and potential estate taxes. Bill concludes that this education has been of value to his policyowners, for they know they will get service whenever they need it. These words were put down in 1956, and since writing this, Bill has put on the books an amount of insurance in excess of $20,000,000. Bill's simple advice—give your prospects an education—is still producing for him more than a million dollars a year.

During the last four and a half years, however, he has devoted the majority of his time to the deferred pension and profit sharing fields, and for this work he has adopted the name of the Shelton Company.

In pension work he uses a visual presentation on flip charts to explain the type of work and service he performs. The great majority of his pension operation is on a joint work basis, and he uses the same procedure that has been described by the famous Sid Thompson and Jack Langan of New York City at various Million Dollar Round Table Meetings, Purdue University Seminars, etc. Bill credits his association with Sid Thompson and Jack Langan and the other successful pension writers in his company, the New England Life, for much of his success in this field in the Los Angeles area.

In the pension area he retains the services of a pension service organization, which is a successor to one which was started by his former General Agent, Rolla R. Hays, Jr., twenty years ago when he was a very active pension agent. Bill pays no direct fees for this business, but after he has designed a proper plan this firm makes all the necessary calculations to determine the total cost and benefits of each participant. If the case is sold, the servicing company becomes an agent on the case to the extent of 10% on commissions. They also service the case when there are terminations and do all the calculations of benefits on each anniversary of the plan. This, in itself, has allowed Bill to devote his time to the sale of pension plans with the actual calculations done by his general agency.

The main reason, however, for Bill's success is that he really enjoys his work. In personal selling, he believes he has a mission to help people accumulate an estate and protect their families. In business selling, he believes he has a mission to provide continuity in business. In designing and administering pension and profit sharing plans, he believes he has a very important part to play in helping an owner of a closely held corporation to accumulate an estate apart from his business in this very complicated world of taxes in which we all live. In fact, Bill reached an income level which was completely satisfactory to him back in 1960, and since that time his objective has been to build his clientele with continual service and to spend more time with his family.

One of Bill's long range plans has always been to put back into this business a part of what he has received and to attempt to explain to others the great emotional and financial rewards enjoyed by successful life insurance salesmen. It was for this reason that in July of 1966 he accepted a new challenge and succeeded his great inspiration, Mr. Hays, as General Agent. The Agency has twenty-two C.L.U.'s and includes such agents as Butch Bearden and George Byrnes and Bill credits much of his success to his association with it. Noting that "you can learn to play baseball better working out with the Los Angeles Dodgers than you can working out with some sand-lot team," he has found that the whole atmosphere of this agency makes one want to be a professional life underwriter, a top producer, and financially successful.

In fact, this atmosphere was responsible for the turning point in Bill's career. In 1954, the year Butch Bearden was to become Chairman of the Million Dollar Round Table, Bill's objective was to qualify for M.D.R.T. so he could attend while Butch was Chairman. Through his determination, his conscientiousness, and driving hard work, Bill made his goal of membership in the 1954 Million Dollar Round Table, and later he also became the youngest man in the history of the New England to become President of the Leaders Association, (*i.e.* their leading agent.)

Bill is very active in the Los Angeles Life Underwriters Association, and served as President in 1964. "I have benefited in a city as large as Los Angeles for my name is known and many life underwriters know that I am attempting at least to do a professional job for my policyholders. And many of my friends in the Life Underwriters Association, when they come in contact with my policyholders, congratulate them on having me as their life underwriter and do not try to move in. In all my cases I do the same thing for the professional life underwriters I have met through the Life Underwriters Association in Los Angeles."

Bill tells us that since 1950, when he decided it was better to have a prepared sales presentation, he has had very few discouraging experiences, for he is never trying to second guess his sales ability when someone does not buy. If this does happen he just goes out to meet two or three new people so he can tell them the benefits of life insurance. Bill knows that lack of activity is the main cause of discouragement, and when you have a pattern which leads to sales you will want to tell your story, for you know the results will be rewarding.

In the January 3, 1965, issue of *Family Weekly*, Bill had an article that was read by an estimated 9,000,000 people. Entitled "The Secret of Buying Life Insurance," it made good reading as well as good sense.

Few of the families I talk with each year are getting their money's worth in life insurance.

What's wrong? Most families buy policies as they would buy clothes, hunting something attractive at a price they think they can afford. This is fine for agents; it makes them money and saves them work. But for the family staking its future on these policies, it can be tragic. Thousands of dollars in protection slip through their fingers.

These people have not learned the essential secret of buying life insurance—buying, not policies, but a plan. Ask any good agent for a policy, and he will ask about your other insurance so he can try to fit your needs and assets into a pattern, to give you a plan.

Bill then gives two case histories and how he planned their programs, concluding:

Aren't both Tom Johnson and Herb Smith putting an awful lot into insurance? Sure they are—if you take the old-fashioned view that insurance is nothing more than a prudent man's hedge against untimely death.

But properly used, insurance is much more. It's the insuring of financial capital in the working years; it's the insuring of a decent, independent retirement in an age where we have a lot of miles left after 65. It is, in fact, *life* insurance—if you put it to work in a plan.

This past year, using plans and pensions, Bill Shelton wrote $4,762,600.

CHAPTER 47

NED SHERA, C.L.U.

NED SHERA, million dollar producer for Schwarz, Shera and Associates, Inc., lives outside of Tacoma, Washington, on American Lake. He and his family, wife Joanne and their three children, have developed an acre home site into a recreational area which even includes swimming and water skiing. Here they spend their summers, and in the winter the Shera's go to Sun Valley and Aspen for snow skiing. Besides being an athlete, Ned says that Joanne is a mother without equal and his best publicity agent in the community.

Ned had an academic scholarship to Yale, and he graduated from there in 1953 with a B.S. in Industrial Administration. At Yale he participated in many student activities, and he also played varsity football.

Ned is now Vice-President of Schwarz, Shera and Associates, Inc., an insurance brokerage firm dealing exclusively in the life, health, pension and group fields. During his first year in the business, Ned wrote $850,000 with an income of $11,000. He became a C.L.U. in 1963, and he has received the National Quality Award for eight consecutive years. Ned's long range objective is to build an increasingly successful brokerage operation.

When he was a boy, his parents would not tolerate a mediocre performance, and this parental insistence on a better than average performance in whatever he was undertaking has given Ned the great drive needed in a career in life insurance. "In my opinion, what makes me tick is a desire for excellence in whatever I undertake. I am very competitive by nature and gain no satisfaction in being second best. When I entered the insurance business, I knew that eventually I wanted to be at the top of the personal producers in this area." Ned has certainly achieved this goal.

Ned spends a majority of his time with group insurance, business insurance, and estate planning. Each month he sends out a mailing called "Financial Planning." His method of operation includes a pre-approach letter, telephone calls, and having the referrer call the prospect and tell him that Ned is coming.

Ned's initial interview is primarily fact finding, and he attempts at this time to know the prospect from many different angles. Ned tries to determine just exactly what the prospect's needs are, and what his goals and objectives may be in the future for his wife, children, estate, and various properties he may control.

Before leaving from this initial interview, Ned explains exactly how he works, that if in analyzing the prospect's situation he should find an evident need for insurance, Ned would expect the prospect to buy it through him, because of his efforts. Generally, this works out well and gives Ned control of the situation.

At the second interview Ned will usually have a written proposal and quite an elaborate outline of recommendations; however, when Ned gets into the actual interview, he generally will use scratch paper and spell it out in that way right in front of the prospect. Ned finds this more effective than placing a batch of written material in front of the man and expecting him to digest it. Even the most sophisticated businessman is often totally lacking knowledge of the life insurance contract and its various forms. Thus Ned tries to make sure his recommendations are understood by keeping them as simple as possible.

Ned maintains a complete file on everything that he and his client have discussed through the period that they work together. Ned calls on these clients periodically, depending on how their needs may change, perhaps once each year or once every two years.

Today Ned makes two calls each day on new people; his first year he made seven calls a day on new people. He now works one night a week; his first year he worked four nights. Today most of his business comes from family programming, business insurance, estate planning, and group insurance planning for corporations. He has many groups and pension plans in force; and he also writes a fair amount of health insurance.

Ned chose life insurance as a career because "I believe no other field could afford me the opportunity to earn the income

I wanted in as short a period of time. That a man is paid just exactly what he is worth in this business also appealed to me. I was willing to put my abilities on the line, knowing that if I did a good job, I would be compensated accordingly. In my opinion, the vast majority of our population do not wish to know what they are worth, because in most cases they are already being paid beyond what they are worth. This is probably fortunate for us in the life insurance field, because it gives the man who is willing to put in a few extra hours a tremendous opportunity. Life insurance as a career offers an opportunity unparalleled in any other selling field."

Ned advises young men coming into life insurance straight out of college to write a great many lives each year, "for these early small clients with potential will grow into your big clients in future years." He also believes a new man needs to learn organization. "Most new men spend a great deal of time spinning their wheels, and if some of this can be eliminated through counsel from an experienced agent or manager all the better."

Ned has learned that, especially in large cases, it is important to get the proper facts of the case as quickly as possible. This is done by a thorough fact-finding interview, first of all to determine at the earliest possible point, whether or not the man is a potential buyer. This will often eliminate becoming involved in a big case that falls through at the last minute, because the people were not good prospects in the first place.

Ned is an active member of his local National Association of Life Underwriters Chapter; he has served as President, Vice-President, Secretary-Treasurer, and Board Member. Ned derives satisfaction in working with this professional organization to uphold the ideals and objectives of the life insurance industry. He believes that the greater the agent's participation in NALU the stronger will be the agent's position in the life insurance industry.

And Ned's former manager, Richard I. Corey, C.L.U., leaves no doubt as to Ned's position in the industry. He says that "Ned would qualify to meet the highest standards called for in our business!" And he certainly does.

CHAPTER 48

PHILIP S. SIRIANNI

To READ ABOUT Philip S. Sirianni takes your breath away! His amazing story radiates hope for those of us who are just about convinced that ours is no longer the land of opportunity. His parents migrated from Italy to seek a new life in America. Phil Sirianni's success is a living example of the fact that the new world does offer opportunity for those of all backgrounds and that it is ours, if only we will use the God-given talents we all possess.

Phil's father was probably the greatest single influence on his life. Money was hard to make, but somehow his father always managed to sacrifice himself so that Phil and his sisters would not want for anything. The lessons Phil learned and the influences his family had on him, especially his father, early implanted the principles and high ideals that have guided Phil to his present day success. Says Phil:

I am particularly grateful that I was taught early in life the value of money and the importance of industry. Everybody in our family worked. For example, as a freshman in high school (age 14), I got a job in a restaurant in Rochester washing dishes after school until midnight to earn extra money. This taught me the importance of using every minute of my time effectively.

My home training and family background indelibly impressed on me in these formative years of my life a real appreciation of the privilege of working in the land of the free, where a man could make of himself anything he wanted to be if he were willing to pay the price. Not having had all of the comforts and luxuries in life that many youths had in their younger years, it was only natural that I could either resent this fact, or use it as a spur to attain these things for myself. I am sure my parents gave me the inspiration to seek the good things in life. Therefore, at an early age, I determined that I would have more of the good things available, and that I was willing to pay whatever price was asked in energy, effort, and self-development. I am everlastingly grateful for the fact that I was not born with a silver spoon in my mouth, but that I had the privilege of building whatever I have for myself.

Now Phil is trying to pass the heritage on to his own four young children, and he can be justly proud of their progress. Phil can also be proud of his wife, Janice. Being active in the life insurance business with Phil as his first secretary has given her a valuable understanding of the demands on him, particularly in terms of the amount of time he must devote to it. It's most helpful, too, that when circumstances require it, she temporarily steps back into her role at the office and gives her able assistance.

As has been revealed about every single man in this book, Phil too is extremely perceptive and sensitive to people—their strengths, their weaknesses, their moods, their unspoken thoughts —how and why they are as they are. Working at an early age just could have been the thing that served to open the door, at least a crack, to reveal many provoking secrets of psychology which have been pursued, studied, explored, and used to great advantage ever since. This is perhaps another instance of ordinary circumstances being recognized by one more young future agent for their true value and not being allowed to pass through their life unheeded.

After high school, Phil attended the University of Rochester where he majored in Chemical Engineering and worked for Hickok Belt Manufacturing Company. When the West Coast Director of Hickok offered to send him to U.C.L.A., Phil lost no time in transferring to the west coast university where he graduated with a B.S. degree and went on to take a post graduate course in business.

Phil knew well his own requirements that would have to be met by whatever career he might choose to follow. There would have to be the opportunity to succeed on his own—not to be hampered by any set limitations (other than those he himself might place)—but where the chance to win or lose would be left entirely up to him.

Phil wanted a career that would satisfy his need to give of himself and to be of service to his fellowman in a manner that would require the maximum use of his abilities and talents.

Walter G. Gastil, now retired Director of Agencies of the Western States for Connecticut General, guided Phil to the profession that met all that he demanded from the work to which he would devote himself . . . the life insurance business. Of Walter, Phil says that "he is one of the truly great men I have had the privilege of knowing."

And Mr. Gastil in turn has many things to say about Phil Sirianni and few would be in a better position to know their subject because he was Phil's first manager. He describes his former protege as "alert, intelligent, restless, optimistic, and possessing a remarkable share of what is probably the most necessary characteristic to any success—enthusiasm. He is completely sold on the product he sells, believing in it wholeheartedly and without reservation. He knows his subject well and speaks with authority, and his clients and associates, as well as audiences at speaking engagements, soon learn to respect and have confidence in what he has to say."

Today Phil operates as Philip S. Sirianni and Associates— Business and Financial Planning. He operates as a financial consultant and markets personal insurance products through estate planning and business planning. His staff consists of two technical assistants and several girls. The men do the detail work involved in analyzing a client's estate and carrying through the recommendations; they do the pension and profit sharing service work and at times they act as a liaison between the client's attorney, his accountant, and Phil's office. Phil's personal secretary sets appointments, writes letters, keeps records of both his life insurance and collateral business interests and, in general, assures that the office is a well coordinated and efficiently run operation. His assistant secretary handles all records, etc. on pension cases, analyzes all documents, and works on summaries.

From 8:00 until 9:00 every morning Phil reviews technical work with his assistants. From 9:00 A.M. until 5:30 P.M. he keeps appointments, mainly with clients engaged in business. "My first client was in business, and he referred me to his friends," is Phil's explanation of his market.

Phil and his staff occupy an attractive suite of offices in the Los Angeles branch of the Connecticut General. A great deal goes on within those office walls when we consider Phil's record, which grows more astounding each year. In his first year, Phil wrote $350,000 to earn $3,600 and his production has grown ever since. For example, his 1961 production was $3,-500,000 on 61 lives; his 1962 production was over $4,500,000 on 125 lives; his 1963 production was in excess of $5,800,000 on 102 lives; and in 1964 he produced over $8,500,000 on 207 lives. In 1965, his production was over $10,500,000 on 330 lives with premiums of $550,000.

To give some idea of how Phil works, let us look at his article, "I Emphasize the CREATION of an Estate," which was published in the January 1964 issue of *Life Insurance Selling*:

In order to earn the right to good relations with my clients, I feel I must deliver continuous and outstanding service, better in quantity and quality than they could get anywhere else.

My clients demonstrate their appreciation for the extra service by referring me to other people. My prospecting problems are solved by these referrals and by centers of influence.

When I approach a referred-lead prospect, I describe my process by showing him a summary of my own estate and illustrate how the problems with which most of us are confronted can be solved. I spend about 90% of the time in this first interview describing the benefits that will accrue to him during his life and only about 10% of it on the problems that will occur at his death. I use case examples to show the ways many of my clients have profited from my service in the past and then explain how he can reap similar substantial gains.

For example, we may discuss short-term trusts for children or grandchildren, a family partnership, pensions, profit-sharing plans, deferred compensation, private annuities, business reorganization, etc. These subjects are far more enticing than a prolonged discussion of imminent death.

I tell my prospects that every man faces the problem of accumulating property, because income from property is the only substitute for earned income. I go on to say that there are factors that combine to defeat or retard the efforts of a person to accumulate property. Some of these are:

1) erosion by income taxes
2) lack of ability to save
3) goals that are too low to encourage the person to do his utmost
4) lack of clearly defined objectives
5) lack of knowledge of how to reach the objectives
6) dissipation of capital—the person living beyond his means
7) obsolescence of investments and failure to shift the portfolio

8) changes in economic conditions beyond the individual's control —inflation, deflation, etc.

9) time itself

I act as a catalyst in crystallizing my prospect's thinking, causing him to identify what he wants out of life for himself and his family. After securing complete data from him regarding his property, his family, and his goals, hopes, dreams, and ambitions, I analyze his assets in the light of his objectives, disclosing any deficiencies. We then determine the amount, character, and time schedule of additional assets needed to meet his objectives.

The careful and orderly analysis that I perform for a client emphasizes the lifetime benefits that accrue from my services. Cooperating with his attorney, I make every effort to be sure that the proper plan for the conservation and distribution of his estate is set up, but this phase is largely incidental to the greater benefits he obtains in building financial security during his lifetime.

My service is devoted to eliminating or reducing the dissipation of property by the owner, the costs of transferring the estate, the losses caused by inadequate management and the erosion by income taxes. More important, I also help him build an estate that he himself can enjoy.

Richard W. Candland, a prominent fellow agent and long time friend, describes Phil as "one of the strongest motivators in our Company for improvement of Company processes and services and improvement of the individual. I have seen Phil grow from a sporadic producer to become the leader of our entire field force and to establish new records for total production in our Company. To me, the qualities which have most contributed to Phil's success are the following: enthusiasm, determination, purpose, gregariousness, ambition, religious and philosophical purpose, and he is a master at the art of motivation. However, of most importance to Phil's success is his philosophy of life. Phil has found, developed, and crystalized for himself a religious belief and purpose for his existence and his work. He has gained understanding of our basic economic principles which guide him in his service to others. This purpose and this philosophy are things which he continually impresses upon his associates and clients, and, thus, he becomes a man with a cause; and, like most men with causes who have the energy and ambition and drive to further these causes, he leaves an important impact upon the lives of others."

However, in setting forth the many talents and assets that Phil possesses, no one should be led to believe that these were so inherent that success came easily. Phil not only had to work hard for his success—and continues to do so—he had much to learn about self-discipline. He has experienced many periods of discouragement and frustration. The same characteristics that carry his enthusiasm to great heights many times lead him to the other extreme into moods of depression—but not for long. The path to success has been no easier for Phil than for any other successful man.

His secretary says, "In view of the enormous volume of clients Mr. Sirianni handles personally, together with his own personal business interests which represent what may be classified as a small 'empire' he keeps a growing staff of people busy—nine in number at this present writing. The people with whom he surrounds himself share his own attitude toward his business . . . in constantly striving to improve methods, systems and the services performed for clients."

Perhaps the most concise explanation of Phil Sirianni's continuing and increasing success is best summed up in the slogan he solemnly works and lives by: "Make every job you do be at one and the same time, the best job you've ever done and the poorest job you ever will do." To young men entering the life insurance field, he says, "The insurance business is one of the last bastions of private enterprise, and we need young men to preserve our system of government" . . . and, "this business, particularly in the sales end of it, is most unique in that while you work for a great corporation, you are actually an entrepreneur in business for yourself and, more than in any other work I know of, a master of your own destiny."

There are few men who have mastered their destinies as well as Philip S. Sirianni.

CHAPTER 49

KAI H. R. SODERMAN, C.L.U.

CAN SWEDEN'S "first teen-age idol" find happiness as a M.D.R.T. agent for New York Life? Can a Swede from Stockholm find success in the new world of Princeton, New Jersey, U.S.A.? Far from being a life insurance soap opera, this was the real life situation of Kai Hans Roland Soderman, C.L.U. He can now answer both of these questions with a resounding yes, for he has qualified eleven years as a M.D.R.T. member and is now Life and Qualifying. In fact Kai's transformation from idol to agent was so spectacularly successful that Kai's brother, leader of Sweden's best known dance orchestra and head of a well known vocal group, sold out to become a life insurance agent. Today this brother at thirty-two is one of the leading agents in Sweden, and Kai is one of the leading young agents in the United States with production in the three millions.

Kai tells us this about his background and goals:

I was born and raised in Stockholm, Sweden, and only went through high school. As I was to begin college, I had some success as a singer and guitarist and decided instead to go into show business. I now recall with humor that I was labeled "Sweden's first teen-age idol."

I decided to stay in show business, only until I was twenty-five. One day a trumpet player with the Vincent Lopez Orchestra called me and said he had left the music business and wanted to sell me a life insurance policy. I told him I would buy one as soon as I, too, got out of show business. The following day the manager with New York Life, Robert W. Quatsoe, called me and asked if I might possibly think of selling life insurance. I said, "No, thank you," but went down to talk to Bob and was very impressed with the business.

Bob Quatsoe helped to give me a lot of confidence that I could succeed, and during my first year I worked five nights a week. My goals, when I started, were to make the Million Dollar Round Table as quickly as possible and to make New York Life's top production club, the President's Council. Since I now have done so each year I have been in this business, my goals presently are to do the best I can and, hopefully, one day to lead New York Life in production at least one year and become President of the President's Council. It is also my goal to earn gross $100,000 each year.

And here are the facts set against Kai's declared goals: His 1963 and 1964 production was $3,000,000 on roughly 90 lives. In 1965 it dropped to $2,400,000 on 82 lives while Kai spent considerable time on finishing his C.L.U. But production by July of 1966 was $1,988,000 issued on 96 cases plus ten cases in the mill for $646,000. Of this production, Kai says, "I hope that a turning point will come, because I have been on a plateau for several years and want to get off to achieve the higher production of which I am capable."

Since Kai is convinced that it is difficult to sell much more than 150 cases a year, he believes that to up his production he must always be upgrading prospects and thus increasing the average sale.

Why is high production important to Kai? "One of the important reasons without question is the necessity to make a large income for a large family (four children, another expected), but this is not the primary reason. Rather it is a desire to do the best I can. I have been given this opportunity to sell insurance for which I am very grateful. I have to get to as many people in businesses as possible to tell them about the tremendous product that I sell—money that will be used at some future date for very important purposes." And Kai always tries to get to enough people in business to make three sales every week.

Kai settled on his major market, that of business insurance, only after several years of package selling. Told that if he could get two people a week to save $5 each, he could earn $250 a week, Kai went out and talked to people about saving money.

In the talk he delivered at the 1963 M.D.R.T. meeting he told how in his first year he sold only "Endowment at 65" but he sold enough policies to make a good living and the M.D.R.T. and formed a valuable habit of producing no less than two applications a week.

If you are new in the life insurance business, I firmly believe that the way to succeed is through one or more package sales talks that you know fully and completely so that when you talk to a man he will feel that you know your business.

Where do you go from package sales and programming in our field? I think the answer still lies in package selling, but to the sole proprietor, the corporate owner, or other people with larger amounts of money. I did not really have more than a smattering knowledge of business insurance, but I was quite sure that the people I would call upon probably would know quite a bit less.

I made use of the New Jersey Industrial Directory and called the prospective buyer on the telephone. My telephone approach went like this: "Mr. Jones, my name is Soderman, Kai Soderman of Soderman Associates in Princeton. We are in the field of estate planning, business life insurance and pensions. I have no idea what you may have done about these subjects, Mr. Jones, but I have some thoughts on how to get tax-free money into your company that I would like to show you. Can I possibly see you tomorrow around ten or would Wednesday at three be better?"

The books that we learn from always say that when you sell sole proprietors there is always someone there to buy the business. Sure. Well, in the ten years that I have now been active in this business, I still haven't found one single situation where there has been someone to buy the business. New York Life's Lou White gave me the idea to get a buyer. If you can arrange to purchase the business from the sole proprietor, you have then found the buyer. I asked the question of sole proprietors as follows: "Mr. Sole Proprietor, if you had died last night, how would your family get any money out of this business"?

In most cases he would say, "Well, I don't know. I don't think they would get anything out of it. It would have to be sold." I said, well, if you have to sell it, that means it has to be liquidated, right? This means that your family would get 30 or 40 cents on the dollar if they are lucky!" He says, "Yes, I guess so."

I would then say, "Mr. Sole Proprietor, how would you like to have someone waiting with money ready to buy your business from your family when you die?"

Now most of them will say, "That's a good idea, but there is no one to buy." Then I say, "Not so. My company and I will buy your business and we'll pay your family exactly the price you tell me that your business is worth today."

"You put aside and save 3% of the purchase price every year (or if he is very young, it is 2% of the purchase price every year). Now when you die, you and I will trade accounts. For that amount of money which you have paid to us, we will give your family the full price you want them to have for your business. But still we will also give them the business. Now, if they can continue the business for any appreciable length of time, well that's just marvelous. But, if they can't, what difference does it make? They have been paid in full. If they have to liquidate, what difference does it make? They have already been paid in full."

In the March, 1962, issue of *Dun's Review* there appears an article called, "The Insurance Nobody Sells." This article emphasizes the need for Key Man Life Insurance and it, combined with my little sales talk which goes somewhat as follows, has been very helpful in placing a few sizeable contracts.

"The name of this article, Mr. Jones, is 'The Insurance Nobody Sells.' I want to tell you right away that this is the insurance I sell, and I would like to give you a copy of this article, but just let me first point out the headline to you. Even the insurance agent may not tell you about this vital policy that every company should carry. (I heard the following illustration from Frank Nathan.)

"I'm certain, Mr. Jones, that you have insured your plant, your machinery, and your trucks against fire, water damage, etc., and for their full value. But as yet you have not insured the human asset which is the most important asset of any business. It is that asset which makes it possible for a business to show profits of 10 to 25% or more."

"Every successful business has one or more key men upon whose skill, judgment, special initiative, etc., the success of the business depends. Have you ever thought of it this way, Mr. Jones? It isn't at all certain that your plant will ever burn down, but it is absolutely certain that your key men will die. No man has a lease on life. It is not a question of if, it is rather a question of when. In all probability, they will live to become 65 or 70 years old—but they could also die today, tomorrow, or next year. Since you have insured against a loss that is really uncertain, doesn't it make sense to insure against a loss that is absolutely certain?"

Kai's method of selling also includes the use of a tax letter called "The Tax Reducer," which goes out each month. Kai seldom uses lead letters but rather has a prospective client on the mailing list for approximately three months; or, if it is a referred lead, Kai will call cold. If his referred lead is from a strong source— what Dan Auslander calls a "power lead" (for instance, from the president of a company that is a good customer of the company Kai is calling on)—Kai will then, of course, use the name and state that he has done some work for Mr. Jones of XYZ Corporation that Mr. Jones found very interesting and helpful.

If Kai thinks, however, that his lead is not from a strong enough source, he does not divulge his source, simply stating that his client felt that Kai should not put Mr. Jones in the uncomfortable position of having to see him because of his friendship to the client. Kai adds that if anything comes of their meeting and if he can serve him, he is sure that he will be free to tell his prospective client who their mutual friend is, but for the present they should meet only on the promise that Kai has some terrific ideas about tax-free money to show him.

Kai uses an attention getting one thousand dollar bill pasted inside his brief case with three pennies around it—an idea he got from Ben Feldman—to drive home the idea that he sells money; no matter what the call is about, whether it is programming, estate planning, money for taxes, or to buy out a stockholder or a partner, it boils down to needing money; and sooner or later he gets to this thousand dollar bill, emphasizing that he sells tax-free money that will cost only three cents per year on each dollar delivered.

Kai's proposals are usually very simple; he uses the company's electronic illustrations wherever possible, and for estate tax purposes he shows only an estate tax table and the form for a Federal Estate Tax Return. Kai discusses the client's taxable estate, what approximately the estate will be, and then he looks up on the estate tax chart to see how much will have to be available to pay the taxes. When Kai presents the proposals, he encases them in a brown binder with the client's name imprinted in gold and all proposals covered by plastic sheets.

Kai uses electronically prepared cash value sheets for all his clients and sends out an annual progress report, an idea Kai credits to Hank McCamish of the Massachusetts Mutual and which Kai picked up from Hank's presentation at a M.D.R.T. meeting.

Kai has also used with success short films produced by the Better Selling Bureau to be shown on a Dukane Flip Top Projector for cases involving partnerships and corporations, estate planning and sole proprietor.

Continually looking for new ways to make insurance come alive to people he sells, Kai is also continually probing the depths of his own values and sharing his ideas with others in speeches.

He has spoken at the 1963 M.D.R.T., the 1964 Toronto Sales Conference, the West Texas Sales Congress, the Atlanta and Dallas Life Underwriters, the 1965 New York Life Underwriters, and in 1966 the Philadelphia Life Underwriters.

In his best known speech "Growing in Life Insurance," he set down the reasons he could wholeheartedly encourage other men to become life insurance agents—in essence, his thanks to the business, the organization, and the men who have given him so much.

We have a lot to count our blessings for—a lot to thank God for. Growing in the life insurance business is not only growing by increasing production with the increased earnings. It is, more important, a tremendous opportunity for growing as a man. In our wonderful business we see more and understand more of human problems than in many other fields. It is up to us to guide, counsel and help, and it brings to mind what a fellow life underwriter once told me. He said, "Either I was going to be a teacher or else I was going to be a minister, but in the life insurance business, I found the only business where I could combine the two."

I am also grateful that we have such a wonderful organization as the Million Dollar Round table. The ideas that I have talked to you about today, the philosophy I have fostered and that has grown to a strong belief has to a great extent come from other fellows in the organization. Over the years I have freely stolen from the minds and hearts of men like John Todd, Ben Feldman, Sadler Hayes, Ray Triplett, Jay Wilcox, John Ames, Jim Bradford, and many, many more. And it has been because they so willingly shared their fine talents.

And so by continuing this tradition of sharing talent with others, Kai is helping to make a career in life insurance unique for its co-operation within the industry.

CHAPTER 50

RICHARD W. SPENCER, C.L.U.

A DESIRE TO BE the younget man in town ever to make the Million Dollar Round Table set Richard W. Spencer's face steadfastly in the direction that saw him producing over $2,000,000 last year. He is an agent for the Provident in Chattanooga and the son of A. De Forest Spencer, one of Provident's most outstanding managers.

Realizing that the sky was the limit as far as earnings were concerned made Richard set his aims high. Beginning with $556,000 production, which earned him $5,500 his first year Richard has now qualified for the M.D.R.T. five times and produced well over $2,000,000 of new business in 1965.

However, Richard would be the first to admit that a career in life insurance is no bed of roses. "There will be many hard knocks along the way, but those who weather the storm and keep working will find it the most rewarding experience in life."

One of Richard's most discouraging experiences occurred in 1958. He had the binder check on a pension plan which would have generated $750,000 of life insurance, and on which Richard was the sole agent. The Trust Agreement was completed and was to have been signed on September 30. On September 25, a bank persuaded Richard's client not to purchase the pension plan from an insurance company, but to allow the bank to suggest an actuarial consultant who would design a plan for them. "That hurt!" admits Richard.

Nevertheless, Richard would unreservedly encourage qualified young men to become life insurance agents. He would suggest that the new agent take a simple package plan, master it, learn to present his package in his own words, know everything there is to know about it, learn to answer any question that might be asked of him, and then go and show it to as many people as he possibly can.

This diligence and persistence which Richard recommends and which he himself learned early has paid off in many ways, perhaps most dramatically in the case of a prospect Richard had all but given up. "I programmed his insurance, changed his beneficiary, and provided all the other services I could. After a two-year period of time, I was still unable to sell him and had just about washed him out as far as a prospect, when one morning the phone rang, and he said he was buying a business. He needed $125,000 of insurance, and asked if I could handle it. After I came to, I explained to him that I thought I could, and since then he has purchased $250,000 of life insurance, plus his group insurance from me."

Richard took insurance courses at the University of Tennessee, and graduated from the University of Chattanooga. These insurance courses gave Richard insight into the life insurance business, and his college fraternity played a big part in giving him contacts to call on during his first years in the business.

However, his introduction to life insurance came much earlier. Richard's father, now Manager of the Home Office General Agency of the Provident and a life and qualifying member of the Million Dollar Round Table, very early took Richard to company conventions. There he could be seen, held firmly by the hand to discourage him from collecting Provident booklets at too early an age. Much later, Richard worked in the Provident Home Office during vacations from college.

Richard credits his father and Mr. Edwin O. Martin, C.L.U., who was manager of the Agency when Richard became a member, with "advice and counsel that has been invaluable to me. They achieved a high degree of success in the industry and this was a real inspiration. They also left me alone."

Richard has now passed his LUTC course and received his C.L.U. Degree, and he believes that these give a newcomer to the life insurance business prestige and knowledge that help him, especially during the early lean years.

He is presently a member of the Estate Planning Council of Chattanooga, as well as President of the Mountain City Hunting and Fishing Club, the Junior Chamber of Commerce, and the Kappa Sigma Fraternity Alumni. He is also a member of the

Chattanooga Chamber of Commerce, serves on the Board of Directors of the Chattanooga Association of Life Underwriters, and is a member of the Chattanooga Chapter of C.L.U.

Richard believes that prestige is important, but he does not use the conventional methods, such as tax letters, etc. to achieve it. He relies almost completely on the monthly newspaper ad which the Agency has run for a number of years; it features the names and pictures of all the members of the Agency and builds community recognition through constant repetition.

His office generates prestige also. It is in the lobby of the Home Office building which is one of Chattanooga's most eye-catching structures.

Richard uses the telephone to set up a definite appointment to discuss life insurance with the prospect. On the second interview Richard presents a written proposal which includes a survey, recommendations, and a ledger sheet of the proposed purchase.

Richard mails birthday cards to his clients and makes a phone call to them on their age change.

His centers of influence have also been of significant importance to Richard. Last year alone these centers accounted for 28 sales producing $504,000 in volume. This was business that Richard most likely would never have written on clients that he most likely would never have met, had it not been for those very important centers of influence.

In a speech he made to the Provident Life Insurance Producers at their annual meeting and in an article published in *Life Insurance Selling*, Richard outlined the three main characteristics peculiar to a good center of influence. "One, he should be a client—a person who has heard your story and who has bought you as well as your product. Two, his daily routine must put him in touch with other people. And, three, he should have an aggressive nature; he should actually be a displaced salesman himself who is doing another type of work, or who is a salesman for another product."

To obtain centers, Richard reviews his clients and measures each of them by these three qualifications, choosing those which fit. Richard believes clients are subconsciously interested in your success anyway; they like to think that their purchase was a good one—that they were very smart in choosing the best underwriter in town and in buying insurance that suited their needs.

Richard's biggest personal motivating force is from within the agency. Five of the seven members of the agency qualified for the 1965 Million Dollar Round Table, and the total agency production was in excess of $11,000,000. Other incentives to Richard's achievement are his thrill at persuading a man to sign an application and check, and his family's personal tastes which cost money to satisfy.

His wife's grand piano and harp may just begin to indicate what he means by these tastes. However, these instruments are certainly not for show. Betty, his wife, teaches harp at the Chattanooga Conservatory of Music and plays with the Chattanooga Symphony, as well as taking care of young DeForest and Mary Stewart.

And what in summary can we learn from Richard? Just this: "Life insurance is not something that costs your client money. At the end of twenty years a man can recover all of his premium dollars should he desire to cash out his insurance. The ledger sheet, which I use almost entirely as my sales presentation, bears out this fact. In this business you can attain a very good income through helping other people solve some of their problems; and by doing so, render a service to them, as well as to the community."

CHAPTER 51

J. LAWRENCE STONE, C.L.U.

WHEN LARRY STONE was given Los Angeles as a scratch agency, few men, even in his own Company, envisioned a five million dollar agency in one year. But that is exactly what Larry and his partner, G. F. Farr, built out of their offices in Los Angeles for the Provident Life and Accident Insurance Company in a twelve months period.

They now have three other full-time agents, and they continuously solicit brokerage from other agents in the Los Angeles area. After five years in business, their agency has over $25,000,000 in force with over 90% of this being Ordinary Life.

Larry entered the life insurance business in 1957 at age 24. In his first full year in the business his paid-for-production amounted to $750,000 and in 1965 exceeded $2,000,000.

Larry became a life underwriter because: "It was the only business I could get into in which I could work for myself without any capital. After comparing it with other businesses, I saw it had all the advantages other businesses do not have."

When Larry entered the business, his goal was to make the Million Dollar Round Table as soon as possible. He attained this goal in 1960 and has qualified for the MDRT six times. His other goal was to make at least $30,000 a year by the time he reached age thirty. He also has attained this. In what other business can a young man write his own ticket, and through hard work and sheer determination achieve an income goal for himself by a particular age?

On a wooded lot in La Canada, California, Larry has a large home with a swimming pool in typical California style. He has achieved these things at such an early age because of the opportunity for rapid growth through the life insurance business.

Prior to entering the life insurance business, Larry attended and graduated from the University of Southern California. After college he worked for a large trucking company, handling their insurance affairs. He continued in that capacity, until he was persuaded by one of his former professors at USC and by his own life insurance man to enter the life insurance field.

How does this man have time to build an agency and yet produce a million dollars of life insurance a year? He makes it a point of seeing new people and not allowing himself to become bogged down with paper work. His weekly goal is to contact two new potential clients, no matter how busy he is. If every agent in the field would contact two new potential clients a week, wouldn't it be possible to achieve, with the proper training, the goal that Larry set for himself—MDRT and an income of $30,000 a year by age thirty.

Larry prospects through the use of referred leads only. He uses pre-approach letters followed with a phone call for an appointment. In initial interviews he always shows an idea to arouse the interest of his prospect. This procedure, according to Larry, has been the one thing most beneficial in his success. If they are interested further in what he has to say, he obtains complete information and then prepares a case. He gives all policyholders a complete audit which he reviews yearly. He also calls them two or three times a year to keep up with their situations and make any necessary changes.

Larry is personable, well-organized, and strongly believes in the business he is selling. "You can do more for people as a life insurance agent than you can if you were in any other business or profession. You should be proud you sell life insurance," Larry asserts.

Another idea that can certainly help an agent improve his average size case, is Larry's plan for closing sales. "After the information interview and upon presentation of the case in the second interview, I make all recommendations based on the assumption that the client desires to solve his entire problem. My recommendations will show what I believe to be the ideal road to solution, and then my alternate plan will solve the entire problem based upon a monthly budget figure, which I always obtain in the first interview. The alternate may include minimum deposit or term. My theory is that you have a duty to show a man the complete solution within his budget. If this means minimum deposit (less than 15% of my production is minimum deposit) and the situation can support this type of policy, I show it. Many times, of course, the prospect doesn't complete his program then and there; however, I would feel pretty badly if something happened, and I hadn't tried for the entire sale."

If all young agents would try for the ideal solution in every case, just as Larry does, no doubt many times we would find that people buy what we have proposed, no matter how unlikely it may have at first seemed.

CHAPTER 52

BYRUM W. TEEKELL, C.L.U.

"GET ONE HUNDRED CLIENTS who are going places and stick with them. These should be young men that you believe have a real opportunity, because of their education, background, or ability to succeed. Some will disappoint you and have to be replaced. You probably will never get your hundred clients, for you will always be replacing them and adding to them. These men will make you wealthy as they gain wealth, if you grow with them and continue to justify their confidence in you and your ability."

The elder Mr. Teekell, himself a successful general agent, gave this advice to Byrum when he first became an agent. Byrum followed his Dad's advice, and he heartily recommends it to others. Incidentally, he is still trying to get those one hundred clients, but he doesn't believe he ever will. "I don't have time to handle the clients I've got," he admits.

But Byrum does say that "if I have succeeded, it is in large measure because of my father's teachings, advice, and my desire to please him. He constantly challenged me by the high ideals and standards he set for me." Byrum's father encouraged him to work at various jobs even in high school such as selling shoes, being a car hop, being a warehouse boy, and having paper routes. He encouraged him in Scout work, and Byrum became an Eagle Scout with three palms. In college Byrum's father encouraged him to be on the Debate Team, while holding various jobs such as waiting on tables, and while working on his law degree.

But, although Byrum got his law degree, and practiced law for a short time, he soon gave it up "to eat" as Byrum puts it. Nevertheless, Byrum says his law degree and legal training have been more beneficial to him than any other single thing in his outstanding career as a life underwriter, with the exception of his father's influence.

Largely because his father was successful, Byrum early in his career had occasion to meet, listen to, and be influenced by other great insurance men. "One who will always stand out is A. H. 'Blip' Hammond of Louisville, Kentucky, at that time Lincoln National's Superintendent of Agencies for the South," Byrum recalls.

Byrum also tells us that Mr. Teekell had a keen sense of humor. "When one of his manager buddies told Dad, after seeing him with my brother and me, 'That's one way to build an agency,' Dad replied, 'It may be, but it's the most expensive way!'"

When Byrum's father passed away in 1961 after being an outstanding agent and general agent for the Lincoln National in Shreveport, Louisiana since 1933, Byrum took over the agency.

Byrum sells all types of life insurance plans from estate planning cases, to business insurance, to group insurance. He does not use visuals, except in pension sales. Byrum has written some 75 group and 25 pension trust cases. He subscribes to the theory that, if you see enough people under the right circumstances and give a convincing presentation, the results will come. The late Albert E. N. Gray impressed Byrum with this statement: "The reason men are a success in this business is that they do things that failures don't like to do." Byrum believes that, if an agent is to be successful, he must pay the price to become more knowledgeable so that he can always "prospect upward" and serve a higher type of clientele. If an agent is in a slump, Byrum believes that he must analyze himself and his operation objectively and relentlessly, be willing to accept the answer he finds, and be willing to pay the price to do something about it.

Jim Irvine, Past President of the Million Dollar Round Table made another point that has been important to Byrum: "The only difference between members of the MDRT and those insurance men who have never sold a $1,000,000 during their career is simply a matter of time and the use of it. If a person could simply work smarter and perhaps crowd one or two more calls into each day, he too could accomplish the job."

The sinking fund idea of insurance has been Byrum's most successful sales idea. He tells prospects who have estate tax problems, "Upon your death your estate will either have to sell or liquidate at a possible great financial loss, or else borrow the money to pay the taxes, if you make no plans." Byrum meets this problem by establishing a permanent sinking fund that will guarantee the principal whenever it is needed at a cost of only 3% on the money. Byrum's clinching question is this: "Which is easier, for you to establish this $100,000 sinking fund now at only 3% or $3,000, or for your family to pay later by liquidating or paying off a $25,000 a year bank note?"

Byrum has made speeches to life underwriter associations and Lincoln National meetings in Louisiana, Mississippi, Maryland, Texas, and in Toronto, Canada. In these Byrum often points out that his remarks are intended for the men who don't want to work for the pennies, but for the dollars—the men who want to make life insurance selling a profession. Byrum also points out that it is necessary to continually keep abreast of all so-called "new plans" so that clients' questions can be answered about these supposed bargains.

One of Byrum's biggest disappointments which occurred at the beginning of his career was a $300,000 business case—$200,000 on one man and two $50,000's on two others. The $200,000 case was turned down by the company, with the result that "my home purchased shortly thereafter suffered a violent change in location."

Byrum has a successful general type of life insurance practice built on ideas, hard work, and sincere service. His secretary adds, "Mr. Teekell prefers that his associates work with him, rather than for him, functioning as a team working toward an established goal. Being his secretary is rewarding, stimulating, and inspiring."

Besides being a General Agent, Byrum is President of Executive Pay Plans, Incorporated, which is a pension, profit sharing, and employee benefit plan consulting company. He is also a member of the Louisiana Bar and past president of his C.L.U. Chapter.

Byrum is a member of many non-insurance organizations too; among them are the Shreveport Petroleum Club, the Shreveport Country Club, and the Ark-La-Tex Tax Institute. He is currently serving as President of a Holiday in Dixie, an annual spring festival held in Shreveport with over fifty events.

Byrum met his wife, Jan, while she was majoring in Journalism and he was in Law School at Louisiana State University. They have four sons. Byrum calls her a "terrific hostess who has a real flair for cooking and entertaining."

A final story that makes good sense to Byrum is one told by Rod Messinger, General Agent for the Connecticut Mutual in Los Angeles, that likens selling insurance to playing golf. "Rod Messinger said that, if you play golf and par is 72, you don't quit in the middle of hole No. 15 just because you've used up 72 strokes. The objective is to play 18 holes. Some people may shoot it in 67, while others may take 95, 100, or more. Selling life insurance is the same way. Some people may have to make three calls to have a sale, while others must make ten or twenty. The objective, however, is always the same—to make the sale. Therefore, a young fellow starting out must not lose sight of the objective, nor think he can get away with the same effort as the old pro par shooter. He must make the ten, fifteen, or twenty calls necessary to finish the game, and as he works on his game he will improve."

Byrum made those extra calls, and today, he is a real par shooter as a Life Member of the MDRT and a General Agent with agency production over $7,000,000.

CHAPTER 53

HUGH G. THOMPSON, JR.

IF YOU HAVE NEVER SEEN an electric dynamo and the power it creates, then you may have difficulty picturing the dynamic Hugh G. Thompson, Jr., agent and often company leader of the Northwestern Mutual Life. During his first ten years in the business, he has sold over $30,000,000 of life insurance and this enormously talented young man led the Northwestern in 1960, 1962, and 1964, with average production of about $6,000,000 on 175 lives per year. In the agents' year of 1963-64 Hugh sold $8,200,000 on 221 lives. It is easy to understand why Hugh says, "I am thankful that I gave this business a chance to show me the opportunities it has to offer!"

Often asked just what qualities an insurance agent should have and what advice is important, Hugh has always emphasized eight points:

1. Everyone says he wants to be successful. But the young man contemplating an insurance career must truly have a keen desire to succeed and not kid himself about it. He must want success more than anything else and have the determination that will not let him quit short of his goal.

2. He must like money. Wanting money doesn't mean that you work just for the sake of earning a dollar . . . and yet, if a person doesn't want the extras in life that dollars will buy, he isn't likely to be as successful as the man who wants an exceptional income for himself and his family.

3. The insurance careerist should really want to be in the business for himself—not just think he does. It takes courage and determination to start in business with no assured monthly income, but every agent knows that a little extra effort in the early years will pay off handsomely in the future.

4. The individual contemplating this business should not have his feelings easily hurt. Many people will say "no" to us through

the years. A good insurance man will not take these turn-downs to heart, pout about them, or feel sorry for himself; rather he will go on to another prospect with renewed effort and continued enthusiasm.

5. He should be interested in people and in community affairs. He must enjoy meeting strangers and feel at home among them.

6. In my opinion he should be a promoter at heart. Most good salesmen are—whether they are promoting themselves or some special community, civic, sporting or social event.

7. The successful life insurance agent must have control over himself. It's easier to sleep late in the morning, or not go out in the evening or say, "I'll make that call tomorrow." Insurance is not sold through good intentions. Success comes from dedication to your business through positive action.

8. Finally, he must be willing to analyze himself and his sales methods and accept advice and help. I have found it to be true that the most successful insurance men are continuously seeking the advice of others so as to improve their own sales ability.

To get the first interview, Hugh normally uses "centers of influence" (friends and clients) to get leads and then follows this up with approach letters and calls for an appointment. He never sees anyone without an appointment. At the initial interview Hugh attempts to create a friendly atmosphere and promises his prospect two things: To be sincere and to offer the best possible service. He tells them what they can expect from him both now and in the future—that he wants to get the facts, answer questions, explain life insurance in general, show them his service and make recommendations. "I solve problems by making our product a 'hero'—showing its flexibilities, both as a tax hedge and as good property. Most important, I try to explain insurance so he can understand it and its flexibilities. If it's a product the prospect wants to own, then the battle is almost over."

Hugh has a filing system that makes him call his clients at least once a year. He also maintains a financial record book as a service to each client. "Service is important," he says.

Asked where most agents fail, Hugh named organization. "We all must have a track to run on. My system makes me work (when I'm working), and lets me work more efficiently. I'm a great believer in planning today for tomorrow, for without such planning there will be no successful tomorrows. When we encounter slumps, we must quit feeling sorry for ourselves and take positive action. One of the best ways to assure continuing production is to develop a way to explain or present insurance so people can understand what is involved. People don't buy things they don't understand—especially intangibles. In presenting our product and in trying to make a hero out of it we must remember two things: Keep the presentation simple, and make our product solve problems. If we will get organized, analyze both ourselves and our methods, substitute positive action for our excuses, and then work, we can not only be successful, but have fun in this business of selling life insurance."

In talking of his personal discouragements, Hugh admits that he has had to learn not to be upset when friends or those for whom he has done work buy from someone else, but to go on to other tasks with renewed enthusiasm. Hugh says, "One of the quickest ways to flunk out of the insurance business is to feel sorry for yourself when you fail to make a sale."

The perennial bachelor until 1964, Hugh often had to explain why as a single man he produced such phenomenal amounts as his production rose from $450,000 to $8,200,000 in ten years. "I guess my drive comes from the pride one takes in being successful —both in his own eyes and in the eyes of others. Of course, I want the things in life that a good income will provide, but money is not the motivating factor for me. I'm happy to say that I have never looked at a commission scale and couldn't tell you what I make on any policy. I know if I sell life insurance, I'll be paid well."

Speaking of his General Agent, Deal Tompkins, Hugh gratefully acknowledges Deal's help, and stimulation "by emphasizing the importance of keeping proposals and presentations simple, by encouraging me to raise my sights reasonably, and by being honest and fair with me."

Hugh also praises his mother for her encouragement and understanding in accepting his independence and by matching his abilities to the life insurance business. It was Hugh's mother who suggested that he consider life insurance as a career.

Growing up in Charleston, West Virginia, Hugh lived with his mother, a younger sister, and his father who was a physician, but who had a limited practice due to a disability. Hugh was active in sports and politics and became president of his class at Charleston High and a four letter man. Beginning at age fourteen, Hugh worked every summer and most Christmas vacation periods. These earnings, some family savings, and an inheritance from his grandfather enabled Hugh to attend Duke University and then graduate from Miami University in Oxford, Ohio.

"One evening during my sophomore year at Duke," Hugh recalls, "my mother asked me, if I had ever considered selling life insurance. At that time I didn't know a life insurance policy from a will." However, his mother seemed to be aware of the opportunities in the life insurance business and suggested that he talk to several companies. Hugh's dad, who was a medical examiner for several companies, echoed her comments and suggested that he consider Northwestern Mutual first. After interviews with twelve different companies, Hugh chose the Northwestern Mutual. His accomplishments with the Northwestern have now made company history.

When Hugh decided on a career in insurance, he transferred to Miami University of Ohio, from which he graduated in 1951 with a degree in business. One college summer Hugh worked with the Northwestern Mutual Life General Agent in Charleston, West Virginia, his home. Hugh says he didn't work very hard, even though he did sell some insurance—almost exclusively of the savings program type. Hugh talked to young college graduates about an insured savings program or to fathers about starting insurance on their sons—programs which would have required savings of $10 to $30 per month. Hugh observes, "Frankly, my reaction to the insurance business at this point was that it wasn't a very high calling in life. I thought: 'Who wants merely to sell a savings program during all his working years?'"

After two years in the Air Force, Hugh entered life insurance on a full-time basis in his home town. It wasn't long before Hugh realized that there is much more to life insurance than savings programs. Soon he was helping young couples plan their financial security programs. Later he began working with young physicians and medical students. Estate planning on a modified basis was then added. Now he is doing a combination of all of this, plus working in the business insurance market. But he still says, "Regardless of whether you work with individuals or businesses, whether you work with professional men, business men or young college graduates, you must above all else keep it simple. Don't get complicated with your proposals or presentations."

Hugh's interests do not stop with the things usually associated with the selling of life insurance. He has conducted seminars for Northwestern Mutual agents for the last three years, which have been attended by about 700 agents. Each agent must pay a fee to attend, but almost without exception those attending the two and a half day seminars have praised Hugh for his efforts, but more important have used this session and the material to increase their own production records.

Hugh is also President of Physicians Nationwide, Inc., an association of Northwestern Mutual agents offering a professional and continuing service to the physician for insurance and financial planning. His outstanding wife, M.K., was instrumental in the formation of a woman's division of this group. He is also co-founder of the Northwestern Mutual Cross Country Study Group. This group meets once a year to exchange ideas. Its members are some of the outstanding agents of the Northwestern Mutual who, like Hugh, were M.D.R.T. qualifiers before age 35—Jim Richardson of San Diego, Dave Foster of Pittsburgh, Martin Polhemus of Spokane, Ed Coffman of Washington, Jim Harding of Portland, Mike Goodrich of Baltimore, Bob Kloppenburg of Milwaukee, Jim Bonebrake of Cleveland, and others.

Frank in appraising his allocation of time, Hugh sells insurance only seven or eight months a year. The other months are spent in community and other activities. "When I work, though, I really work," Hugh emphasizes. "This means many nights plus some weekends."

They say all work and no play makes Jack a dull boy, but obviously they have never met Hugh Thompson whose work is his play, and who is anything but dull!

For Hugh doesn't separate his work from his recreation. Selling insurance and talking to fellow agents about insurance is fun and relaxing to him. Combined business and pleasure trips are extensive and restful; last year he made forty such trips.

Hugh also enjoys his wide range of work in community and church affairs for he believes that "we should all lend a helping hand to our community." He devotes almost three months of each year to his work with the Junior Tennis players around

Charleston. He is the founder and President of Tennis, Inc. of Kanawha Valley, National Co-chairman of the National City Team Tennis Tournament, Vice-Chairman of the United States Lawn Tennis Association (he has won West Virginia State Men's Doubles Championship four times), and is Vice-Chairman of the Charleston Park and Recreation Commission. He has been active with the United Fund, Morris Harvey College in Charleston, and numerous other community endeavors. Hugh and his family have been active in the First Presbyterian Church of Charleston, since he was a small boy. He is now a deacon and a few years ago was president of the Men-of-the-Church.

With his work for play, Hugh sells for pleasure. "I have always loved selling and the field of promotion. I am a perfectionist and have always had much ambition."

How does Hugh achieve such spectacular success in life insurance while spending great amounts of time in other interests? He is always superbly organized, whether selling or playing, which enables him to sell fantastic amounts of life insurance when he works. He has had a number of months which have exceeded $1,000,000—in fact, one month exceeded $3,000,000—and these months have included no policies over $100,000. Therefore, when he is going at what is his normal pace, he can accomplish in one month what it takes another man a year to accomplish. He has the sensational ability to write an extraordinary number of lives in a given short period of time. During the month when his production was $3,300,000, he sold 87 lives.

Hugh's first ambition in the life insurance business was to make the M.D.R.T. Next it was to sell $2,000,000, and later to lead the Northwestern Mutual. There was always a goal. Two years ago when he sold over $8,000,000 to lead the Northwestern Mutual for the third time in five years he said, "This is my last year to lead the Northwestern Mutual." Few believed him. As one agent said, "I'll bet he will set a goal of $12,000,000, so he can average a 'million a month.'" Don't ever bet against his doing it—especially if you challenge him, and if he sets this as his goal, for he has never failed to reach a goal yet, no matter how big.

CHAPTER 54

STAN B. TOWERMAN, C.L.U.

Mr. Gordon Harper, C.L.U., Director and Agency Vice President of the Phoenix Mutual Life Insurance Company, describes Stan B. Towerman, C.L.U., as a "young man with a solid future." And this is in part what he means. Stan finished his first year in the business as the number one first year agent in the Phoenix Mutual, and today he is a repeating member of the Million Dollar Round Table with production last year of $1,400,000. He is also a past chairman of the Council of Field Underwriters, which is a liaison organization between the St. Louis Association of Life Underwriters and the insurance agencies in St. Louis. He serves on the Board of Directors of the St. Louis Association of N.A.L.U. and the Society of Chartered Life Underwriters.

Stan graduated magna cum laude, with a B.S. in Commerce from St. Louis University. He had held a four-year honor scholarship, had risen to A.F.R.O.T.C. group commander, and had been awarded the Chicago Tribune Gold Medal Award and designated a Distinguished Military Graduate. After graduation, Stan completed his military service and then spent three months as an executive trainee for a lingerie manufacturer before coming into the life insurance business.

Foy Dean, C.L.U., who was a M.D.R.T. member and a Phoenix Mutual agent in St. Louis before his death, impressed and inspired Stan during his first year in the business. "Foy Dean always made time for me and would counsel me, as if nothing else was so important. He was a great man and stands as an example of what the life insurance counselor should be."

Stan's training has included L.U.T.C. courses, C.L.U. courses, and Advanced School on Pension Planning, the latter held at the University of Connecticut and sponsored by the Phoenix Mutual. He has also attended C.L.U. Institutes.

Stan did his studying for these courses, as well as reading and rereading his many insurance services and books, in the elaborate office of his home. In this office he has a desk, reclining chair, phone, built-in library, file cabinets, and piped-in hi-fi.

His wife, Elaine, helps Stan by taking care of all personal financial affairs in addition to taking care of their home and three young children.

Stan's major method of operation is "exposure." For an individual with many holdings, Stan explores the idea of trusts. After Stan gets the interview, he usually shows a sample of his work. He uses his own program, to which he has attached his will and his life insurance trust. "I merely point to them, whetting his appetite," Stan adds.

Stan sends each policyholder a letter one month prior to his age change, enclosing an annual review check list. Stan informs the client that he expects to call him to discuss the check list, in order to update his program. If in conversation it appears advantageous, Stan steps up a personal interview. "It is amazing how often they ask me to come out to sell them additional insurance," notes Stan. He also requests referrals in conjunction with the check list.

Several years ago, Stan decided to stop working nights. In order to make what Stan considers a sufficient number of calls during the day—a minimum of 40 calls a week—he keeps careful records. He duly records all seen calls, policyholder calls, fact-finding interviews which include service calls, and closing interviews. Stan keeps track of these things on a daily work sheet, and he tallies the calls cumulatively, day by day during the week, so he knows if he has to accelerate near the end of the week. He also makes a minimum of 20 telephone calls for appointments per week to clients and prospects.

He likes to have a luncheon appointment every day. He also keeps a card file in his car. The card file is set up by area, and in it he keeps the names of people he does not consider referrals. He uses these for fill-ins, if he finds himself between appointments with nothing to do in a particular area.

Every night Stan lists the people he intends to see the next day, the telephone calls he intends to make, and he puts on his dictating machine letters and instructions to his secretary. He goes into his office three days a week, limiting his stay to as short a time as possible. He sets aside Friday mornings for planning the next week and reviewing policyholders' files. Wednesday afternoons are reserved for golf or squash.

Stan believes that he is only now beginning to reach his stride and that the idea which is helping him most is this time control with the discontinuance of night work. "I have confidence that I am in control—that I am captain of the ship, running on a course that I have set toward a known objective, rather than a piece of debris being tossed about by this wave and that." Stan emphasizes, "My success formula is time control plus education."

Stan's business was, until a few years ago, essentially split between the medical market and the business insurance market. Stan got started in the medical market by concentrated circularization of lead letters to interns whose names appeared on a list. However, Stan now finds the business market much more intriguing and is concentrating his efforts there.

Stan adds this advice for those starting in the business: "You have to close your ears and eyes to all distractions. Say to yourself, 'This is my life's work, and I must be a success at it.' Then work day and night on simple approaches and presentations. Don't look for big cases, but merely aim for consistent, steady effort. If you make a sale, forget it; assume you made none and go on to the next."

Stan believes that activity—getting out to see the people—is the key. "Don't let failure discourage you. Keep going and play the numbers. Feel good about going out and seeing a man, without concerning yourself too much about whether he buys. Remember, you are that much closer to a yes, if he says no."

Mr. Allan Kent, C.L.U., Managing Editor of *Life Insurance Selling*, describes Stan's approach to the sale of life insurance by emphasizing how well he lives up to the C.L.U. professional pledge. "Stan gives his clients the service which he would have applied to himself, if he were in the same circumstances."

And Mr. John A. Sinning, C.L.U., Stan's Phoenix Mutual manager, adds, "This man has success built within him. He is a hard worker and sets goals for himself. He continually tries to improve his techniques, knowledge and skills in our business, and as a result has developed a method of success that can be an example to all men in our business."

CHAPTER 55

JACK BRAME TURNER, C.L.U.

"THE AFTERNOON I CAME HOME and told my wife I was going into the life insurance business, she couldn't believe it. But being the wonderful wife she is, she finally responded, 'Well, anything you want to do will be satisfactory with me.' Recently she made the confession to me that her heart nearly broke, when I told her what I was going to do. She said all she could think about was that wonderful college education going to waste. Now she loves the business almost as much as I do, and she's convinced that it was the best thing that ever happened to us."

And the honors and accolades that have been given twenty-nine year old Jack—his C.L.U. designation and M.D.R.T. membership, his election as President of the Life Underwriters Association of Clarksville, and President of the Tennessee Life Underwriters Association; being named "Man of the Year" by the Tennessee Association; and being featured speaker at the Southern Agents Management Conference at Vanderbilt, featured speaker at the Georgia Independent Insurance Agents Convention, a speaker at many of his Company meetings, and a featured speaker at the M.D.R.T. 1965 Broadmoor meeting— these honors partly tell why Jack's becoming a life insurance agent has been such a terrific thing for the life insurance industry, for Jack himself, and for his wife, Margie, and their four children.

If we go back to Jack's senior year of college, when he began thinking seriously about his career, however, we find that he was not even considering life insurance. As a boy Jack had pushed a big soft drink truck around town peddling pop every Saturday, for his father was in the wholesale beer business and a Double-Cola distributor. All through high school and college summers, Jack had delivered a regular beer route. Although he was not particularly interested in going into beer and bottling,

Jack values these years of experience for he says that it was here he learned the true meaning of hard work. "My exposure to long laborious hours on the truck and my exposure to people in all walks of life proved to be a valuable education for me. This point becomes more apparent day by day as I continue in life insurance, and I am convinced that these early years of hard work were invaluable to me." Jack also recalls that during his grammar school years when he lived on a farm, he had the pleasure of rising at four o'clock every morning in order to milk forty Holstein cows. "And would you believe it . . . I even enjoyed it at the time!"

But neither drink distribution nor farming interested Jack enough for him to make it a full-time career, even though he had a wonderful opportunity to make a good income and become a partner almost immediately in his father's business. "I was familiar with his wholesale beer business and was very much interested in the business except there was some spark missing and this upset me considerably," Jack recalled recently.

The only thing he was sure of was that he wanted to go back to Clarksville and work, and he wanted to be engaged in some general aspect of selling. So, out of frustration, Jack decided to go to job interviews on campus. He walked into an insurance interview and for the first time Jack was shown the vast scope of the life insurance business.

To get advice, Jack went to see Arch Northington, who at that time was Tennessee Commissioner of Insurance and Banking. He shoved a book into Jack's hands and told him not to talk to him any more, until he had read every word of it. The book was Bettger's *How I Raised Myself From Failure to Success in Selling.* Jack stayed up all night long reading that book, and after it was finished, all he could think about doing was going into the life insurance business.

In reflecting back on these early experiences recently, Jack recalled several factors were instrumental in his selecting life insurance for a career. First of all, he wanted to live in his home town. Secondly, he knew that he wanted to sell and life insurance seemed to be the most rewarding selling job possible . . . rewarding not only from the compensation that was available, but from the satisfaction that results from truly being of service to mankind. It's important for Jack to believe that through his efforts, he is helping to make the world a better place to live. He sincerely believes that every successful life insurance salesman has an obligation to widows and little children, and an obligation to be of service to all clients. "I know that without this sense of dedication, I would never have made it in the life insurance business," he concludes.

As Jack became more and more captivated by life insurance, his production soared, going from $1,235,000 on 58 lives in 1962, to $1,653,682 on 73 lives in 1963, to $1,203,500 on 56 lives in 1964 and $1,519,172 in 1965.

"Although recognizing that money is always a motivator, Jack did not believe that it could ever serve as a permanent source of inspiration—at least it could not for him. "I've not found any consistent motivational strengths in thinking of a sale as so much commission!" he said.

The desire that has given him consistent motivation, however, is to be the best in his field and to be thought of as "Mr. Insurance" in Clarksville. He knew that the only way he could do this was to be successful in the business and to show that he was a top professional career life underwriter who was a competent financial planner. Thus each year he sends out the M.D.R.T. announcements and encloses the story of the M.D.R.T., and the Provident runs congratulatory M.D.R.T. advertisements.

The C.L.U. has also added immeasurably to Jack's standing among the professional men in the community. Routinely with mailing pieces, letters, etc., Jack sends a copy of the little booklet "What is a C.L.U.?" so that today in Clarksville most people know that C.L.U. designates professionalism.

These announcements and mailing pieces help Jack to live by his motto—first a friend, then a client. Jack prefers to work only with people he knows personally; therefore, personal contact is almost 100% his approach for interviews. He attempts to make friends with a man, before asking for a business interview. When he does ask he says simply, "Would you have any objection to discussing your life insurance program with me?", an approach used by others in this book.

When a new man moves to Clarksville, Jack makes it a point to serve as a one man Chamber of Commerce, to really make the man feel welcome, see that he meets as many other people as possible, and really tries to make him feel at home.

Thus, Jack's initial interview, whether with a long time resident or with a newcomer, is usually a meeting between friends. Jack places primary emphasis upon selling himself and his unique services. Jack lets the man know that he is interested in working for him and earning the privilege of serving as his life insurance counselor. Jack makes it a point to tell the prospect that he is not interested in peddling a policy, but that he is applying for the long range job of handling the prospect's complete comprehensive program. Jack generally either describes the type of audit and estate analysis work that he does, or else shows the prospect a sample copy—maybe even Jack's own.

Jack then likes to complete a confidential information sheet and pick up the policies. He gets policy authorizations signed and proceeds to do a routine audit. Jack always writes to the respective companies to make sure everything is in order.

In his audit work, Jack always attempts to get the prospect's health insurance policies and bring him up to date on these along with presenting him what Jack considers to be a most valuable addition to his audit, the college cash sheet. Jack shows the cash value of all policies as each child reaches the age of seventeen. "I've found that the wives are particularly impressed by this, since they are most anxious to have some systematic accumulation plan for college."

In his estate analysis procedures, Jack has stopped typing out lengthy recommendations to leave with the prospect. Instead, he uses a regular yellow pad to make handwritten notes which he heads "Observations and Recommendations" and he takes these along with him to the interview. He has found that this handwritten sheet of notations has a very dramatic personal appeal to the prospect for they show that Jack has devoted considerable time and thought to the prospect's particular problems.

Jack tries to have two interviews a day to get two sales a week, but he admits that he has difficulty keeping his goal going on a regular basis.

In his interviews, Jack regularly uses a Provident audio visual on business insurance, and he has found it quite effective. Just recently Jack has started experimenting with homemade flip charts and is very excited about continued use of them. Jack uses a regular flip chart pad and a marking pencil to organize any presentation in a logical sequence. "I've deliberately done this by hand," says Jack, "to avoid any package looking approach. I've found that this flip chart presentation captures a prospect's interest and understanding much more effectively than anything I've tried before." And Jack now plans to use the flip chart for all of his sales.

One type of sale that Jack discussed in his M.D.R.T. speech last year was Juvenile Life Insurance. He pointed out that it is useful to the new agent because he can utilize it without having a gigantic knowledge, and useful to the established agent who can use it as an idea that will be fresh as well as fun. Another tremendous advantage of this particular type of sale is its simplicity of presentation and the relatively quick sale which usually results. This entire sales plan is in the 1965 Proceedings of the M.D.R.T.

Jack thinks other men should become life insurance agents "if—and only if—they know exactly what they are getting into. Life insurance selling is no bed of roses, and it is most certainly one of the most difficult businesses in the world." One of the things that caused Jack to go with the New England originally— Jack was a special agent with New England until he joined Provident Life & Accident as a general agent—was because Tom Harrison, the General Agent in Nashville, was one of the few who gave him the true facts. He actually told Jack that he probably wouldn't succeed in the business for it is such an extremely tough business—particularly for a young man out of college. He plainly said that statistically Jack's chance of success was not good at all, and he advised Jack of the real possibility of failure. But Mr. Harrison went on to tell him that if he could stick it out for three years, then in all probability he would go on and be successful in the business and that the rewards for those who succeed are quite satisfactory.

Jack believes that one reason the mortality is so high with new agents is that no one tells them the truth about this tough business.

Jack also points out the need for the agent of any age, if he is to remain successful, to keep acquiring knowledge; "Knowledge is a vital instrument in our business, and knowledge yields confidence. With confidence, this job of selling life insurance becomes a lot easier." But Jack would be the first to caution that knowledge in and of itself does not insure success and that a man must be willing to pay the price in terms of hours spent before prospects.

Jack would advise agents not to anticipate overnight success, but to establish realistic goals, with the help of their general agent, which can be attained within a certain period of time. When I entered the life insurance business, I was determined to give "it at least three years," Jack told us. If, at the end of the three year period, I was not well on the road to being a success, I decided that I would get out of the life insurance business and try something else. I had several goals I wanted to achieve very badly; among them was completion of LUTC, starting my C.L.U. exams, and a minimum income of $10,000 per year by the end of the third year."

Long since accomplished, these goals may seem easy now, when compared to Jack's actual achievements and his future hopes, but drop by drop the ocean was made, and goal by goal the underwriter becomes successful. Jack and the others in this book know there is no other way!

CHAPTER 56

THOMAS J. WOLFF, C.L.U.

IN HIS FIRST TWELVE MONTHS in the life insurance business (1957), Tom Wolff wrote $1,200,000, and he has qualified each year since that time for the Million Dollar Round Table. He has also earned the National Quality Award every year, is a C.L.U., served as an LUTC Instructor, led the Hartford Agency of the Aetna for the past nine years, produced in excess of $2,000,000 of ordinary volume in all companies in 1959, 1960, and 1961, and in excess of $3,000,000 in 1962, 1963, 1964, and 1965. In each of the last three years his new paid ordinary premiums have exceeded $100,000.

In fact, this young agent is so good that he was able to sell the Aetna Life Insurance Company key man insurance on the life of the Chairman and President. This is a real sales feat, because no one knows better than the man in the field how hard it is to sell executives in the home offices of life insurance companies.

Tom has also served as president of the Hartford Life Underwriters Association and vice-president of the Connecticut Life Underwriters Association. His speaking engagements to underwriter groups around the country have taken him into twenty-five states. He has lectured many times at the University of Connecticut and has addressed such industrial groups as the IBM Schools on frequent occasions. Perhaps his most cherished invitation came in 1964 when he was invited to address the annual meeting of the American Medical Association in San Francisco. Still, he has found time to serve as president of his Rotary Club; he is immediate past president of his country club, and is one of the organizers and vice-presidents of his Chamber of Commerce. Thomas Wolff has done all of this, and he still manages to play golf every day of the week during the spring, summer, and fall.

He has also authored a book entitled *Life Insurance, A 9%*

Investment which has sold over 75,000 copies to date, and he is one of few life insurance men to be listed in Marquis' *Who's Who in the East.*

What is Tom's secret? Although this young man does play golf or engage in some other recreational activity every day of the week for seven months of the year, during that time he gets up at 5:00 or 6:00 A.M., is in the office between 6:00 and 7:00 A.M., and works until 12:00 or 1:00 P.M. Only after he has put in his day does he find time for leisure. This means he must be very efficient, well organized, and self-disciplined, and that is exactly what he is.

Tom has a very sincere belief in the product of life insurance, and this was instilled in him by two professors to whom he gives much credit for his success—David Ivry and Dean Laurance Ackerman of the University of Connecticut. These two professors have constantly served as sounding boards, counselors, and friendly guides throughout Tom's career. With his thorough background, clear explanation of principles, and persuasiveness, Tom has been able to convey ideas to his prospects in such a way that he is able to sell large amounts of life insurance with the use of a simple, oral presentation. In fact most of his presentations are oral, although he sometimes uses a blackboard.

Tom Wolff once gave a speech entitled "Two and a Half Million in Two and a Half Calls per Week." Actually, Tom averaged about three interviews a week and wrote in excess of $3,000,000.

Tom is very generous in his praise of others and especially likes to credit Al Granum, C.L.U., of the Northwestern Mutual with giving him the magic words that have become his one and only approach. The approach is: "Mr. Prospect, would you have any objection to discussing your life insurance program with me?" He has been using this for seven years and has never at any time had anybody object to discussing their life insurance needs.

Tom's secret of success is best defined in a law he calls Wolff's Law: "Two agents of equal ability given the same amount of output—namely, work—will earn life insurance commissions in direct proportion to the earning power of the market in which they are selling." Unless we do a good job of selection, the approach even if successful will do very little good. His success in selection is the real key to Tom Wolff's record. In a recent speech, Tom said that ten years ago he knew no one who was earning over $5,000 a year. Now, he sells no one who earns under $15,000 a year. Why? Because if you want to triple your income, you must triple the income of your clients. Tom definitely decided if any money was to be made in this business, prospects with larger earning power would have to be found.

How did he find these prospects in an eight year period? He became well known in his community, taking civic responsibilities in which he was genuinely interested. When he was given these responsibilities, he did the best job conceivably possible. This is evidenced by his many community and civic offices. In each instance Tom undertook responsibility, worked his way through the ranks, and became head of the organization in which he was interested. These organizations have given him an opportunity to show people he can do things and do them well. And large numbers of important people, seeing Tom at work and liking what they saw have given him the clientele he was seeking. Now, Tom sells only friends, and he approaches these friends with the simple Al Granum words, "Would you have any objection to discussing your life insurance program with me?" In each instance the approach has been on a strictly business basis, a simple approach which not even a distant friend could take offense at.

Thus Tom's way of doing business has become almost a Utopia. He plays golf a half day for seven months of the year; he is able to take an active part in his civic clubs, his country club, and his community; and he is able to sell $3,000,000 of life insurance by calling on friends and acquaintances he has met in his civic work.

You may be thinking and saying to yourself that you can't afford to take the time to get involved in community activities the way Tom does. Well, you know what Tom's answer to that is —the same as you would give a prospect, if he told you he couldn't afford life insurance. Tom says you can't afford not to. You can't afford not to take time away from your business and help your community for two reasons. First of all, you owe it to your community; and, secondly, it will help you double or triple your income.

And what keeps Tom enthusiastic, wanting to double and

triple his income? He says, "The real inspiration in my life comes from my beautiful Norwegian wife. Bette was my childhood sweetheart at the age of fifteen, and we were both only twenty when we married. Whenever discouragement comes, Bette is there to help me weather the storm. Life is only worthwhile because of the love and affection of my wife and three children."

CHAPTER 57

LOUIS E. WOODWORTH

LOUIS E. WOODWORTH was a million dollar producer his first full year in the business. He was until recently the leading member of the George H. Plante General Agency in Cleveland, Ohio, which represents the John Hancock. Today he is an outstanding independent insurance broker in Ohio.

Lou early showed the will to win in a difficult situation. His mother died when he was three years old. And although housekeepers tried for a time to keep the family together, this eventually became a financial impossibility. Lou's father was a wealthy man in nonliquid assets, but by 1935 all his properties had been sold for taxes.

Lou and his family then moved to East Moline, Illinois, and at nine years of age Lou began caddying at the Short Hill Country Club. From the age of twelve until he was twenty, Lou worked for the golf pro there, Mr. Waldo H. Johnson. During his senior year in high school, Lou was awarded the Western Golf Association's Chick Evans Scholarship. On this full scholarship Lou attended Northwestern University, planning to become a professional golfer.

However, he married Ritha Jean Plante, daughter of Mr. George H. Plante, in February of 1954 on his 21st birthday, and they decided to spend their summer vacation in Cleveland. Lou had planned to get a summer job in the golf business; however, because of his late application no positions were available. He then rather reluctantly went to work in the outer office of the John Hancock. By September he had decided to stay in Cleveland, and Lou petitioned the Board of Directors of the Western Golf Association to transfer his scholarship to Western Reserve University, Cleveland, Ohio, and permit him to change his major field from education to business. This was approved, and Lou graduated with a B.B.A. in 1956, with his major field of study banking and finance.

Lou's entire five years of education had been completely paid for by an annually renewable scholarship. It was difficult for a young man to be accepted initially under this scholarship, and it was even more difficult to continue beyond the first year. But, even with attending regular day classes as well as evening classes during his senior year to make up business credits, Lou kept the scholarship and graduated on the Dean's list.

And on top of all this, he began his career in life insurance on a part-time basis, because "money was needed and this was the only way I could get it."

After writing in excess of $1,000,000 his first full year, Lou has continued to write this amount and more, so that he is a Life and Qualifying Member of the Million Dollar Round Table, having qualified each year consecutively, since entering the business full time. Lou's production in 1963 was $1,750,000, approximately $2,000,000 in 1964, and $3,750,000 in 1965.

Lou's tremendous production begins with the interview, and to get one he uses referrals and the telephone. These referrals, however, are usually not solicited by Lou. Rather they are solicited for the most part by a number of Lou's own policyholders, who believe the work Lou has done for them is something their friends and associates should have done also. Lou has several centers of influence who are continuously on the lookout for him; and all referrals are done strictly on a gratuitous basis.

Sometimes when the name of a prospect passes across Lou's desk without a referrer, Lou telephones one of his clients who does the same work and asks for an indirect referral. "I call Joe Smith, C.P.A. and ask, 'Do you know Fred Doe, C.P.A.? His name has come across my desk. I would like to know something about him, so that I can call upon him. What do you know about him, and how should he be approached?'"

After obtaining information about the prospect from his client, Lou's client frequently will volunteer to call the prospect and arrange an introduction. If not, Lou asks his client, if he would be good enough to call and tell the prospect the kind of insurance man Lou is. From this, a case usually develops.

Since nearly all of Lou's fact finding is done over the telephone, prior to the first interview, he can present a written proposal for his first interview presentation. In most instances, he would use the trust approach which is actually a sophisticated use of the old will approach:

"I personally have an A & B Trust at one of the large banks in Cleveland, and I do sell a great deal from this simply by showing my clients what I have done for myself. It obviously requires a substantial amount of insurance to fund an A & B Trust. I, therefore, find more substantial sales can be made to people who will appreciate what an instrument such as this can do." Incidentally, Lou does not sell the idea of using principal and interest to pay an income to a beneficiary; rather he sells the idea that it requires a large sum of capital to pay a moderate income. For example, $130,000 at 4% interest will produce only $5,200 per year interest, which will pay an income of $100 per week to a beneficiary. Therefore, if a person does not have at least $130,000 net after all expenses (mortgage, education, etc.), it is not possible for them to see that the family has even a minimal standard of living ($100 per week income) in the event of their death.

After Lou has presented his ideas, and they have been tentatively accepted by his client, he usually reviews the plans with the trust officer at the client's bank.

Lou says that a good part of his business is conducted by telephone. Endowed with a good memory and an ability to retain facts about people, Lou can converse with his policy-owners about most phases of their insurance program from memory, although he does maintain notes and records to which he can refer. He has found that telephone contact, in most situations, is better than personal contact, because he can cover more ground more rapidly.

He simply finds out if the person is free to talk, and if so, wastes little time with preliminaries.

Mr. William E. Warnkin of Warnkin and Associates, Cleveland, Ohio, who is well known from his appearance in the Pictorial Publishers Recruiting Film entitled "The Best Paid Hard Work," believes Lou has a sure fire telephone approach. Says Mr. Warnkin, "Lou's voice and mental attitude when using the telephone is one of his greatest assets." Mr. Warnkin, himself a Life Member of the M.D.R.T., also comments on Lou's excellent follow-up service to clients and the sales that result from them.

Lou writes a considerable amount of health insurance. He finds that it is an absolutely necessary part of his operation, and his premium production in health insurance annually runs from $8,000 to $10,000.

A substantial portion of his market is dentists, and during the past six years Lou notes that at least 50% of his sales have come from this area. Lou says he has one center of influence, an orthodontist, who has personally been responsible for over $3,000,000 of production with dentists. Another referrer, a C.P.A., is also one of Lou's "multi-million dollar centers."

The major goal, that Lou is now well on his way to accomplishing, is to own $500,000 in marketable securities. He has a definite plan to acquire this. It is, briefly, to be systematic via a net worth increase each year. This is not too different from putting money into insurance except it is obviously on a larger scale. A great deal of these marketable securities are, at the moment, being acquired by Lou in the area of insurance companies.

A concept Lou often uses in selling is tied in with accumulating marketable securities. He presents insurance as representing a device for accumulating venture capital with the idea of withdrawing money from it at an opportune time. The accumulation is done in convenient denominations.

Lou's reasoning goes something like this: It takes money to take advantage of an opportunity, for an opportunity seldom presents itself without requiring money. And money can be available only to the extent that money has been accumulated. Insurance is a means of accumulating money. Thus, if you buy insurance you have money. If you have money, you can take advantage of opportunity. And it seems that the more money you have the more opportunity presents itself.

The relationship between the marketable securities and insurance as venture capital is related to trading on the equity. It is possible for Lou to use his own funds to acquire securities by borrowing on his insurance, if necessary, to first get the securities and then repay loans from earned income. As Lou increases his equity through loan repayment, he will, at opportune times, again borrow from the cash values to finance new acquisitions.

Lou believes that there are unlimited opportunities for men in the life insurance business. He believes that if at a standstill, you should find a successful insurance man and emulate his operation, and that you should freely exchange ideas with other successful insurance men. To a young man just out of high school or college, Lou would say: "Work twelve hours a day, seven days a week!" And Lou did just that, knowing hard work in the early years would pay off in high income later.

A young man who from the beginning had an insatiable thirst for knowledge of the life insurance business, Lou has never ceased seeking advice and know-how from other successful life insurance men. Regardless of his own accomplishments, he knows that others have done more, and he is never satisfied until he knows why.

Lou has an excellent command of the English language and talks sincerely about his subject. When he speaks, people listen and are impressed. This fact plus his manner inspire confidence from most prospects with whom he talks. Even as a young man of 21 just starting in the business, he was able to sell life insurance to men considerably older than himself.

Lou still plays golf with a scratch handicap, and although he is always trying to perfect his game, Lou never lets this distract him from his work in the life insurance business. Even when he takes vacations or attends business meetings, Lou puts in extra hours working both before and after his absence. The harder he plays, the harder he works!

And as we watch his now three million a year production soar still upward, we will continue to marvel at how Lou Woodworth seems to do everything well.

QUESTIONNAIRE

1. Name.
2. Birthdate.
3. If married, wife's name.
4. List children, names, ages.
5. Residence address.
6. Do you own or rent?
7. Is there anything of special interest about your apartment, home or homes?
8. Describe anything special about your home life that would be of interest to others.
9. Does your wife take any part in your business affairs as such? If so, describe.
10. Describe your wife. (Background, education, interests, etc.)
11. Please describe your wife in terms of anything unusual she does that fits into your business situation.
12. What is your present title? (Example: General Agent, President of Consulting Company, Special Agent, Supervisor, etc.)
13. What year did you first acquire this classification or promotion, etc.?
14. Date entered life insurance business.
15. List years you have made MDRT.
16. MDRT Classification for 1962, 1963, 1964, 1965, 1966.
17. Production (approximate) 1st full year in life insurance business.
18. Income (approximate) for 1st full year in life insurance business.
19. What are your activities outside life insurance business? (Social clubs, business clubs, civic activities)
20. Please list any offices, boards, titles, etc. that are noteworthy in the above (No. 19).
21. How do these activities, if they do, help you in your work?
22. What do you do for relaxation?
23. How often do you take a vacation? How long does it usually last? Where do you go?
24. Please give a brief sketch of your early life, college and degrees, and your family.
25. Did an activity, subject, or anything else in college help you as a life insurance agent? What and how?
26. What do you feel really makes you tick? What gives you your drive or momentum to continue to produce at such an outstanding rate?

27. How do you create your image? (For example: Tax letters, newspaper ads, etc. Enclose sample.)

28. What methods do you use to get an interview with a prospect? (For example: Lead letters, approach letters, cold calls.) Describe any unique methods.

29. How do you handle the initial interview? What do you do when you get there—show sample of work, visual aid, etc.? Enclose sample, if possible.

30. How do you solve the problem? (Written proposal, estate survey, use of company forms, develop own forms, etc.) Enclose sample if possible.

31. What do you do after you solve the problem? (How do you keep up with the people through the years?)

32. What else do you do, especially in regard to some unique method, that is beneficial to your sale of insurance?

33. Perhaps you have an unusual operation to which none of the preceding questions apply. If, for example, you sell pension trusts, groups or unique tax-saving ideas, please describe your specialized operation in these areas.

34. How many calls do you make a day? Now _____ Your first year _____

35. How many days a week do you work? Now _____ Your first year _____

36. How many hours do you work a day? Now _____ Your first year _____

37. How much night work do you do? Now _____ Your first year _____

38. Do you have a work organization pattern for successful production? Describe briefly.

39. From what market do you get the greatest per cent of your business? How did you get into this market? Would you mind sending me something that describes your operation or approach, etc.?

40. Have you developed any work organizers or work systems which could be helpful to others? If so, please explain or enclose.

41. Did you have business experience of any kind before you became a life insurance agent?

42. Who makes up your office personnel? Briefly describe their duties.

43. Who are your associates or partners? What are their duties as compared to your own?

44. Did anything unusual cause you to enter the life insurance business? Why did you pick this business for a lifetime career?

45. What was your goal or goals when you started into the life insurance business? Has this goal changed since you have become successful? Explain.

46. Is your office layout or building, etc. that you feel it is especially outstanding? Describe.

47. Do you have any other related interests? Briefly describe.

48. Please give the following information:
    (a) 1961 Ordinary Production—1961 Number of Lives
    (b) 1962 Ordinary Production—1962 Number of Lives
    (c) 1963 Ordinary Production—1963 Number of Lives
    (d) 1964 Ordinary Production—1964 Number of Lives
    (e) 1965 Ordinary Production—1965 Number of Lives
    (f) Give total number of groups you have in force.
    (g) Give total number of pensions or profit sharing plans you have in force.
    (h) Do you write any other type of insurance other than life? Give details.

49. Are there any unusual sales procedures or presentations or material you have developed you would be willing to share with other young agents? If so, may I have a copy to use as a description?

50. What two people have given you the most inspiration and help in this business? Explain.

51. What person or idea has been the most beneficial to you in your climb toward the top? Describe.

52. If you have spoken at insurance meetings or other large or important gatherings please list places, dates, titles, brief summary or copy of speech.

53. If you have written any articles on insurance please indicate whether they were published, where they were published, and title. Please enclose a copy/copies of the article; if impossible, please give a brief summary.

54. What are your long-range objectives?

55. Would you advise other young men to become life insurance agents? Why?

56. What suggestions could you give a young man who is at a standstill in his life insurance career and/or is eager for success or greater success?

57. What advice would you give to individuals who are just entering life insurance selling upon graduation from high school or college?

58. What advice would you give to agents entering life insurance after previous business experience?

59. Is there anything especially unusual in your operation that could be helpful to a young man just entering life insurance? If so, describe.

60. What can other young agents and potential agents learn from you? Describe. Suppose a man asked you for two hours of your time—what would you show him or tell him?

61. Is there any other advice you would like to give to young men in our business that has been beneficial to you?

62. I would like to have a short summary from someone who could be objective about you and yet emphasize your good points. Could you give me one or two names and addresses of persons who could be contacted for a very brief comment about you?

63. Please ask your secretary to describe you. Please enclose her description.

64. What one word or one sentence best describes you as a life insurance agent?

65. What brief comment best describes your life insurance operation?

66. Write down the qualities which best describe your life insurance operation. Smart, shrewd, personable, well-organized, steadfast in purpose, charming, tactful, persuasive, diplomatic, clear-thinker, self-disciplined, will to win, self-reliant, colorful, work long hours.

67. What are you best at doing in your operation? Describe.

68. In your opinion, what has been your greatest accomplishment in the life insurance field?

69. What would you say was the real turning point in your career?

70. What training have you had to better prepare you for life insurance?

71. If you had to do it all over again what training or courses would you take?

72. Is there anything noteworthy that your General Agent or Manager has done for you that would be of interest to others?

73. Are you a NQA winner? If so, how many consecutive years?

74. What professional honors, degrees, awards, etc. do you hold? Date each received.

75. How active are you in your professional organizations? Are they of any benefit to you?

76. What were/are your most discouraging experiences? How do you overcome their effects?

77. Are there any interesting stories about you or your career? (For example: My Biggest Case, The Event that Made Me a Life Insurance Agent).

78. Are there any "Rags to Riches," "Horatio Alger" or other events that apply to you which would be of interest to an outsider?

79. Please make any other comments or include any other material that you think could be helpful.

80. If you were to share one sale idea with other underwriters what would it be? Please present in detail.

CONCORDANCE

A

B

C

D

E

F

G

I

J